COMPARE PRICES

pence per pound	pence per kilogram
10	22
11	24
12	26
12½	28
13½	30
14½	32
15½	34
16½	36
17	38
18	40
22½	50
27	60
32	70
36½	80
45½	100 (£1)
54½	120
63½	140
72½	160
82	180
91	200 (£2)

AREA

1 Hectare = 10 000 square metres = 2·5 acres
4 000 square metres = about 1 acre
1 square metre = 10·8 square feet

TRAVEL

miles	kilometres
5	8
10	16
	48
	80
	120
	161

4½ litres = 1 gallon

SOME USEFUL LENGTHS

inches	centimetres
1	2·5
6	15
8	20
10	25
12 (1 ft)	30
14	35
24 (2 ft)	60
36 (1 yard)	90
40 inches	100 (1 metre)
4 feet	1·2 metres
5	1·5
6	1·8
7	2 metres

FABRICS

Fabric will be measured in centimetres; these are the new widths

inches	centimetres
36	90
45	115
55	140
60	150

ROUGH SHOPPING GUIDE FOR LIQUIDS

Them (Metric system) cc or ml (or g for gramme)	Us (Imperial system) fl oz (or oz for ounce)	
600	21	
570	20	1 pint
540	19	
510	18	
500 480	17	17½
450	16	
420	15	¾ pint
400	14	
370	13	
340	12	
312	11	
300	10½	½ pint
255	9	
230	8	
200	7	
170	6	
140	5	¼ pint
114	4	
85	3	
50 57	2	1½
30	1	
0		

SHEET AND BLANKET SIZES
Ancient British

Sheets should be at least 108 ins long.
Blankets should be the same width but need not be longer than 72 ins if you have a narrow turnover at the top.
2 ft 6 ins (·76 m) need sheets 64 ×108 ins (1·68 ×2·74 m) beds
3 ft (·91 m) beds need sheets 70 ×108 ins (180 ×260 cm)
4 ft 6 ins (1·37 m) beds need sheets 90 ×108 ins (230 ×260 cm)
5 ft (1·52 m) beds need sheets 100 ×108 ins (275 ×275 cm)
The new Metric size is:
Single: 100 ×200 cm
Sheet size 150 ×250 cm
Double: 150 ×200 cm
Sheet size 200 ×250 cm

HATS

inches	centimetres
5	41
5½	45
6	49
6½	53
7	57
7½	61
8	65
8½	69
9	73

Glove sizes continue as before

YOUR WEIGHT IN KILOS

stones	kilograms
0	0
2	
4	20
6	40
8	
10	60
12	80
14	100

INTERNATIONAL SHOE SIZING

The new 7 Mondopoint sizing will give (a) foot length, and (b) foot width at joint, like this: 250/92

Mondopoint																					
110 120 130 140 150 160 170 180 190 200 210 220 230 240 250 260 270 280 290 300																					

English children: 1 2 3 4 5 6 7 8 9 10 11 12 13
adults: 1 2 3 4 5 6 7 8 9 10 11 12 13

SUPERWOMAN
Everywoman's Book of Household Management

SUPERWOMAN

*Everywoman's Book of
Household Management*

by

SHIRLEY CONRAN

Introduction by Mary Quant

Illustrations by Jan Mitchener

SIDGWICK & JACKSON
LONDON

First published in Great Britain in 1975
by Sidgwick and Jackson Limited
Reprinted July 1975
Reprinted September 1975
Copyright © Shirley Conran 1975

ISBN 0 283 98163 6

Printed in Great Britain by
The Garden City Press Limited
Letchworth, Hertfordshire SG6 1JS
for Sidgwick and Jackson Limited
1 Tavistock Chambers, Bloomsbury Way
London WC1A 2SG

For my mother
IDA PEARCE
with love and thanks

Contents

CONTENTS

Introduction

by

Mary Quant

I HATE housework.

I LOVE cooking, bathing children, brushing dogs, polishing things and even occasionally scrubbing floors. But not housework.

I NEED an immediate return on work done—congratulations or even violent criticism. But no one mentions a squeaky-clean bath and I would have thought a dirty bathroom means a clean me.

Most of my life has been spent running away from household management without much success. A busy working life may be a good excuse for not doing it but it remains undone nonetheless. The inevitability of it appalls me, but here we have somebody who can laugh at it, do it, or dodge it.

I have known Shirley Conran since we were first grown up. The quantity and originality of the domestic catastrophies that have beset her can only be matched by the brilliance with which she has dealt with them and the funniness of her accounts of them.

She is clearly uniquely qualified to write such a book as this.

If only this book had existed when *House and Garden* came to photograph my first flat! I was inordinately proud of it but the editor glanced around and asked, 'Are you moving in or moving out?' Shirley is always either moving in or moving out but it never shows.

INTRODUCTION

She advises on a great many problems I never knew existed but I live in a bit of a mist. I am the only person I know who can happily not answer the telephone; I never open letters unless they are from lovers and I didn't read a book about childbirth until after the event.

However, having laughed my way through *Superwoman* I am going straight out to buy a filing cabinet. I can't find my passport or my cheque book, I am no longer allowed a key to my own house and there is a terrible smell in the basement.

Thanks to Shirley Conran's *Superwoman* all this is going to change.

I am most grateful to
Katharine Whitehorn
for reading the typescript and suggesting
alterations, improvements and additions.

Acknowledgements

I would also like to thank:

George Seddon for his unfailing encouragement, support and criticism.

The editor of the *Observer* and the editor of the *Daily Mail* for their permission to include material written when I was woman's editor on those newspapers.

Margaret Lecomber for typing on and on and on with interest and enthusiasm: Celia Brayfield for her valuable assistance, Jennifer Ware for her criticisms and Audrey Slaughter for her patience.

Liza Kendall, Iris Wade of Elizabeth Arden, Jean Medawar, Barty Phillips, Mrs Smith, Jean Southern, Betty Jakens, Ruth Francis, Janet Seed, Barbara Kelly, Pamela Lewis, Lotte Berk, Shirley Lowe, Sheila Black, Janet Fitch, Dee Wells, Prudence Raper, Phoebe Hitchen, Doris Grant, Barbara Sussman, Alexander Weymouth, Sid Field, Dr Jonathan Gould, Dr James Cyriax, Sebastian Conran, Jasper Conran, Robert Lacey, John Laughton, Michael Bateman, Tony Fairhurst, Phillip Dalton, Tony Wilkins, Alan Murphy, Albert Locke, Noel Ritchie of the Press Association, the Automobile Association, *Do It Yourself Magazine*, the Food Information Bureau, the Metropolitan Police, the R.S.P.C.A., St Thomas's Hospital, Messrs Sandersons and the many other people and organizations who were kind enough to help me.

I am grateful for the help of the British Standards Institute in checking the list of metric conversions.

THE REASON WHY

WHAT is a home ? A home is a myth. A home is the Forth Bridge, one damn long, never ending cleaning job, which nobody notices unless you don't do it.

No matter what they claim, no one can tell you how to make washing up a sensuous experience. Until women's lib comes up with a mechanical Sarah Jane, *someone's* got to do the dirty support system work. The purpose of this book is to help you do the work you don't like as fast as possible, leaving time for the work you enjoy. It is for women who have to housekeep but might prefer to do something else.

I don't pretend that housework is fun because on the whole it isn't. Some parts of housekeeping are pleasant. Getting up early, getting breakfast, laying tables, darning, spring cleaning, and doing the flowers would never be a strain for me. But I find routine cleaning tedious at the best of times and clinically depressing at the worst. Because it is so dreary it is quite easy to forget to do it, or even forget *how* to do it. Twenty years of blood, sweat, toil and tears haven't helped me to eliminate housework but they have taught me a few tricks to lighten the load.

Parts of this book are taken from my own home notebooks. Parts of it are the summed up experience of ten years as a home editor on Fleet Street. Where there is an excellent book on a subject which I cover briefly, I recommend that book for further reading, but only if it is exceptionally good.

I have mentioned prices and costs as little as possible for the obvious reasons. World prices are going up and up and up, and will continue to do so.

It's doubtful whether *all* the advice in this book will apply – or appeal – to any one woman, for it was not written for a specific woman and in any case a woman's circumstances constantly change. Some women go out to work, full- or part-time, some don't. A few start a little business on the side. Some have husbands, some have lovers, some have both. Most have children, some don't. Some have the worst of all worlds with no husband, no lover, several children and a full-time job. For this reason I have tried to cover problem areas from mild to extreme. For instance, in 'How to Spend Money' my suggestion that you try having two purses may help you solve a housekeeping money muddle. The same chapter shows you how to do a cash flow forecast. Dig into the book as you need it.

To get the best out of this book it's important to know your own limitations, allow for your weaknesses, and ignore the impossible, milk and honey standards of the impossible TV housewife.

I make no secret of the fact that I would rather lie on a sofa than sweep beneath it. But you have to be efficient if you're going to be lazy.

Most women don't like organizing themselves because it involves some forethought and self-discipline. But organization needn't mean a rigid plan brought to the fine pitch of a royal visit. There must be a plan, a loose plan, but scrap it whenever it doesn't fit in with life. Life is like a British summer – you have to grab it while it's there. This means being flexible enough to drop everything and get out into the sun while it's still shining – which it never does to schedule.

A routine helps you to know what you haven't done. You must also learn what will galvanize you into action to get that work done, what carrot will coax you into doing it. Katharine Whitehorn, the writer, asks friends in at least once a week because that's the only empirical method she knows of getting herself to tidy up the home. In half an hour's whirl of activity – which she enjoys – she does it all : it then becomes not a boring routine but a double bonus activity. Of course if you like your home tidied daily this could get a bit expensive and you might even run out of friends.

Her methods are not mine. My methods are probably not yours. There may even be those who think my methods appalling. Fine. What works for me might not work for you, but one of the tricks of sorting out what's best and fastest for yourself is to criticize someone else. Then, WHAM! you may have suddenly analysed and perhaps improved your own system. *So please deface this book.* It is a working book. Add to it, cross things out, make notes in the back and scribble your own ideas in the blank areas provided throughout. (They were the easiest parts to write.)

Finally, no one should waste her life on the treadmill of housework. So decide how much you're prepared to do, and when. Four hours a day ? One day a week ? None ? (A high aim, I feel, but good luck to you.) Decide how much mechanical help you want, how much it will cost, and how you're going to get the money to pay for it. Don't use that help to raise your housewifely standards. Use it to get more free time to get out and enjoy yourself. Remember that the whole point of housework is to keep the place functioning efficiently as a cheerful background for living – so live! Decide on something positive, or simply pleasurable, to do for *yourself* with the time you save. Otherwise life ... just ... slithers ... a-w-a-y ...

CLEANING

HOW TO CUT DOWN ON HOUSEWORK

Keep it to the minimum and keep it underfoot. No one's going to strangle you if the mantelpiece is dusty. Your man doesn't love you because you can tell the difference between whitest and whiter-than-white. Your children won't remember you with love in twenty years' time because your floors had such a fantastic shine.

A TV producer and mother of two small children recently asked me, 'Now that I can afford some home help, how much cleaner should my home be?' I was astounded. A home should be as clean as you can get away with. On the whole, nobody except you cares how the place looks. If somebody does, then press him into service. Always, charmingly, press any critic into service: they either help or stop criticizing or, ideally, both.

If your mother-in-law is about to call, don't dust; she'll win that status game hands down and *you* shouldn't want to. Organize some modern luxury such as a crackling log fire or fresh flowers, or home-baked bread. Serve her a cold meal (which you won't worry about) and give her a delicious drink as fast as is decent, whether it's home-made lemonade, a cup of tea or scotch on the rocks.

WAYS TO SAVE TIME!

The only way that never fails is to get up earlier, but you're not going to, are you? So the other thing to try is cutting out anything which isn't essential. The secret is . . . *elimination.*

19

CLEANING

So make your list of things which no one will care much if you don't do. (Some of these suggestions need money, so they might have to be tucked away at the back of your mind until the piggy bank is feeling better.) No one is forcing you to give up anything, but if something has to go consider these *timesavers*.

1 DON'T wear nail varnish.
2 DON'T keep pets.
3 DON'T polish floors. Seal them.
4 DON'T scrub the bath. Unless anyone in your family is allergic to detergent keep a bathroom bottle of liquid detergent and get everyone to pour in a capful before turning on the water.
5 DON'T dry dishes. Buy a second drainer and stand it in front of the first, or else spread teatowels on the table or a trolley to provide more drip-dry surface.
6 In fact, if life gets unbearable, DON'T wash up at all. Get the family to washup, Elizabethan style. That is, each person has his own mug, plate, knife, fork and spoon and manages with these, then washes them up and resets his own place at table ready for the next meal. This always happens in our family towards the end of the school holidays.
7 DON'T lay a tablecloth or use table napkins.
8 DON'T make beds. Use continental quilts or sleeping bags.
9 DON'T scrub dirty collars and cuffs. Wet them and dip in a saucerful of detergent; leave for ten minutes then wash.
10 DON'T iron handkerchiefs. It's more hygienic to use disposable paper tissues.

11 DON'T iron pyjamas or night-clothes (smooth and fold them).
12 DON'T iron teatowels, pillow-cases or sheets.
13 DON'T sew. Mend sheet tears with press-on tape. Stick patches on with Copydex.
14 DO cover kitchen shelves with self-adhesive, wipe-clean plastic. You will save cleaning time.
15 DO line the grill pan and the tray under the gas burners with aluminium foil.
16 DO roast in foil, which cuts out basting and oven-cleaning; unwrap for the last fifteen minutes to brown nicely.
17 DO use non-stick pans, which cut the horror out of washing up, as well as a lot of the time.
18 DO get your family to tidy up after themselves or else stand a cardboard box under the kitchen table and dump everything you find in this lost property office. After a bit they prefer to tidy up their own possessions rather than sort them out of the tangle.

DAILY LICK AND SPIT

AIM to get through the routine housework in the minimum time. Try to keep to a routine which starts with getting up at the time you planned. If you get up late you'll probably do everything late all day, and snap at people.

Decide how long your daily routine will take and realize, if you are over-running, that you will either have to abandon the job unfinished or sacrifice whatever other, possibly more enjoyable occupation, you had planned for the afternoon.

It's amazing how much better a room looks if you *don't clean it at all*, but simply tidy it, straightening the cushions, emptying the ashtrays and shoving every odd thing into a large basket and standing it in a corner.

Allow time after breakfast to empty wastepaper baskets, ashtrays and kitchen dustbin; put everyone's clothes where they ought to be; throw away dead flowers or renew water if necessary; swab washbasins, sweep the kitchen floor; make the beds: you can't tidy a bedroom until you've made the beds.

In spite of my mother's traditional horror, although I clear the table I always do last night's washing up the next morning, because I haven't the strength to cope with it after the evening meal (see 'How to Wash Up', p. 39). In the evening I like to lay breakfast as this is one less rushed job for the morning.

SUGGESTED ROUTINE

On Monday: Clean up the kitchen after the weekend, defrost the fridge, clean the oven, scrub out dustbins, and deal with any other strictly kitchen jobs, plus household desk work.

On Tuesday: Do the clothes washing and mending and shopping, including a trip to the dry cleaners.

On Wednesday: Do the ironing in the company of the transistor. You'll risk backache if not a slipped disc, if your ironing board is too low and you have to stoop over it.

On Thursday: Clean other rooms. If you can get away with it, this is the day you can take off with a free conscience. Use it for odd jobs such as turning out cupboards, washing down paintwork, cleaning ceilings (light fittings and cobwebs), cleaning the pram, polishing the silver if you have any and so on. Or just leave the house at 10 a.m. and do something interesting.

On Friday: Do the weekend shopping; clean the bathroom and lavatory thoroughly; clean one room (see 'How to be a Housemaid', p. 25.) or passages or hell holes such as a basement area full of dustbins.

If you're doing a full-time job you probably won't have time for a daily routine but rely on one thorough weekend cleaning swoop. In which case, still use the list above, and for further ideas turn to p. 153 for 'How to be a Working Wife'.

SPRING CLEAN FASTER

Spring cleaning is rarely necessary if you stick to a good weekly schedule. But one day when you are feeling strong and rich you could finger through the yellow book and get a professional carpet cleaner to estimate for your carpets. It's amazing what they can do. If you still use open fires call the chimney sweep; send all the curtains to be cleaned. In London you can telephone specialists, Pilgrim Payne, to collect them (01-969 3093). Look at your list of things to be mended, things to be bought and things to be overhauled.

I do this in the first week of January. It's anti-climax time and the weather is horrid, so you might as well do the nasty jobs and try not to do anything else for the rest of the year. Nobody seems to notice. The rest of the year I just make notes in the back of my diary of things to be mended or replaced, as the home inexorably disintegrates about my ears. Don't do anything that can be postponed until spring cleaning time.

Not everyone agrees with me but, temperature permitting, I believe that the best, private, spring cleaning outfit is a bikini. You can always wriggle into a sweater as well if you're not warm enough.

Spring clean with a friend (who doesn't talk *too* much) to spur you on, cheer you up, patch you up or wipe you down and – ideally – complete the job for you when you get stuck or bored. Do the same for her.

> WARNING! Mutual help is best done on an hourly basis. Her home might be twice as large and take twice as long.

PLAN A METHODICAL CAMPAIGN

Decide what you can afford to do in terms of time, money and interest.

1 Inspect your home, yet another notebook in hand, and list all the things you'd like to see clean – you'll feel so virtuous when you tick them off as each job is finished. You'll feel virtuous just making the list and doing nothing.

2 Decide what to clean and what to renew. It's only a little more trouble to paint a wall than just to scrub it. Paint costs more than water, but achieves more exciting results.

3 Check if any small jobs, such as mending electrical plugs, sash cords or chimney cleaning, have to be handled by professionals and, if so, arrange for them to be done before anything else.

4 Check that your ladder is strong and firm, that the first aid box is full, and that your paint brushes are not stiff.

5 Check your cleaning cupboard. Are your brooms balding? Is your vacuum cleaner listless? Have you got enough dusters and a ceiling broom?

6 Decide in what order the rooms will be cleaned. Clean one room at a time because you can stop right there if time runs out or you get bored. *Stop* half an hour before you had planned, because then you won't be too exhausted to clear up properly.

7 Plan the simplest catering for your family, but don't live on bread and cheese – a grilled chop and salad is almost as easy as making sandwiches.

8 Tell your nearest – who won't even have noticed that you are spring cleaning – that you'll expect him to provide a night out, say next Monday, and you'll be having a bubble bath and going to the hairdresser beforehand.

CLEANERS TO BUY

Here's a minimum list of ten household cleaners, which save money as well as shelf space.

> WARNING! Keep all these liquids away from children.

1 Household soap, in solid bar or soapflakes.

2 A biological washing machine

detergent (such as Ariel) which you can use for almost anything that's washed with water and also soak off burnt saucepans.

3 A cleansing powder which contains bleach (such as Flash).

4 Washing up liquid (such as Fairy Liquid). Alternatively, a gallon can of 'Tepol' concentrate, which you can dilute. You might also acquire a jar to put chopped left-over soap in, topped with boiling water. This results in a soft soap jelly for washing up.

5 Steel wool scouring pads (cut in half to last longer).

6 Household ammonia. Add to water for cleaning windows, pictures, glass, mirror. Also adds sparkle to silver.

7 Washing soda. Add 1 tablespoon to warm water and detergent to wash paintwork. Add 2 tablespoons to water when soaking burnt saucepans or oven racks.

8 Household bleach. Use cautiously to whiten yellowed, scorched, mildewed or stained cloth (see 'Hello Goodbye Washday', p. 49).

Bleach removes colour and acts as an antiseptic and deodorizer. It is useful for cleaning any surface that it will not damage (such as the lavatory). Shop-bought household bleaches such as Brobat are a strong mixture of chlorine bleach and disinfectant and should not be used for stain removal.

Peroxide is a mild bleach (buy 20 vol. 4 per cent hydrogen peroxide). If you dilute this 50/50 with water, you will have a very mild bleach to use for removing stains from delicate fabrics (see 'Stain Removal', p. 42).

9 Disinfectant, such as Dettol.

10 A spray oven cleaner, such as Shift.
11 Polish for floors and furniture.

CLEANERS TO MAKE YOURSELF

Partly out of interest and partly because of the high cost of convenience cleaners, I've included throughout this book quite a lot of simple, cheap 'do-it-yourself' ideas as used by Great-Grandmamma.

Window cleaner: Mix 1 cup paraffin, 1 cup water and 1 cup methylated spirit. Shake well and bottle. Rub on glass, polish off when dry. This recipe is a real winner.

Polish for chrome and paintwork: Mix 2 cups paraffin with 1 cup methylated spirit. Rub on with damp rag.

Non-slip linoleum polish (don't make near a naked flame): Place a wide-necked jar in a bowl of hot water, add 1 pint methylated spirit and 3 fl oz brown shellac, stir until dissolved, then tightly screw on lid. Wash and dry linoleum then brush on polish and leave to dry.

To remove grease stains and dirt from furniture: Mix $\frac{1}{4}$ cup methylated spirit, $\frac{1}{2}$ cup vinegar, $\frac{1}{2}$ cup turpentine and $\frac{1}{2}$ cup paraffin. Bottle and shake. Apply with rag and polish off immediately. Test first on an inconspicuous part of anything old or valuable.

Great-grandmother's furniture polish: Mix 1 cup turpentine, 2 cups linseed oil and 1 cup water. Takes a lot of rubbing, but you get a good shine.

White House furniture polish: 1 cup turpentine, 1 cup linseed oil, $\frac{1}{2}$ cup methylated spirit, $\frac{1}{2}$ cup vinegar. Mix

CLEANING

together and shake well before using. For leather and furniture. Apply with soft rag, then polish with duster.

Cooker cleaner: Dissolve 1 tablespoon caustic soda in ½ pint hot water. Separately mix 1 tablespoon flour and a little water to a thick cream. Add to soda solution, stir and bottle. Apply to cooker with mop.

> WARNING! Take great care not to spill mixture. Wear rubber gloves and don't bend over it.

Wood ash, that is left after a fire, makes a good scouring mixture and can remove stains from metal and china. Keep a jar near the sink.

Silver cleaner (given to me by a canny Scots housekeeper): Mix 1 tablespoon ammonia, 1 tablespoon powdered whitening, 1 pint boiling water. Leave for fifteen minutes. Don't bend over mixture, because it fizzes and fumes. Saturate a piece of old towelling in it and let it drip dry. Instead of using an ordinary drying up cloth, dry your silver with this and it will rarely need cleaning.

Tip from the Ritz: The Ritz cloakroom has the most sparkling silver hairbrushes in London. 'Use a spot of meths by itself on a piece of cotton wool to brighten up silver in a hurry,' says the cloakroom lady.

HOW TO BE A HOUSE~MAID

I CAN'T claim to be a comprehensive cleaner. I would no more want to read a comprehensive domestic encyclopaedia than I would want to write it. For thoroughness and idiosyncratic problems with a faint aura of mothballs I recommend *Modern Domestic Encyclopaedia* by Dorothy V. Davis, published by Faber and Faber. Just to pick at random from the index, it covers such specialist cleaning areas as hamster urine stains; elastic corsets (shouldn't go for two weeks without washing, they advise); knickers, weighty; panama hats; piano, ivory keys to whiten; serge, to remove shine from; teddy bears; swansdown; suspender belts (for when they bring back stocking tops); and wedding dress, clean to store (never know when it might come in useful again).

I learned most of what follows from a parlourmaid called Louise who had been in service after the First World War at Panshanger, one of the great Edwardian houses of England. Her two awesome tips were:

1 Work at a steady, rather fast pace. Time yourself to work up to it. A steady worker does the work in half the time.
2 When you have finished cleaning a room, stand in the doorway and look round it, slowly and critically from left to right.

CLEANING A ROOM

Close all doors and windows.

First deal with the fireplace: Rake out ash (unless it's a wood fire in which case leave it to build up a good base

25

for your fire through the winter), and remove anything solid with tongs. Brush soot from grate, remove ash pan, put in old newspaper and carry to dustbin. Sweep hearth and wipe with spongecloth.

Light a fire (or lay it ready for lighting): You need matches, newspapers, twigs, old wooden boxes or cardboard, logs or coal or smokeless fuel. In a smokeless zone you must use a smokeless fire lighter. The method I was taught came from a girl guide who insisted that fire lighters were smelly and not always to hand.

Put *loosely* screwed up newspaper balls on top of the cinders. Lay a lattice of kindling on top and around the sides. Pile on wood or coal, keeping it firmly balanced so it won't topple out of the grate. Light paper at bottom in several places so that it burns evenly. The trick is to get lots of air into the paper and kindling. Never leave a fire when it is starting and never leave it without a guard.

> WARNING! Always use a fireguard in front of a fire, whether coal, electric, gas or oil stove. After visiting a children's burns ward I wouldn't have an open bar electric fire or oil stove in the house. (A gas fire is safer because it is firmly wedged in the grate, and as it changes the air in the room frequently it does not dry the air).

Now tidy and clean: Carry a bucket or basket containing all the things you will need and a screwtop jar to empty ashtrays into (then wipe them with a clean sponge). Keep the jar in your cleaning basket, and empty it straight into the dustbin.

Dust with soft cloth folded into a pad so that there are no loose corners to catch. Carry damp sponge cloth in left hand to remove dirty or sticky marks. Dust from top downwards (highest surface first), first using a feather duster for tops of bookshelves or picture rail.

Vacuum, swab or sweep floor.

Wash paintwork if necessary. You are supposed to wash paintwork from the bottom up, but I've never understood why, and, gravity being what it is, I've always done it the other way. Use two pails, one for warm water with detergent and a spongecloth, one for rinsing with a bit of old towelling. Use a soft scrubbing brush for moulding or skirting.

Check that all the pictures hang straight.

Rinse out cleaning cloths after use and hang to dry. Don't leave damp cloths in a cupboard or they will smell sinister.

Hang brushes up *on hooks.* Never stand a brush on its bristles or the bristles will turn sideways. When brushes are dirty, wash in warm water with detergent and rinse thoroughly in clear, warm water, then cold water.

WINDOWS AND WALLS

To clean windows: Take down or draw back the curtains. Clean frames first: dust them, then wipe clean with warm water and Flash. Wipe with clean water and dry.

If window glass is very dirty, use a little warm water and 1 tablespoon methylated spirits, plus a chamois leather, finishing off with a dry chamois leather. If not very dirty use Windolene, which also cleans mirrors and picture glass. Better still, make your own! Try Old Mother Conran's amazing window cleaner (p. 23).

For luxury window cleaning there's an instrument with adjustable handle that lengthens your reach by two feet. It has a hinged sponge head which adjusts to clean all sizes of window.

Curtains: Dirty curtains will rot, so remove hooks, release gathers. Soak overnight in the bath in lukewarm water and biological washing powder. Let water out and refill bath with cold water to rinse. Let water out again, gently squeeze surplus water out, then, if necessary, wash in the correct way for the fabric.

If you allow room enough to run a rod through the bottom of your hems, net curtains will hang straight, drip dry, and possibly not need ironing.

Blinds: To clean venetian blinds *wear gloves*, rubber or otherwise, as you can hurt your hand, especially with metal blinds. Clean with warm soapy water and sponge. Dust holland blinds. Wipe specially treated blinds with detergent and water.

Don't send delicate blinds to the laundry. My coffee lace ones were wrecked by London's most expensive hand laundry. You'll do better washing them in lukewarm water gently by hand yourself. (That's all they do.) Rinse clean.

Wallpaper: Goddard's Dry Clean, which is an aerosol powder, works wonders on greasy marks. If that doesn't work, rub the stain with white bread or a soft india rubber. It's possible to cover a badly stained part with another piece of the pattern cut to fit and pasted over, but the wall-paper may have faded so the new patch may not exactly match. In fact, this is undoubtedly what will happen.

FLOORS

Ceramic tiles, terrazzo or marble: Sweep. If necessary wash by hand or mop, using hot water and synthetic detergent such as Surf.

Remove stubborn marks on quarry tiles and terrazzo with fine scouring powder (e.g. Vim) or fine steel wool.

Use Cardinal liquid polish for unglazed tiles, brickwork and cement.

Linoleum: Wash with Flash and very hot water and don't leave it soaking wet as it will crack. Dry with mop or cloth.

Cork: Sweep, vacuum or damp mop. Occasionally mop with warm water and Flash. If it has been sealed, don't polish it. Otherwise use a non-slip wax polish, using a little polish and a lot of buffing. If sealed, it can be resealed as required. A tough abrasive will rub off the costly sealed layer, so don't use one.

Remove a build-up of old wax polish with a lot of elbow grease, fine steel wool and white spirit, or liquid Ajax with ammonia. Leave fifteen minutes. Rinse, dry and rewax. Alter-natively, it can be sanded by machine (for nearest sanding firm look in your yellow pages).

Rubber, thermoplastic or vinyl: Sweep, vacuum clean or mop. Avoid rubber solvents (such as dry-cleaning fluid) and coarse abrasives. Use warm water for washing and polish with wax or plastic emulsion polish. For special cleaning use scrubbing brush or mop with hot water and detergent. Carefully remove stubborn stains with steel wool and scouring powder, then repolish. Remove a build-up of wax polish on vinyl as for cork.

Wood: pine, deal or parquet: Sweep, mop or vacuum. Wash with as little

27

warm water as possible, with detergent. If *oiled*, sweep or use an oil-impregnated mop, when required. If *wax-polished*, remove build-up of wax, as for cork. If *sealed*, you can sweep or damp-mop with water and detergent. Reseal as required. Allow about two years for heavy wear (as in a kitchen), longer in a sitting room. Can be sanded by machine.

White wood: Scrub, using hot water and detergent. Rinse with cold water, then polish when dry.

Fitted carpet: Use a good underlay. Don't use rubber underlay for a seamed carpet because it drags the seaming. Don't use it where you have underfloor electric heating.

Vacuum regularly. Use the little vacuum cleaner attachment on the edges of the carpet or they will get exceedingly grubby. You're not supposed to vacuum or carpet sweep new carpets for two weeks in order to allow the loose fibres to bed down: brush it gently, if you feel you must.

To wash a carpet: Test trial patch with shampoo. Move furniture, then:

1 Vacuum carpet.
2 Use proper carpet shampoo, with a hired proper carpet shampooer, which stops the carpet getting too wet.
3 Start at wall farthest from the door and don't replace furniture until dry.

For bad stains call a professional carpet cleaner. I've seen them work wonders.

An expensive but incredibly effective, almost magic carpet cleaner for small carpets or rugs is Johnson's Glory aerosol foam cleaner. Turn the can upside down and spray one small area at a time, then swab it with a damp sponge. Test-cleaning a 10' × 8' Persian carpet was a positive pleasure, and I felt like a TV ad housewife as I stroked away years of dirt in twenty minutes.

Carpet stains: Remove normal stains fast with mild detergent, such as '1001', well rinsed afterwards then dried by hitting with your fist wrapped in a towel. For oil, paint, polish or tar, soften with a little eucalyptus oil, then try a cleaning solvent such as Beaucaire. Start at the outside edge of stain and work inwards. If stain doesn't shift try liquid Ajax or the following carpet stain solution, which can be used for alcohol, coffee, tea, wine, food, soot, ink and fruit stains.

Carpet stain cleaner: Add 1 teaspoonful white vinegar to 1 pint made-up carpet shampoo. Lather with sponge. Rub gently until stain has gone. Rub gently with clear water.

For owners of unhouse-trained puppies or babies who are still at the stage of being amiably sick over your shoulder, there is one thing that will get rid of that rancid smell: soda water. If you take your whisky neat during this stage and don't have any soda water, just dip your handkerchief in Alka Seltzer solution or bicarbonate of soda and rub it on the spot.

To repair fitted carpet: Cut a square of damaged carpet and remove it. The golden rule is always to work from the back. Cut a square from the ½ yard of extra carpet which you thoughtfully ordered when you bought it. Cut a square of hessian 1 inch larger all round than the carpet square. With Copydex stick the new carpet centrally on the hessian square and leave to dry for five minutes. Now cover the surrounding hessian with Copydex, lift the fitted carpet square with a finger or a knife blade and slide the square into place. Then put a newspaper on top and sit on it for five minutes. The patch may look newer than the rest of the carpet, because, of course, it is. You could try rubbing a little dirt around to blur the joins.

Stair carpets: Carpet which is the full width of the stairs and continues round the stair turns looks best, but is extravagant as it will wear on the edge of the treads and you will not be able to move it up a bit – so it will wear out about *six times faster.* Keep your stair carpet as wide as possible (for good looks) but the same width throughout. Then allow an extra 18 inches rolled under at the bottom, or top, of the stairs so that you can move it up or down as it starts to wear. Use the best contract quality that you can afford and have it professionally laid, if you can. After a lifetime spent trying to skimp on stair carpet, I promise you that money saved here is money fast wasted. It's the only carpeted surface in the house on which you shouldn't economize. If you can't carpet your stairs sensibly and expensively, don't do it at all. Cover them with haircord or stain the treads, which will then be very noisy.

Old, valuable carpets: Antique shops don't shampoo them. They hang them over a line and beat them. Sorry about that. Seriously, if you have an expensive rug don't risk washing it yourself. Send them to real experts (look in the yellow book) who will wash them with Johnson's baby soap and rinse them in gallons of specially purified water, then put them on special racks to dry.

Cleaning long-haired rugs: Handwash in lukewarm water using a mild detergent. Rinse thoroughly with a fabric softener and allow to dry

naturally. (It will take ages.) Brush pile gently.

How then do you clean a fur rug like white sheep or goat skin? Same way as you would a white sheep or goat. With lots of hot water and soap. Try Stergene. Rinse thoroughly (in the bath?).

FURNITURE

If you put antique or modern furniture too near any heat source it may crack or shrivel. This often occurs after installing central heating unless humidifiers or bowls of water (with flowers in them, perhaps) are placed in the room. If it's a centrally heated house I always stand a jug of water by a bowl of flowers. Then you can dash forward and top them up as soon as they wilt.

If you put furniture in a damp atmosphere (such as a bathroom) it may swell. Drawers might therefore be difficult to pull open. Rub soap or candle grease on the runners of the drawers which stick.

Dust furniture and occasionally wipe clean with a damp chamois leather followed by a dry duster. To remove stickiness or fingermarks use a damp chamois cloth or a cloth wrung out in warm water and detergent.

DON'T polish on a damp surface or white patches will appear.

WOOD

Much modern furniture is not solid but uses a sandwich of wood veneer on plywood or blockboard (which is built-up strips of wood). Plywood is particularly useful for curves and blockboard is unlikely to warp. Wood is very absorbent, and must be treated with a finish which protects it from moisture, grease and dirt. These protective finishes determine the final texture of the wood, whether it has a high gloss, a dull gloss or a matt look.

Wax-polished furniture is treated with beeswax made into a stiff paste with turpentine and rubbed well into the wood. You can use a standard wax furniture polish instead.

For mass-produced wood finishes, apart from satin, matt, oiled, or French-polished surfaces, occasionally rub with a soft cloth and a cream or liquid polish. Johnson's aerosol Pledge is a good polish for wood (also leather and vinyl upholstery, porcelain, enamel and glass).

An oil finish is generally achieved with linseed oil and turpentine, rubbed into wood. You should continue to dust, then rub with an oily rag, if you want to keep the same appearance. Use teak oil, which you get from a classy furniture store such as Heal's, or Johnson's teak cream, from a supermarket. Don't use much oil. Try not to use any other oil as it goes horribly sticky.

If a *permanent seal* finish has been applied, then don't waste your time polishing it.

Layers of shellac dissolved in spirit have been lovingly built up and rubbed down to get the gleaming finish of *French polish*. It only needs dusting, although you may occasionally apply a little cream or liquid wax polish.

Don't polish a *satin* or *matt* finish or it may become glossy.

To remove polish from furniture use a solution of 1 tablespoon vinegar to 1 pint warm water. Dry and repolish.

How do you clean the *brass inlay on a polished antique* when you don't want to use some vicious modern brass cleaner for fear of what it might do to the surrounding wood? Use a neutral shoe cream, such as Meltonian.

Painted furniture: Can be washed with detergent and warm water.

Perspex and Acrylic: Clean with spray-on Windolene or Perspex Polish No. 3 from Habitat.

Plastics: Can be washed with warm water and detergent. Don't rub dry, because this increases static, which collects dust. Remove stains by rubbing with a damp cloth dipped in bicarbonate of soda.

Slate: Clean with warm water and detergent, then, when dry, rub with a rag moistened in cooking oil, then rub off with a dry cloth.

Marble: Can stain because it's porous. Clean with soapy water; whiten by rubbing with a lemon. Also clean with Bell 1967 Cleaner (1). Polish with Bell's Marble Polish (2). For stained marble use Rustic Marble Cleaner but this will dull the polished surface which can only be restored by expert polishing. All from A. Bell and Co., Kingsthorpe Works, Northampton (tel. 0604 22821).

UPHOLSTERY

Leather upholstery: Clean with a soft cloth dipped in warm soapsuds, followed by a soft cloth in clear water, then dry with a soft cloth. Leather is skin and needs polishing with furniture cream to keep it supple and prevent cracks. Or use saddle soap.

Plastic upholstery: Use a car upholstery cleaner such as Groom or Valet from Halfords. Don't use abrasive cleaners on any plastics as they may scratch. Reinforced plastics can be repaired with car body repair kits, then repainted with polyurethane paint.

Fabric-covered upholstery: Clean by taking out the cushions and vacuuming or brushing out the corners. Shampoo periodically with carpet shampoo or a detergent with warm water and gentle scrubbing brush – working on one area at a time and being careful to overlap each area with the next. Avoid using too much water.

Loose covers: Dry clean if possible, as they are less likely to shrink. Otherwise wash in lukewarm water. Make sure washing powder has dissolved before putting in fabric. Treat gently. Squeeze or spin damp-dry. Don't twist or wring. Iron, on wrong side if possible, while still damp and immediately replace on chair, while the seams are still slightly damp; they will then stretch out. (I never bother to iron.)

Wickerwork and Cane: Wash in hot water and detergent (in the bath is a good place) and rinse three times more than you thought necessary. Otherwise the cane will quickly split.

LIGHT FITTINGS AND PICTURES

If possible, remove fittings to clean. Alternatively, get a steady stool or ladder if they are at ceiling level. Wear rubber gloves. Turn off switch. Wipe bulb. (You can lose 25 per cent of your light with a grimy bulb.) Dust with a feather duster, especially paper shades.

Try to remove dirt marks with a gum eraser, or try a (just) damp cloth. Wash acrylic shades with warm soapy water (I wash them in the bath). Let them drain on a towel: don't rub them or you will increase static, which attracts dirt. (It's worth telling you this twice.)

Clean glass and frames of pictures with a chamois damped with methylated spirit.

FURNITURE STAINS REMOVAL

Light stains left by glasses on marble: Try 2 teaspoons borax in $\frac{1}{2}$ pint water. Dry and polish.

Ink stains: Rub with fine dry steel wool or glass paper. Dab with a hot solution of weak acid and rinse. As you have now removed both colour and polish, rub in linseed oil to darken. Leave to soak in, then the next day or so give it a coat of polish and buff well. It's best to try this out first on a bit of the wood which doesn't show.

Rust stains: Remove with Rust Eater or Naval Jelly, both from Halfords.

White rings and heat marks on a French-polished surface: Try a very little methylated spirit rubbed on with a soft cloth. Repolish with brown shoe polish while the surface is still soft.

Cigarette burns: Rub down with fine steel wool or glass paper. Then rub in linseed oil and proceed as above.

Wine or spirit marks: You can rarely remove these if they have been left on a table too long.

Candlegrease: Scrape off as much as possible with a blunt knife. If the grease is on the carpet or upholstery cover it with tissue or blotting paper and hold a hot iron just clear of the paper, so that it warms the wax, which you blot, using a fresh bit of tissue each time. If it is on fabric, place between two bits of blotting paper and iron. Then clean with dry-cleaning fluid. Work from middle of stain to edge.

Grease marks on sofa backs and arms or bedheads: Rub gently with cloth and dry-cleaning fluid. Work from outer edge of stain inwards. Then (if necessary), repeat with chamois leather wrung out in a solution of warm water and a liquid detergent. Rinse well.

To remove scratches: White shoe polish can hide scratches on white woodwork. For dark scratches try touching up with iodine or shoe polish or try to eliminate bad marks by rubbing down gently with finest wirewool, then resurfacing. Alternatively, try darkening with iodine or olive oil on the end of a nail file wrapped in cotton wool. A much scratched item can be professionally sanded or resealed.

To destroy woodworm: You can either buy a special insecticide and apply it or holler for help from an expert, such as Rentokil. I wouldn't take any chances here as woodworm spreads to other furniture, window frames, floorboards, beams, etc. Never import any bit of furniture into your home without checking it for those sinister tiny holes.

BEDROOMS

Cupboards and Drawers: Empty cupboard, wipe with spongecloth dipped in detergent and warm water, then wrung out. Don't get the wood too wet. When dry, line cupboards and drawers with paper to prevent bottoms getting dirty again; wallpaper or lining paper is often prettiest. If you haven't much

storage space, stack shoes on plastic racks piled on top of each other, as in a shop; keep underwear and small articles in clear plastic bags; hang hooks inside doors and stretch elastic between two drawing pins to hold ties and belts.

Mattresses: Take the polythene wrappings off mattresses and pillows or they may eventually mildew. A flock, feather or hair mattress should be turned from end to end daily (thought I'd let you know). A spring interior needs turning only once a month.

Sheets: Mark the corner of each sheet 'S' for single, 'D' for double, 'K' for kingsize and so on. Although you can feel the difference in weight, one has days when one isn't certain of *anything* and they certainly aren't improved by unfolding and folding up clean sheets for half the morning. Reasonably, the middle of a sheet is the part which somebody puts his foot through first, when it's wearing thin (the sheet that is). Try to anticipate this. When sheets are showing signs of wear but before they get too thin, cut them down the middle and join the two outside edges together with a flat seam, then hem the two outside edges.

Darn holes in sheets by sewing a square patch on either side, considerably bigger than the hole.

Sheets can yellow through too warm storage. Send them to the laundry with a note or wash using a mild powder bleach, not a strong household bleach, which might rot the fibres.

Blankets: Before washing, soak really dirty blankets in the bath in cold water with added softener such as Calgon. Blankets can be turned sides to middle, like sheets, when they have become thin and worn. Another use for aged blankets is this old campers' trick. Use three thin blankets underneath the bottom sheet and you will never need an electric under-blanket.

Hair brushes: Wash in warm water with detergent, but expensive wooden-backed teak, rosewood or ebony hair brushes shouldn't be *immersed* in water. Rinse in clear warm water then finally slosh in cold water to harden the bristles, and wave fiercely and quickly to flick the water out, before lying on their backs to dry, away from direct heat.

BATHROOM CLEAN-UP

Clean bathroom routine: Owners of small children might find it worthwhile to keep a brush, dustpan and wastepaper basket in, and exclusively for, the bathroom, so you can deal with those sweet papers, old lavatory rolls, empty detergent packets, and foot and talcum powder.

Remove hair spray from mirrors with a mop soaked in surgical spirit.

The Bath: I find a hand shower invaluable for bathing children, getting boys to wash themselves and rinsing hair, but *especially* for cleaning the bath.

More backs may have been put out cleaning baths than in any other activity. If you have serious stain problems that just won't yield to elbow grease, these tips from *Ideal Standard* may help.

Don't use an abrasive cleaner on the bath, because it may scratch the surface. Try liquid Gumption or dry detergent powder. Never use lavatory cleaner in the bath, it's too harsh.

For coppery green and tan stains, cut a lemon and smear the juice (citric acid) on the offending areas. Leave for a couple of minutes and wash off thoroughly.

For general grime and dinge, run a full hot bath and empty biological washing powder into it. Leave the foamy mess for at least six hours, then rinse out the bath with cold water.

Blizzard removes even lime stains as well as scum and rust.

Clean chrome bath taps with cloth and soapy water. Polish with a soft cloth. If stains persist, rub on dry bicarbonate of soda with a damp cloth. If that doesn't work use Duraglit for chrome, or Salo Autosal, a German product.

The Lavatory: Keep your lavatory brush in water with a little disinfectant. You don't have to buy a smart holder. I keep mine in a stone marmalade jar.

Clean lavatory by lifting the seat and pouring down a bucket of hot water with bleach or detergent and a disinfectant such as Dettol. Brush with the long-handled lavatory brush and swab outside of lavatory and seat with spongecloth. A dirty lavatory pan can be cleaned with shop-bought Harpic or chlorine bleach (never both, because it produces chlorine gas vapour). Alternatively, for very bad stains on lavatory or bath, use RB70 from Selfridges. As a last resort, wipe with one part spirits of salts to five parts water. *Wear rubber gloves* as this can be dangerous. Rub stain quickly with a mop or brush dipped in spirits of salts which can then be thrown away. Flush three times.

You can buy a disc which you can attach to the inside of the bowl in order to turn the water blue (or sometimes green). Similarly discs which create a miasma of mothballs. You might try to dissipate unwelcome odours by opening a window or use freshener such as Airwick.

33

HOW TO BE A HOUSEMAID

Lavatories are meant for human waste and nothing else. Anything else is likely to block a lavatory and that includes large wedges of toilet paper, newspaper, sanitary towels or tea leaves. If your lavatory gets blocked holler for a plumber (in yellow pages).

Similarly exterior *drains* must be kept unblocked. Don't let leaves block them up. If they threaten to do so, get a wire cage (a bit like a beekeeper's bonnet) fitted round it. Occasionally *flush the drain by pouring boiling water* with a handful of washing soda down it. If there seems to be something badly wrong or a smell which gets worse, or you see a rat (or smell one), telephone the local town hall and ask for quick help from the sanitary department.

KITCHEN CLEAN-UP

Clean kitchen routine: Put food away, check larder and tidy everything on to trolley. Clean windows, ledges and working surfaces, then the equipment.

To clean a cooker: Turn off electricity at main or all gas pilots. Turn off taps or switches, remove any utensils. Half fill sink with hot water and detergent. Remove grill pan, burners, shelves and trays and put in sink to soak if there is room. Wipe enamelled parts with warm damp sponge cloth. Use liquid Gumption for stubborn dirt on cooker enamel (or sinks). You're not supposed to use a harsh abrasive or a caustic cleaner on enamel areas or the inside of an oven, but if you are faced with a filthy oven buy a spray cleaner, such as Shift, or make your own (see p. 23). Otherwise clean oven with hot water and detergent. Scrub burners (if you have a gas cooker), grill pan, shelves or trays (if you have an electric cooker), rinse and dry, and then replace. Remember to light gas pilots and test or turn on electricity at the main.

To clean a solid fuel cooker: Wipe spills immediately. Regularly brush out oven. Wipe enamel parts with damp cloth and rub dry, or use liquid Gumption or a spray cleaner if really dirty.

Cleaning a grill pan: Unable to find out how to clean the exterior of a really filthy oven and grill pan I eventually telephoned the manufacturers. 'You shouldn't have let it get filthy,' they chided me severely. Apart from it being none of their business it was an unhelpful answer, because I had just bought the filthy oven along with the filthy flat.

If the handle is plastic remove it. (You may need a Philips screwdriver. Remember, they hitched it on somehow; all you have to do is find out what they did and reverse it.) Now attack with Flash and Brillo pads and to hell with those gentle warm water instructions.

The kitchen sink: Clean the sink with hot water and washing up liquid. Don't use a scourer on a metal sink or you may scratch it. Clean the sink outlet by dissolving a handful of washing soda in warm water and pouring it down the sink and the outside drain. Alternatively, you can use household bleach.

Anything, except water, is likely to block a sink (unless you have a fitted electrical waste disposal). That includes matchsticks, tea leaves and vegetable peelings. So use a sink drainer and buy a sink plunger, which is a stick with a black rubber hollow breast shape on the end of it.

If the sink blocks, turn to p. 119

34

for HOW TO UNBLOCK A SINK.

The kitchen floor: Brush, mop or wash. By all means have a sponge mop, but you will not, when operating it, be able to see clearly how dirty the kitchen floor is. Again, disregard the magic ads on TV. What do you do ? Scrub it when it's dirty like your mother did, but now with Flash, which is the eighth wonder of my world. (See also FLOORS, p. 27.)

Refrigerator care: A refrigerator won't do its job of keeping food fresh if you leave the door open or jam in so much food that the cold air can't circulate around the food. If the cooling unit gets clogged up with ice it can't do its job efficiently. Don't leave a refrigerator shut if you turn off the gas or electricity when you go on holiday. The inside may be spotted with nasty green mould when you open it on your return and the rubber ice trays may have perished. Rubber ice trays are the sort which allow you to take out one cube when you feel like it, without holding the thing under a tap or hitting it on the bottom with a hammer.

Wrap all food in polythene bags or keep in covered boxes or bowls, or wrap and cover with Saranwrap. Otherwise the kippers may impart their flavour to the raspberry mousse which may in turn add an interesting *je ne sais quoi* to the camembert, which you shouldn't keep in the refrigerator anyway, because it is a soft cheese.

If you haven't an automatic defrosting refrigerator you should defrost the fridge once a fortnight. Turn off the refrigerator. Take all the food out and throw away anything from the back which is growing whiskers or looks too small to survive. Now take out the shelves and empty the ice tray. Wash the shelves and plastic boxes and bowls with warm water and a little bicarbonate of soda. You shouldn't use detergent, because it can leave a soapy smell if you don't rinse it off thoroughly.

Wait for the ice to melt. You can hurry this up by leaving the door open and putting a washing up bowl of hot water in the middle of the refrigerator. You had better put a tray or folded towel or both on the bottom shelf or melted ice will run all over the kitchen floor.

.

LARDER CARE

Don't put away jars or tins with drips on them. Clean floor and shelves with warm, damp spongecloth. Fold packet tops over *before* putting away and regularly wipe out bread, cake and biscuit tins.

EATING EQUIPMENT

Pans and Dishes: If you are left with a nasty burnt mess in your saucepans try soaking them overnight in lukewarm water and a handful of biological detergent. Before using a pan for the first time, wash with spongecloth and warm soapy water, or whatever you cook first may taste rather odd. Don't put pans straight on to a high heat. Don't leave empty pans on burners or in the oven.

If Teflon parts discolour, try mixing 2 tablespoons baking soda, $\frac{1}{4}$ cup of household bleach and 1 cup water. Boil solution in the stained pan for five minutes. Wash, rinse and dry. Wipe with oil before using.

35

Non-stick pans: Don't use abrasives and scourers or you may remove the non-stick surface. Don't use metal implements such as spoons; use wood or plastic spoons. Don't store non-stick pans in each other or they may scratch.

Aluminium pans: Don't scrape with a metal spoon, as it scratches the surface. Don't use washing soda, which is bad for aluminium. Don't use a harsh scouring pad. If you shove a hot aluminium frying pan into water it will hiss and perhaps buckle. Cool it first. If food has been burnt or fish cooked in it boil up a little water with washing up liquid in it *before* you take it off the stove. If the insides of aluminium pans discolour, boil up some water in them with a squeezed lemon, or rhubarb leaves.

Copper pans: Should be lined with silver, nickel or tin. Unlined copper develops poisonous verdigris so reline when necessary and use wooden spoons for stirring. Antique shops can often quote for relining copper pans.

Clean copper with half a lemon dipped in salt and vinegar and rubbed on. Alternatively, use Goddard's long-term brass and copper polish. You don't end up with a smelly rag to throw away if you use Duraglit wadding metal polish (it also cleans pewter). Rub corrosion spots with salt and vinegar or a lemon rind dipped in salt, then wash. Treat bad marks with fine steel wool and liquid polish.

Vitreous pans: If they discolour inside, fill with a solution of bleach and leave overnight, then wash thoroughly.

Ovenproof dishes: Not necessarily flameproof, so don't use on top of the stove unless you are certain. I lost a wonderful Worcester fish dish that way. Play safe and always use an asbestos mat on an electric hob, but on no account try any of these tricks on a naked gas flame because the cooker enamel could be damaged.

Always check whether your dishes are ovenproof. Unless they are stamped 'ovenproof' assume they are *not*, however ovenish they look.

Don't put anything plastic or with plastic handles in the oven or it will probably start melting.

Hot dishes and plates straight from the oven can mark wood, plastic, tablecloths, painted surfaces. Don't ever risk it. (Plastics aren't magic and can scratch, burn and chip.) Buy cheap, natural cork table mats.

Pyrosil ware: Not non-stick, but you can freeze dishes in it and then take it straight from the freezer to a hot oven and the dish won't crack. That's why they make rocket nose-cones with the stuff. There's a hook-on handle which enables you to use dishes as saucepans.

CLEANING ORNAMENTS, UTENSILS

Brass and bronze: If it's lacquered it doesn't need cleaning, only dusting. If it isn't lacquered and not for cooking, why not lacquer it with brass lacquer? Ask in a hardware shop for cellulose clear lacquer. It dries very fast – in about ten minutes – and hardens in an hour. If it is for cooking, treat as copper pans. Clean with Brasso or Bluebell.

Pewter: For heavy stains try cleaning with a brass polish, such as Brasso or Bluebell. Don't use silver polish. For mild stains and everyday cleaning use Aquinas Pewter Polish from the Pewter Centre, 87 Abingdon Road, London, W.8. (tel. 01-937 4118).

Silver: Goddard's Long Life is an excellent fast silver cleaner. Alternatively, make your own (see p. 23).

If possible, keep a silver bag. Smart stores like Harrods sell yard long baize bags with divisions for each different implement. This also means that silver is stored in the minimum space. You might make your own.

Never let bleach get near silver, the result is a disastrous stain impossible to move.

Brides have been known to burst into tears as yet another wedding gift, thinly silver-plated sauceboat, turns irrevocably, uncleanably black before the first anniversary. Having had the same trouble myself I won't bother you with pages of tedious chemical reasoning. Eventually, after rubbing my sauceboat with all sorts of never-fail Kwick Kleen preparations, I had it replated.

If you wish your sauceboat to gleam when its donor comes to dinner, then you should always wash the relevant item as soon as possible after the meal. *Never* leave sauce in a sauceboat; not gravy; not mayonnaise; not vinaigrette; never. Similarly, never leave sauces in any other silver container, such as a bowl, or on spoons. I lost a lovely rat tail teaspoon through leaving it in a jar of chutney. The silver was eaten away.

Get egg tarnish off silver by using Goddard's Silver-Dip for quick results. For general cleaning, however, try Goddard's Long Life.

To clean a silver teapot, fill it with boiling water and add 1 teaspoonful denture cleaner. Leave overnight and rinse well.

Cutlery: Vinegar, lemon juice, egg and salt can mark cutlery, so wash as fast as possible. Don't use Silver-Dip on stainless steel because it pits it.

Keep knives in a drawer or jar by themselves and you are less likely to cut yourself or scratch other implements. Don't leave ivory or plastic handled knives in hot water or put in the washing machine. Carbon steel knives should be wiped clean after use and rubbed with cooking oil before putting away. Remove stains with emery paper. Sharpen on carborundum stone.

Don't use abrasive powders on trays with a printed pattern (especially tin trays) or you risk scratching the pattern off.

China and glass: Don't pile things in a cupboard unless they are designed to stack. China is at risk if stored too high, too low, or too far back in a cupboard. Things which are difficult to reach are more likely to get broken.

Remove tea stains from china with a damp cloth dipped in bicarbonate of soda, or borax. Butlers clean glass decanters or narrow-necked glass vases by swilling them round with brandy and lead shot. *You* can soak them overnight in biological detergent and warm water. Best to avoid stains by rinsing out the decanter as soon as possible after use.

Natural materials are not static. They expand with heat and contract with cold and damp according to the way they are treated. If you hold a glass under the hot tap it may crack. If you pour hot water into a glass, put a spoon in first to absorb the heat.

Wood: Don't leave in too warm a place, and never dry near direct heat, or it may split. Don't leave soaking in water. Don't put in the dishwasher.

Scrub chopping boards and untreated wooden working surfaces clean with Vim or Flash and scrubbing brush. Rinse well with cold water.

Wipe salad bowls with paper, then the oil will soak into the wood. If it smells, wash in warm soapy water, then rinse thoroughly.

GETTING RID OF THE GARBAGE

An electric waste disposal unit in the sink eliminates the sludgy smelly stuff. Get the sort that unclogs itself when you push a button, otherwise you may have to call a mechanic every time it clogs itself up. Whatever brand you use and however careful you are, you will need four times as many teaspoons as you had before. They seem to trap them, like insect-eating orchids.

Pedal bins drive me scatty because they generally have inadequate base balance, and are therefore unsteady and tip drunkenly towards me every time I tread on the pedal. And they don't take enough of my rubbish. I use plastic, waist-high kitchen bins, which stack when empty. I have four of them. I keep one of them in the kitchen and the rest, whether empty or full, in the dustbin area. (I don't have dustbins). Or use one bin with disposable plastic sacks.

Wall-mounted litter sacks: I haven't the patience to push each one into place. Also, everyone in the family, except me, invariably overfills them so that the bags fall downwards out of their holder, and then there's a mess on the floor to clean up.

Dustbins: Metal ones make a noise and get bent, plastic ones get split; hence my choice of kitchen bins. Paint your name on them (use emulsion paint) if you don't want them pinched. I wash mine in the bath with warm water and detergent and a stiff brush, rinse with clear water and disinfectant, and then tip them upside down to dry, still in the bath.

Keep a pack of plastic dustbin liners in your kitchen paper drawer for those moments when all your dustbins are full and you need a sack for further rubbish.

GETTING RID OF NASTY SMELLS

How do you get rid of a persistent nasty smell, such as in a bedsitter that seems to have housed a dozen cats ? It's amazing to think that our ancestors dealt with this problem before anyone thought of disguising the odour with synthetic daffodil spray. They used to open windows and doors to create a draught, and you can continue the tradition. To help the smell on its way buy an Airwick, burn joss sticks, incense, burning perfumes from Floris and Mary Chess, or scented candles.

You can avoid those nasty cut-out circles in windows which are expensively let into the glass and create draughts by installing an electric ventilating fan in your kitchen (get a strong one).

To rid clothes of cooking smells or tobacco fumes, hang them in the open air for several hours. To get rid of the smell of perspiration on clothes, wash, rinse thoroughly in warm water with a little added vinegar, then rinse in clear lukewarm water and dry, if possible in the open air.

To remove a persistent smell of onion or fish from knives, push them to the hilt in earth (your kitchen window box of herbs).

Add 1 teaspoon mustard powder to the washing up water to get the smell of fish off silver and add 1 teaspoon vinegar to remove it from china. If you can't get rid of a smell in a saucepan, try boiling a little neat vinegar in it for a minute.

For cutting down a paint smell, cut an onion in two and put it cut sides up in the room while you're painting. Then throw it away.

HOW TO WASH UP

With two sinks, or a sink and a rinsing bowl and two washing up racks, you rarely need to dry up, although you can polish glass and cutlery. Breakages happen if too many things are crowded into the bowl or piled up to drain. If you are right-handed and planning a kitchen from scratch, remember that you will wash up from right to left, so plan to have the draining surface on the left.

If there's only one drainer and not much space round the sink use a nearby table to stack and then to drain, or pull up a trolley behind you (or to one side) on which to stack the dishes. (Glasses and cutlery, plates and cups on top, serving dishes on lower shelf and cooking pots beneath.) As you clear one surface use it for draining. Spread a tea towel on any drying surface which doesn't drain into the sink.

Washing up starts with *proper stacking*. Helpful men tend to pile things into a sink, higgledy piggledy, run warm water on them and then leave them. These men probably never have to reach into the greasy cold water to remove the dishes in order to put in hot water to start actually doing the washing up. If they do wash up, men never remove mustard from the undersides of plates and they think that saucepans, baking tins and vegetable dishes don't count or get done by leprechauns.

Empty coffee grounds or tea leaves. Scrape bits off plates and stack crockery and utensils according to size and greasiness.

Put cutlery and table silver to soak in a jug or saucepan of hot water and detergent. Keep bone or wooden handles out of water.

Wash articles in this order: glass, silver, cutlery, non-greasy china, non-greasy serving pans, greasy china, greasy serving pans, cooking pans. Wash glass in warm water and detergent and rinse in clear warm water. Use a soft nail brush for cut glass.

Clean sink outlet. Empty sink basket, then wash it. Wipe cooker and grill pan, drainer, sink. Rinse dishcloth and spread to dry.

For the cheapest possible washing up liquid, buy a concentrate called Tepol, in a gallon can, and decant it into a bottle or squirt container. If you want to make it 'kind to your hands' dilute it with water.

NOTE: Never put antique or hand-painted or valuable china or bone-handled knives (or wood or plastic anything) into a dishwasher. Probably the manufacturers are cautiously covering themselves because I have heard of a family which eats entirely from Melaware and uses a dishwasher for it. You might risk a trial run with a plastic article, if it is not valuable.

Read the instructions book *before* using the dishwasher for the first time.

CONFESSIONS OF A DRY CLEANER'S DAUGHTER

Speaking treacherously as a dry cleaner's daughter, I would say you can save yourself a lot of cleaning bills if you equip yourself with a stain removal kit (see p. 42). Keep it in a drawer out of reach of children. Label all bottles.

Whatever the stain, if there's nothing available with which to treat it, act immediately by soaking in lots of *cold water*. If cold water doesn't remove the stain try using lukewarm water and ordinary soap. *Never use hot water or you may permanently set the stain.*

The seven golden rules of stain-shifting are these:

1 Treat stains as fast as possible.
2 Never use hot water.
3 Treat from the wrong side of the fabric, if possible, so that the dirt needn't be pushed right through it.
4 If coloured, check effect of remover on an unimportant part of the fabric. Test all chemicals first on an inconspicuous area.
5 After using a chemical, rinse well in lukewarm water.
6 Use a weak solution several times, rather than one strong solution.
7 Avoid leaving a ring in place of the stain by this old trick I learned at my daddy's knee known in the trade as 'spotting'. When using a chemical always make a ring larger than the stained area then gradually work in towards the stain, never vice versa. Treat potential water rings in the same way. After treatment, place the still wet article on a towel and thump the fabric dry with another towel, working *round the*

edge of the treated area, and towards the middle.

The theory of stain removal is to either dissolve the stain or wash it out. If you don't know a specific treatment choose one of these three main rough and ready treatments.

Water-soluble items (from kindergarten paint to toothpaste): Sponge or rub gently under cold, or at most lukewarm, water, with soap if it's persistent.

Protein stains: Soak for several hours or overnight in cold water in which has been dissolved a little biological enzyme powder (such as Ariel). This breaks down the protein molecules in stains such as urine, sweat, blood, milk, egg, tea, coffee, fruit, vegetable and wine stains. Enzymes are ineffective in water hotter than 140°F (hand-hot water is 122° F).

> WARNING! Fabrics which are wool, silk, flameproof or not colour-fast shouldn't be soaked. Wash quickly in a solution of warm water and enzyme detergent.

Fat, oil and grease stains: Dab with a cotton wool pad soaked in dry cleaner's carbon tetrachloride on the dry fabric. It dissolves rubber, so don't use on rubber-backed items. Work near an open window so that slight fumes evaporate fast.

Don't use grease solvent on plastic or expanded polystyrene as they may dissolve. Try washing in a solution of warm water and synthetic detergent.

A friend of mine, who runs a hotel and whose life is filled with nameless stains, always tries a dab of eucalyptus oil on unknown old, dried-out stains and leaves it to 'lift' the stain, then removes the eucalyptus oil with dry-cleaning solvent.

To remove stubborn stains such as scorch, mildew or make-up marks: Test fabric on a seam which doesn't show, then damp garment and immerse it in a 50/50 solution of peroxide and water. Watch it: don't walk away. Wash thoroughly, then rinse and dry. I once scorched a beautiful pink suit, gave it to a friend for Oxfam and, to my chagrin, saw her wearing it the next week without the scorch mark. This was the method she used to remove it.

Bleach should never be used on a fabric which has a special finish, such as drip-dry.

If you don't know what a mystery stain is and you don't want to risk removing it yourself, take the garment to a dry cleaner, point out the stain (otherwise it may not be noticed and it will be returned to you) and firmly state that that stain is the only reason you want the garment cleaned. If you are on friendly terms with your dry cleaner, ask him how he's going to treat it. At least he will have to stop and think about it. Try to patronize a cleaner who cleans in his own shop; then you will also know where that lost button is most likely to be.

Never buy anything white that *must* be dry cleaned; it will always come back from the cleaners pale grey, because dry-cleaning spirit isn't white in the first place, and when your Wimbledon white wedding dress has been whirled round in a machine with a lot of seemingly demob suits, it will never regain its first, virgin bloom.

STAIN REMOVAL KIT
(A real money-saver)

General: A bucket and a box containing the following:

packet of tissues; two small sponges; two old handkerchiefs; ordinary clothes brush; wire clothes brush (use gently, it's a ruthless weapon); Sellotape (for wrapping round knuckles, sticky side out, then dabbing at fluff on a dark suit); spray can of Goddard's anti-wrinkle 'Smart'; spray can of Goddard's aerosol dry-clean spray (removes spots without leaving a ring, and especially good for ties); heavy pudding basin (not plastic); biological **detergent**.

Water soluble stains: bicarbonate of soda; bottle washing soda; small jar of soapless detergent; salts of lemon or Noval; Steradent false tooth cleaner.

Fat, oil and grease stains: methylated spirit; glycerine; benzine; turpentine; eucalyptus oil; Polystripper (to soften hard paint); Polyclens oil paint remover; white spirit; grease solvent such as carbon tetrachloride or Beaucaire (use near open window to blow away fumes).

You may also need the following: india rubber (for wallpaper); blotting paper (for sealing wax); acetone (for nail varnish); powdered denture cleaner (for stained teapots).

HOW TO SHIFT THE STAINS IN YOUR LIFE

(Please forgive some repetitions, I want a quick, comprehensive reference.)

Adhesive tape: This leaves sticky patches on your injured finger. Use carbon tetrachloride or acetone.

Animal messes: Sponge with borax solution (1 pint water to 1 dessertspoon borax). Won't smell as much if you squirt the area with soda water.

Ballpoint pen: Soak with methylated spirit.

Beer: Sponge immediately with plenty of clear cold water.

Bird droppings: Dissolve in half a bucket of warm water, a handful of washing soda and 1 tablespoon soapless detergent. Scrub the droppings with it.

Candlewax: Although any manicurist or Latin lover will tell you never to use them as weapons, scrape as much wax as possible off with your fingernails. If the wax is on wood do the best you can by rubbing with fingernail and ball of finger. If the wax is staining a cloth, place blotting paper over the stain, iron over it with a hot iron and attack any remaining stain with carbon tetrachloride.

Carbon paper: On fingers or clothing. Use carbon tetrachloride.

Chewing gum: To freeze-harden the gum rub with a cube of ice (in polythene bag to prevent wetting the material), scrape as much as possible off with a fingernail, then use carbon tetrachloride.

Coffee, tea (and – I discovered recently – curry on pink dressing gown): Instant action essential. Sponge with borax and warm water.

Dandelion: Use biological detergent.

Emulsion paint: see under Paint.

Felt pen: Water-soluble. Soak immediately, then use soap and water.

Fruit (including tomato sauce): Wash out immediately in cold water, then warm water with biological powder. Wash delicate fabrics in cold water, then work glycerine into stain and leave for one hour to 'float' the stain off, then wash out with detergent and warm water. On non-washable fabrics leave glycerine for several hours, then sponge with liquid detergent and water. Better still, always tuck your napkin in your neck when eating spaghetti napolitaine or peaches, regardless of the company, because a fruit stain is potential disaster.

Grass or seaweed: Spot with methylated spirit, then wash thoroughly.

Hair lacquer (on mirror): Wipe with methylated spirit.

Ice cream: Use carbon tetrachloride and then wash.

Iron mould: Drip on a solution of salts of lemon (2 teaspoonfuls to $\frac{1}{2}$ pint warm water), rinse well, then wash. Or rust remover, such as Noval, from Boots.

Jam: Soak in warm borax solution (1 pint water to 1 oz borax), then wash.

Latex adhesive: Can be removed with special remover made by Copydex.

Lipstick: Use carbon tetrachloride, followed by soap and warm water.

Make-up: Mostly grease. Remove even the powder round your neckline with carbon tetrachloride followed by soap and water.

Mildew: Brush off as much as possible, then sponge with hydrogen peroxide and rinse thoroughly.

Paint: If you are painting, buy 2 pints Polyclens or 2 pints white spirit – when you need it you need it quick and plentiful (as when you've upset a tin of paint on the Chinese carpet).

A pool of paint: First spoon up all you can of the free liquid, working from the edge inwards so as not to enlarge the area affected. Then mop with newspaper, then tissues.

Emulsion paint: Wash *immediately* with lots of cold water. If stain has set, try methylated spirit, but I don't hold out much hope on an old stain. You could pick at it with a comb or thumb and forefinger.

Oil paint on natural fibres: Mop up.

Soak immediately and liberally with Polyclens, then wash with lots and lots of cold water. If you have no Polyclens remember the way an artist cleans oil brushes. Wipe with newspaper, rub with a rag soaked in turps or white spirit, then wash in warm soapy water.

Oil paint on artificial fabrics and most plastics (including patent floor tiles): Soak with white spirit until all traces of paint are gone, then wash with lukewarm water and detergent.

Oil or emulsion paint which has set: Cross fingers, and apply a little Polystripper – this will quickly soften the paint. It may soften everything else as well so stand by with lots of water to stop the rot. Once softened, old paint stains can be treated as fresh paint stains. Polyclens is wonderful stuff for taming oil paint (and varnish, polyurethane sealers, etc.). The only snag is that it dissolves any plastics and also adhesives, so if you don't watch out you can really come unstuck. It is also good for cleaning paint brushes – just dunk thoroughly in Polyclens for five minutes then hold under the cold tap.

Rust: Dab with a commercial rust remover such as Noval.

Scorch marks: Rinse immediately in cold running water, sponge with borax and water. If this has no result try a weak solution of hydrogen peroxide.

Seawater:

1 On fabrics: Sponge with warm water to dissolve salt. If stain persists, spot with methylated spirit, then launder or dry clean.

2 On shoes: Try 2 teaspoons methylated spirits to 1 dessertspoon milk. Rub on, leave to dry, then repolish. If unsuccessful buy and apply overall shoe dye of the same colour.

Soot: Brush off excess and sponge with carbon tetrachloride.

Tar: Scrape off with the back of a knife or thumbnail. Swab with turpentine, then carbon tetrachloride.

Float tar off a dog or cat's paw by rubbing in eucalyptus oil, leaving for half an hour, then washing off with warm water and detergent. Repeat until tar is completely removed.

Tea (inside the teapot): Fill the teapot with boiling water, add 1 teaspoon denture cleaning powder and stir. Leave for several hours, then rinse thoroughly. Alternatively, don't let anyone look in the teapot.

Tea (on china or glass): Wipe with a damp cloth dipped in bicarbonate of soda and rinse. Or soak in a biological detergent.

Tomato: see Fruit.

Urine: Sponge or wash in warm water. Sponge remaining stain with a solution of vinegar and water (1 tablespoon vinegar to 1 pint water).

Vomit: Sponge with borax solution. If on a carpet remove vomit with a cloth, then squirt with soda syphon to get rid of smell.

Wallpaper marks: Try to avoid clean wallpaper–nobody minds a spot here or there (could you hang something over it?) but you risk leaving a large, obvious 'clean' patch which will show how grubby your wallpaper is. If spongeable, wipe with a damp cloth or sponge. Otherwise, try a soft india rubber or a piece of soft bread. For grease marks try a proprietary dry cleaner, such as Beaucaire.

Wine: Stretch the stained bit of fabric over a pudding basin and keep it in position with a rubber band or a bit of string. Push material down into borax and water solution in the basin for half an hour. Then launder or dry clean.

Yourself: Try clear acetone for stains you can't get off your skin, such as Elastoplast marks, emulsion paint or tar on feet.

WHY NOT DYE A LITTLE?

You don't need much equipment to transform all your underwear and become a scarlet woman. With a little effort you too could sleep between coffee sheets like a film director. Or make sure that all your towels match by dyeing them French blue.

You'll only need a plastic bucket or a sink for cold dyeing. For hot water dyeing you will need a wooden stick or spoon, rubber gloves and a flameproof bucket, although any big tin container will do. I use an old Victorian fish kettle.

Know what fibre you are dyeing before you start. Just in case you're confused by mad scientist trade names, here is a guide.

FABRIC GUIDE

Fabric	Fibre Group
Acetate	Acetate
Acrilan	Acrylic
Bri-nylon	Nylon
Canvas	Natural
Cashmilon	Acrylic
Celon	Nylon
Cotton	Natural
Courtelle	Acrylic
Crimplene	Polyester
Crimplene/cotton	Polyester mixture
Dacron	Polyester
Dacron/cotton	Polyester mixture
Darelle	Viscose Rayon

Fabric	Fibre Group
Delustra	Viscose Rayon
Dicel	Acetate
Diolen	Polyester
Dralon	Acrylic
Elaston	Polynosic (a regenerated viscose)
Enkalon	Nylon
Enkasheer	Nylon
Evlan	Viscose Rayon
Fibreglass	Glass Fibre
Helanca	Nylon/Polyester
Lancofil	Acetate
Lancola	Acetate
Lancolene	Acetate
Lansil	Acetate
Leacril	Acrylic
Linen	Natural
Lycra	Elastomeric
Neo-spun	Acrylic
Nylon	Nylon
Orlon	Acrylic
Perlon	Nylon
Raycelon	Viscose Rayon
Sayelle	Acrylic
Sarille	Viscose Rayon
Shareen	Nylon
Silk	Natural
Spanzelle	Elastomeric
Tendrelle	Nylon
Tergal	Polyester
Terlenka	Polyester
Terylene	Polyester
Terylene/Cotton	Polyester mixture
Trevira	Polyester
Tricel	Triacetate
Tricelon	Triacetate
Vincel	Viscose Rayon
Viscose Rayon	Viscose Rayon
Wool	Natural
Zantrel	Polynosic

If you aren't certain what fabric you are trying to dye . . . DON'T GUESS.

I doubt whether you are going to cut bits out of your underwear in order to identify it but if you want to know what you should use to dye those curtains that look like silk but which you suspect to be rayon and which actually turn out to be terylene . . . send a snippet of fabric and have it analysed *free* by Dylon's laboratory. Write to Annette Stevens, Consumer Advice Bureau, Dylon International Ltd., Worsley Bridge Road, London SE26.

As together we dyed an assortment of coloured tights to a hopefully alluring black, Annette told me the mistakes which women make most frequently.

As always, the main complaint is that women *don't read the instructions*. I submit that that is because the instruction books are generally badly written, unclear, boring and confusing.

DO wear rubber gloves.

DO weigh your article and obey the instructions for that weight.

DO thoroughly wet the item before dyeing it.

DO wash the garment first (unless you're using Wash'n Dye, of which more later).

DO remove all stains beforehand or they will dye a different shade from the rest of the item.

This applies particularly to carpet dyeing, which incidentally is rewarding but extremely hard work and involves lots of elbow grease.

DO stir constantly with a wooden stick or spoon when you are dyeing by hand. Take the telephone off the hook and don't answer the door.

DO expect to blend colour. If you dye a yellow nightdress with blue dye it will not turn blue . . . it will turn green.

COLOUR ARITHMETIC

Red	+ Yellow	= Orange/Red
Blue	+ Yellow	= Green
Yellow	+ Pink	= Coral
Green	+ Yellow	= Lime
Lt. Brown	+ Med. Red	= Rust
Red	+ Blue	= Purple
Pale Blue	+ Pink	= Lilac
Yellow	+ Brown	= Golden Brown
Dk. Brown	+ Lt. Red	= Reddish Brown

Dyeing patterned material is tricky and I personally wouldn't do it.

In overdyeing patterned material, the *strongest colour in the pattern should be used as a guide.*

For example a red, yellow and pale green pattern would be suitable for overdyeing in red, this colour being the strongest of the three colours named.

DON'T use a too small vessel or the colour will be patchy.

DON'T dye glass fibre or acrylic, which simply won't absorb the dye. Some acrylic trade names are Courtelle, Acrilan, Dralon, Orlon, Neo-spun, Leacril, Sayelle and Cashmilon.

DON'T expect magic. Your beat-up, worn-out, old, cheap sweater won't be suddenly transformed into a new, fresh, smart, expensive-looking, different-coloured sweater – all for 17p. It will still be old and beat-up but a different colour.

DON'T try to overdye a dark colour with a light colour. You can't transform a dark blue bra into a pale peach one although you can metamorphose a yellowing white one into palest peach. You can also turn it white again by using Dylon Super White.

The following advice refers to Dylon dyes because they are ubiquitously simple to use.

There are four basic dyes: Dylon Cold, Multi-purpose, Liquid Instant, and Wash'n Dye.

BEWARE special finishes such as drip-dry, which can result in blotchy home dyeing.

WARNING! Don't wash home-dyed articles with biological powder such as Ariel or the colour will come out. Use a detergent soap powder.

For dyeing wool do not use Dylon Cold unless you want a very pale shade. Use whichever of the other three dyes is appropriate, but do not allow to boil or the garment may shrink. Turn the heat down when it reaches simmer point. You can use Superwhite for whitening wool.

Dylon Cold: For all natural fibres (except wool). Dye fading cotton, towels, jaded teatowels, boring bedspreads and sheets, over-familiar blouses. You simply buy a little tin with a packet of dye fix, mix the dye powder with water and add four tablespoons salt to each tin of dye. Dissolve the dye fixer in boiling water. Add both to a bowl of cold water. Now submerge the item for sixty minutes, stirring for the first ten. Then wash, rinse until water clears and dry as usual. They shouldn't bleed afterwards. ('Bleeding' is when the garment discolours the water.)

Multi-purpose: A teeny tin of dye powder intended for the odd pair of gloves, tights or pants. After using this dye, always wash a garment immediately, to make sure that it bleeds thoroughly.

You dissolve the dye by stirring in boiling water, add 1 heaped tablespoon salt, then the garment, simmer for twenty minutes, rinse thoroughly, wring, and dry away from direct heat or sunlight.

Liquid Instant: A hot water dye which will dye up to 2 lb dry weight. It is convenient because you don't have to dissolve any dye powder and you can keep it for years and use it as you please. I once dyed all my sad white nylon underwear Madonna Blue, which is a bit stronger than baby blue, not the standard Vatican shade. Use as Multi-purpose.

Wash'n Dye: For using in a washing machine because it washes the article as well as dyeing it. Useful for big items, such as rayon curtains or sheets or loose covers.

You just chuck in the dirty items. Don't add soap powder. Run the machine for twelve minutes (or the full cycle on automatics), rinse, then dry away from sunlight or direct heat. Will dye up to $2\frac{1}{2}$ lb dry weight.

> WARNING! Terylene, Tricel and Crimplene will need three times the dye quantities and you can still only dye them to pale shades.

SWIFT SEWING BOX

I used to have a great big EFFICIENT Mother-type sewing box with pretty rows of different coloured cottons and so forth. I used to have a basket grandly labelled SEWING which was generally overflowing with grey flannel school clothes that I couldn't summon up the energy to attack.

Then I realized that when travelling on business I take my tiny travel sewing kit and always immediately

repair anything that bursts. So I put this kit on the television in the sitting room and pointed it out to the men of the family, and now anyone who has anything to sew goes and does it themselves. I never asked. I just don't sew for anyone over seven, but I do see that the sewing kit is stocked up. If the men in your life travel, get them a pocket sewing book from the Co-op: smaller than a passport, it costs 40p at the time of writing. I've just given one to each of the men in my life and you'd have thought I was dishing out gold cuff links; they seemed pathetically grateful. I almost felt guilty.

Basic sewing kit
needles, large and small
tin of pins
small scissors
thimble
tape measure
reels of cotton in black, white, mid-brown, pale blue
black button thread
knicker elastic
trouser band hooks
hooks and eyes
seam ripper

I also have a transparent plastic button bag and an odd sock bag and keep an old pair of jeans to cut up and use for patches.

Zip tip: Zips are less likely to stick if you close them before cleaning the garment. If your zip sticks it might be because a thread has caught in it. On the other hand it might need lubricating; try a light touch of cooking oil or grease – even your face cream might unstick it. If your zip won't stay up, and it's not because a garment is too small for you, pull up zip end, slap a bit of Sellotape horizontally across it, or vertically up the zip, as a temporary measure.

HELLO, GOODBYE
WASHDAY
(Short guide to the weekly wash)

How to lose your laundry efficiently:
Laundries are wonderful if you are
rich enough, even though they can
beat hell out of your linen. Decide
which things always go. I currently
send sheets, big towels and shirts.
I have to face the fact that I'm not a
ravishing blonde, I can't speak six
languages and I can't iron shirts. Sort
into piles: white shirts, coloured shirts,
sheets. See that everything is marked
with your initials, using an indelible
laundry pen. Write in laundry book
as you put in laundry box. Always
mend sheets before laundering, for
even a small tear may return a major
calamity.

All over Britain laundry vans are
collecting the wrong boxes and taking
them back to be mechanically rubbed
on stones at the riverside (explains
how the holes get into the sheets) then
redistributing them back to even
wronger doorsteps. When it comes to
chasing a missing load you have no
proof because the laundry list is in the
lost box. So I bought a little office
duplicating book, the sort that gives
you carbon copies, which I keep with
a ballpoint pen in the bottom of the
laundry basket, where nobody nicks it
to keep the bridge scores.

Not since the invention of double
entry book-keeping in the fourteenth
century has there been such a revo-
lutionary idea. I write the laundry list
in my book, tear out the top copy and
send it with the laundry and tick off
the items in my book when they are
returned. If anything is missing I
report it to the laundry immediately,
and as my laundry is a member of the
British Launderers' and Dry Cleaners'
Federation, they play the game properly and *compensate* with *replacement*
value for anything which they've lost.
(Watford Model Laundry, please take
a bow.) I've also started to use it for
when I take a load to the dry-cleaning
shop, as those easily lost little slips
with their mad hieroglyphics mean
nothing to me.

How to be a laundry maid: If you're
doing it yourself, here are some
suggestions.

Don't do it on a Monday when you
have all the clearing up from the
weekend. Use gloves to protect your
hands when laundering; a must if
your skin is sensitive to washing
powders.

Whether you go to a launderette or
do it at home the routine is the same.

Before washing: Empty pockets,
mend tears and remove stains. Hot
water sets stains so they cannot be
removed. Ever. Sort into piles of

1 white cotton and linen.
2 coloured cotton and linen.
3 nylon and other synthetics.
4 rayon and silk.
5 woollens.
6 items whose colour you suspect
  might run.

Wash each pile separately.

Always read the label on the
garment. Use *very* hot water for white
and fast cottons (cheap cottons are
not always fast). Use hand hot water
for synthetics, warm water for woollens
and anything that you're a bit dubious
about.

Fastness: Wash all black things
separately as it then doesn't really
matter if they're not fast. Never wash
pale colours with dark colours in case
the colours bleed. Never wash white

49

with any other colour. Coloured sheets and towels should be washed separately for the first few times as surplus dye may come out. (It doesn't mean that they will get paler.)

You can tell whether or not a colour will run by wetting a corner of it in hot water and squeezing in a white towel. Anything brightly coloured or printed might run. Yellow dusters don't only run, *they gallop.*

Woollens and other delicate fabrics (e.g. lace): Always handwash unless such garments are definitely marked differently.

Wash woollens in warm water with Stergene or Lux soapflakes. Do everything gently. Rinse in warm water, squeeze gently, then press damp-dry in towel.

Damp-dry items by gently squeezing the water out (wringing can ruin the shape) and spreading them on a towel, rolling it up and banging gently on the roll, and repeating the process with a dry towel.

Don't peg up woollens: lay them out on a towel, pull into shape and leave to dry over the back of a sofa, or on the table or somewhere else flat, and warm, but not hot.

Many garment manufacturers now produce treated wool garments, which are labelled 'Superwash'. You can wash such an item in a washing machine and spin-dry it and it will still retain its shape. Be careful to obey the manufacturer's washing instructions.

Fabric softeners: They work by coating the fibres with a thin, invisible layer of the product, which includes silicones which prevent the fibres from adhering to each other and tend to make each item feel soft and fluffy as opposed to thick, compressed and 'felted' (a bit like blotting paper). Comfort is a good fabric softener for woollens, especially blankets.

Elastic: Wash in lukewarm water, never boil. Don't iron. Don't let it get too dirty. Don't wring it out: pat dry in a towel and proceed as for woollens. Remember, however, that the average male does not consider it glamorous to see a pair of elastic knickers drying on the back of a sofa.

Don't wash

1 Angora sweaters unless you have a tumbler drier. Dry clean.
2 Anything cheap which you like in crepe, satin or corduroy. You risk the garment losing shape. Dry clean.
3 A pleated skirt, unless the label says you can. Take it to the dry cleaner.
4 Ties. If you must try, do so in warm water and detergent, rinse well and pat dry in towel. Press under damp cloth. The more expensive a tie, the easier it seems for a dry cleaner to ruin it. There's no solution. Buy ties in dark colours and regard them as expendable.

The rule is: if in doubt, dry clean.

Electric washing machine: A twin tub washing machine takes about two hours to do my family laundry and I quite enjoy it, because the lot gets finished in this time. Most other women prefer an automatic because it washes, rinses and spins dry without any attention, but the load takes much longer to deal with. You are somehow cheerily advised to 'spread the load and banish washday'. This seems to mean doing some washing every day, instead of the lot at one go.

Don't put more things in the washing machine than it will wash. You don't pack it like a suitcase. If you don't feel like weighing the sheets or you haven't anything to weigh them on, fill it two-thirds full, as a rough guide. Always put stockings, lace and underwear in a pillowcase so they don't catch in the machine.

After using a washing machine, rinse with clear water, disconnect machine from electric supply unless it is permanently installed, *then dry it inside and out with an absorbent cloth.* Through not doing this and not using the machine for several months while I was away, I turned a trusty into a rusty seventeen-year-old twin tub, and had to scrap it.

Soaking: (see also p. 53 for biological products). There's a rumour that one person in five is sensitive to biological washing powder, so make sure you dissolve it properly to begin with and rinse it out thoroughly and off your hands.

I used to be very mean about water. Then an Italian laundry maid saw me in action and told me that you can never get anything clean if you wash it in grubby water. Simple, really. She told me to keep on rinsing until the water is clear, otherwise you risk a grubby wash, a soapy smell and a sticky feel.

Boiling: Boil nasty handkerchiefs or baby or invalid linen or similar in a boiler or an old saucepan, or something big enough. (Why boil nappies if you can afford disposable ones?)

Boiling for about ten minutes will often get out stains which ordinary washing won't and it also kills germs by sterilizing, so is good for face flannels, dishcloths and teatowels. If you have a stubborn stain, send it to a good laundry with a note safely pinned to the item.

Bleaching: A very mild household bleach solution will often whiten your white nylon, and remove stubborn stains such as scorch, mildew or make-up stains at the same time. If your white nylon goes grey you can buy a whitener. Try Dylon Super White on most synthetics and on all natural fibres (linen, silk, cotton, wool). Adding bleach to the water keeps white linen and cotton white. Use carefully according to directions, but remember that it shortens the life of any fabric. With coloured items try it on a bit of the lining. Damp the garment and immerse it for a few minutes in an equal mixture of water and household bleach. Remove and rinse well, then dry (see p. 23 on household cleaners).

Drying: You can buy a drying cabinet or a folding frame to drip dry overnight in the bath but NEVER dry in front of an open fire. The fierce heat is dangerous and bad for clothes.

If you dry your washing outdoors wipe the line first and stand with your back to the wind so the wet things don't flap in your face.

I bought a drying machine in the year when it rained 361 days *somewhere* in this country (meteorological department figures). Especially if you haven't a garden I find a drier is more important than a washing machine. A good tumbler drier can also reduce ironing by 80 per cent. Don't fill it too full, half capacity at most, and for drip-dry results remove articles, shake out and hang or fold immediately they have finished tumbling. Pillows and other feather-filled objects can be washed whole and tumble-dried.

Starching: You can buy a costly spray tin, such as Robin, which you use when you're ironing. (Alternatively buy a powdered starch such as Robin and mix exactly as it says on the packet.) Spray starch tends to leave a nasty brown deposit on the base of the iron which you transfer to the next white blouse. So spray starch last. Then unplug the iron, cool it and clean base with a damp brillo pad.

Use plastic starch if you want a rock-hard finish like nurses' cuffs.

Ironing: The secret of ironing is to avoid it. If you can't avoid it put the iron on something flameproof, such as the asbestos pad on the end of the ironing board.

Any old ironing board will do. For years I had a cheap wooden one which I covered with pretty materials at intervals, sticking it on with drawing pins. Then I bought a super galumptious enormously expensive ironing board which I hadn't got the patience to manage. It was always collapsing on my toes because I hadn't put it up properly. Now broken, it is too heavy to carry to the shop, or to send back to the manufacturers, etc. Moral: Keep life simple.

Get a sleeve board: you can't iron a sleeve without it unless you mess around folding clean teatowels into arm-shaped pads.

If you're going to iron, do it somewhere near a radio or record player. Or carry the transistor to the ironing site.

If you're going to iron, do so while it is still damp. If you can't iron at once, either roll up the clothes while still damp (I once accidentally left some sheets like this for a week and they went grey-green in parts) or else, just before you iron, wet with a flour shaker filled with water. The very best thing for damping-as-you-iron is a

pressure sprayer which releases a fine mist. They are generally sold in garden shops for spraying plants, although some enterprising ironmongers now sell them.

It is important to know what you're ironing. Read the label first and don't expect drip-dry not to need some ironing. Silk, or any synthetic, can fall apart under your eyes if you use too hot an iron. If you *know* it's cotton or linen, use a hot iron. If you don't know, take it gently. Start ironing on a part which won't show in case you're about to burn it.

Always try and iron clothes through a damp cloth. Many cheap fabrics, such as boutique crepe and satin, should always be ironed through a damp cloth so the iron marks don't show.

The point of ironing on the wrong side is that ironing makes the materials shiny. On the other hand it's fiddly to turn things inside out and back again and you risk creasing them more than they were in the beginning.

Never iron velvet, or velvet ribbon; steam it. Put on your electric kettle of water, and when boiling, point it at that which you wish to de-crease. Wear rubber gloves or you may steam-scald yourself. If you haven't a kettle try hanging the velvet in the bathroom over the hottest possible bath, and if that doesn't work take it to the dry cleaners.

Pressing: Is the same as ironing only you do it over a damp cloth and push hard. I once knew a minor TV personality who always pressed his trousers before wearing them – every single time – because it stops them knee-ing and bagging.

Airing: If you put ironed things away when warm but still a little damp (which is very easy) mildew will sprout. Also, damp clothes are unhealthy. So air things after ironing them, in the sunshine (best of all – but not for white woollies or you will probably have yellowy woollies), in a drying cabinet, on a clothes horse before a radiator, or in a warm, slatted cupboard. Don't air things in front of a fire even with a guard. May I remind you how fast you can burn to death? In fifteen seconds.

SUPER WASHERWOMAN
(Which washing product?)

They really ought to print the washing powder instructions on the cornflakes pack because everybody *reads* the cornflakes pack. For washerwomen who are bewildered by manufacturers' claims, descriptions and instructions, here are the encapsulated facts about washing products.

The word 'detergent' is derived from the Latin for 'cleaner'. Pure soap was the original detergent for washing people, clothes and homes. Synthetic detergents are a mixture of chemicals, each one with a different purpose, such as scum-inhibiting. There are two sorts: *strong* (such as Surf or Tide) for heavy-duty cleaning of fabrics such as cotton, and *weak* (such as Dreft) for more delicate materials, like silk. Anything which is 'kind to your hands' is weak. You would use a good quality (as opposed to household quality) solid soap, rather than a detergent for maximum gentleness, i.e. on your face.

There are three *textures* of cleanser: (1) solid, (2) powder or flake and (3) liquid. A liquid detergent like Stergene does the same job as a light duty powder or flakes. It is liquid for convenience.

The cheapest nationally available detergents are Surf and Tide, which should sell at 20 per cent cheaper than other brands, mainly because the manufacturers save money on promotion (so now you know how much the free, plastic daffodil may be costing you). *The cheapest biological* detergent you can get is probably the own-brand selling in your local, good quality chain store, such as Sainsburys.

All British detergents were made biodegradeable in 1964. This means that when the foam residue goes down the plughole it immediately breaks down before reaching the sewer, let alone a river.

How much to use? Whatever you use, it is important when washing clothes to maintain a good lather throughout the wash (except for special, low lather products used with front-loading automatic washers).

Synthetic detergents generally work very well in hard water, but if soap is used in a hard water area, a limestone scum will form.

If a new washing machine isn't giving as good results as handwashing and you are in a hard water area, try checking the washing instructions on the packet or using a lot more of the washing agent.

Too much soap powder or synthetic detergent cannot harm a fabric, so long as it has been properly dissolved before washing starts (except for some fully automatic washing machines when the manufacturer tells you to put the dry powder in the machine before the clothes). If the detergent hasn't been properly dissolved you risk a patchy garment. So never sprinkle washing powder on clothes; dissolve it separately beforehand.

Another way to counteract hard water is by using a water softener, such as Calgon.

Biological washing powders, such as Radiant or Ariel, contain a blend of soap (for mildness) and synthetic detergents (for power) and enzymes, which break down proteins by chemical action during soaking, so that the garment can then be washed by detergents in the normal way.

Natural body proteins include blood, sweat and urine as well as most food stains, such as egg yolk and cocoa. (Stubborn old stains may need several soakings.)

NEVER soak wool, silk, fabrics which are not colourfast or specially finished fabrics, such as drip-dry, in anything at all.

It is important to remember that the enzymes need time to act. It's no use just handwashing a garment quickly in a basin with a biological detergent because it won't work.

The longer the soak, the cooler the water can be. Soak garments overnight, eight hours in cold water with biological powder, or soak for an hour in hand-hot water (50°C or 122°F to be precise). If the water is too hot the enzymes will not act. Refer to the packet to find how much enzyme detergent to put in the washing machine. If your machine needs a low-lather washing powder, then presoak suitable clothes as suggested above before machine-washing them.

GOOD TIP: You can use a biological washing powder in water to soak overnight such kitchen irritations as burnt milk or scrambled egg in saucepans or for cleaning narrow-necked decanters or vases.

'If God had wanted women to stay in the kitchen he would have given them aluminium hands'—BETTY FRIEDAN.

TO BUY OR NOT TO BUY (Household Gadgets)

I took my first unconscious step towards female emancipation and away from martyrdom when I decided that, instead of teaching the au pair girl to cook for the children, it might be a better investment of time to teach the children to cook for the au pair. After all, I don't change the children every year. For the first time they always ate what was put before them and they eventually asked to do the shopping, a task which they performed far more frugally than I.

The next step was to find a new job for the au pair, and to invest the money saved on wages in anti-drudge machines. One was the fridge-freezer, the other was the dishwasher, and any working woman with a family could regard these as business investments to offset against her wages in the family budget. The cost of both machines was equivalent to the au pair's wages for eighteen months, not taking her keep into account. Furthermore, I'll never have to do the freezer's homework and the dishwasher is hardly likely to have an affair with my husband.

You need all the help you can get and afford. But even if you can pay for it, manufacturers don't make it easy to choose, blinding you with marketing science and glittering extras which you won't need. You can get along fine without a surprising amount of equipment. I always considered a washing machine an essential – until I was without one for six months. I didn't even notice the loss but simply soaked everything in biological detergent in bath and basin overnight, then rinsed them out the next morning.

However, here's my biased list of what and what not to buy – what to look for when you do decide to invest in helpful equipment.

TO BUY	WHY?
A good transistor radio	It entertains and informs when you're doing the washing up and says good morning cheerfully.
Continental quilts	They simplify bed-making and are lighter and cosier than trad.
Good quality, drip-dry, non-iron linen, underwear and shirts	They save time and trouble.
A steam iron	It irons more efficiently.
An ironing board to suit your height	Otherwise you will get backache, if not worse.
A shower in the bath	A shower uses less water than a bath; children love it; it encourages people to clean the bath and a cold shower is invigorating.
Mixer taps	For painless temperature control.
Electric blender	It makes soups, purees and puddings in a trice and grinds coffee as well. Escoffier would have given his sous chef for one.
A good steady stool which converts to a stepladder	You'll use it constantly.
Anglepoise lamps	For close work, study, shaving or even make-up, and washing up.
A solid non-rickety trolley	It's a movable, working or stacking surface for kitchen, study or workroom.
A double sink with swivel mixer taps	It's half-way to a washing-up machine.
A self-cleaning oven	It eliminates a filthy job.
A front-opening deep-freeze	Top-loading ones can be awkward and confusing to use.
A tumble drier	It rained in Britain somewhere or other 350 days last year and a tumble drier gets things bone dry.
Electric knife sharpener	If you need knives you need sharp knives. Blunt ones are dangerous.
Three good kitchen knives	They are basic kitchen equipment.
Cheap non-stick saucepans, casserole and frying pans	They take the strain out of washing up.

56

TO BUY	WHY?
A Cooper's roasting thermometer	You'll never overcook a joint again.
A pair of kitchen tongs	To save your fingertips.
Shopping basket on wheels	Carrying bags is exhausting.
Rubber ice trays	Plastic ones break. With these you can simply remove one cube at a time without hitting the thing or holding it under a tap.

NOT TO BUY	UNLESS
An electric floor polisher	. . . you have acres of parquet, P.V.C. or linoleum floor.
An electric mixer	. . . you make cakes three times a week.
An expensive sewing machine	. . . you know how to use it. All those extras only frighten a novice. Buy a secondhand, cheap, hand-operated model.
Electric frying pans } Electric toasters }	. . . you want to accumulate mechanical clutter in the kitchen.
Extractor fans	. . . there's no window to open.
Electric kettle	. . . you're using it outside the kitchen, i.e. for morning tea, or in an office.
Tupperware	. . . you can't find cheaper plastic containers at your local large store.
Exercise machines	. . . you know someone who's used one for over a year.
A waste disposal	. . . you live in a seventeenth-storey flat with little room for a dustbin.
A flimsy lightweight dish drainer	. . . you don't mind the lot crashing to the floor.
A plastic colander	. . . you don't mind replacing them regularly. They seem to melt disgustingly before your eyes.

Most people, however biased, would like certain basic equipment, such as cooker, dishwasher, refrigerator, vacuum cleaner and washing machine.

Cooker: Choose your cooker with care because you'll probably be spending over five hundred hours a year at it, cooking a thousand meals per annum.

It is possible to buy a secondhand cooker (reconditioned) through your local gas or electricity showroom, although they don't always like to own up to this fact. Insist and persist.

The basic choice is gas, electricity, or solid fuel, such as an Aga.

All the professional cooks I have ever met use *gas* cookers when possible because the heat of the burners is instantly adjustable. The top of a gas oven is hotter than the bottom, which can be a culinary advantage because you can fill the oven with

57

different foods and cook economically.

The advantages of *electricity* are the lack of fumes and an even oven temperature. The disadvantages of electricity are clumsily controlled heat, possible danger to children if you can't see that the burners are switched on and non-performance during power strikes.

A *solid fuel* cooker is cheap to run, can heat water and provide limited central heating, and is delightfully cosy to have in the kitchen. But they are comparatively large and dirty, are clumsily controlled and have no grill.

Other points to consider are size of grill, size of oven, self-cleaning oven, timeswitch, spit, roasting thermometer, number of burners, simmerstat (so that milk or sauces don't boil over), see-through oven doors with light-up interiors.

Eye-level grills (providing your eye is on that level) often mean red-hot grill pan handles, but you can have a grill (Cannon) fixed apart from your oven. You can also have a gas and/or electric hob separated from your oven (Advance Domestic Appliances).

Double ovens are a good idea especially if you are cooking several meals at once. They also ensure enough warm plates. Remember that if you choose a coloured oven you will be stuck with that colour, even if at a later date you want to change your kitchen colour scheme.

Dishwasher: Once, after a New York party, I saw my hostess, apparently blind drunk, stagger zigzag across her kitchen to a pink washing up machine, shovel the dishes inside, and kick the door shut without so much as squinting to check whether it was properly loaded. To my surprise everything came out clean and unbroken,

since when that pink machine has been my personal yardstick for dishwashers. The only ones in Britain that I have found to measure up to it are the Miele (quietest) and the Westinghouse, from Advanced Domestic Appliances, 18 Berners Street, London W1P 3DD (Tel. 01-580 9991). It's the only machine I've ever tested which never involves an inspection of dishes and glasses afterwards. I prefer it to more expensive machines.

Don't expect a dishwasher to dispense with your washing up problem, but it will halve the job and also seems to provide a painless, built-in discipline for clearing up immediately. People with dishwashers always seem to have tidy kitchens. Try to buy a dishwasher with a built-in waste disposal unit, because it cuts out possible maintenance trouble. Nevertheless, scrape plates before putting into the dishwasher.

Try using Finnish washing powder in the machine. If you are in a hard water area, use whichever water softener is recommended by the manufacturers of your machine and Rinsaid. Seek further guidance from the Food Freezer Committee, 25 North Row, London W1 (Tel. 01-499 0414). Buy only dishwasher-proof china and cutlery, even if you haven't a dishwasher. You never know. Dishwashers may easily ruin wood, bone, horn, hand-painted or delicate china or cut glass. Wash these by hand. Manufacturers say that you shouldn't put plastics in a dishwasher although I know people who do so with no consequent melted plates.

Refrigerator: People always buy a too small fridge when buying the first time. Allow $1\frac{1}{2}$ cubic feet per member of household – minimum.

Minimum 4 cubic feet even for a bachelor.

Absorption models are silent but use twice as much electricity as compressor machines, which purr.

Useful things to have in a refrigerator are:

1 Well organized, back of door storage, with enough height for hock bottles.
2 Adjustable shelving.
3 Plenty of room to make ice.
4 A worktop, if you need a small model.
5 Deep-freeze space, if you're not buying a freezer.

But ignore flimsy ridiculous egg holders. (You shouldn't keep eggs in the refrigerator anyway or they will crack when you boil them, and you can't always make mayonnaise with them unless you take them out half an hour before using them.)

Vacuum cleaner: Don't bang it about, it's a sensitive machine and not magic. Pick up hairgrips or pins by hand because they might damage the engine. Empty the bag before it's full. Service it regularly, because repairs are expensive, and *stop using it* if you suspect that it's faulty.

There are basically three types of vacuum cleaner:

1 A hand-held, heavy upright model, which will be necessary for acres of carpet.
2 A small upright model, light enough to carry upstairs (even if you currently have a flat, people move house on average once every eight years).
3 A cylinder model, easily stored, for small areas and stairs, with special attachments for curtains and upholstery.

There's also a portable model (spherical) which follows you like a dog. I use this; it's light to lift and cleans *everywhere* easily. Try Black and Decker's Majorvac.

Washing machine: Do you want an automatic, a semi-automatic or a twin tub? An *automatic* does everything unsupervised while you go out to the cinema but the washing programme isn't always adaptable and each load takes a long time and can use a lot of water (up to 30 gallons). If your hot water is limited buy a self-heating model. A *semi-automatic* machine will wash by itself but you have to operate it in order to rinse, and spin dry. A *twin tub* needs constant attention but you can probably do the family wash in two hours.

You have to bend down to a *front-loading* machine but you have to lean over a *top-loading* model and heave out the damp load. Short girls with weak backs should avoid them. Obviously, you can't build a top-loading machine into a laundry 'wall'.

Roller-type wringers can leave you with a damp floor and backache. Try to get a spin dryer, which leaves clothes damp-dry. *Drying cabinets* are heated and ventilated cupboards fitted with clothes racks. Useful if you haven't a tumbler drier.

Do not be swayed by glamorous advertisements. Before buying household machinery trot along to your local library to see which model is recommended by *Which*. If you want to subscribe to *Which* the address is Consumers Association, 14 Buckingham Street, London WC2.

When buying machines don't forget to consider three points:

Installation: Will it need new wiring, plumbing or a ventilation fan and if so is it possible and how much will it cost?

Will the shop you're buying the machine from arrange to have it installed, or will you have to arrange it yourself? If so, who does the maker recommend in your area?

Maintenance: Is this the responsibility of the shop, or the maker? If the latter, how long is it likely to take for repairs to be done and how much might they be?

Guarantee: Is the shop or maker guaranteeing your purchase? How long does the guarantee last? Does it include the cost of spare parts and labour? Does it include standard 'visit' charge and VAT?

Before you buy anything ask to see it demonstrated or ask if the store can suggest one or two satisfied customers who have bought the same item. It may be worth asking recent owners if they are satisfied with what you're about to invest in. You're likely to get a quicker reply if you telephone but if you write it is polite and sensible to enclose a stamped addressed envelope.

Repairs: Stand over the man who's repairing your tumbler drier and see what he does and make a note of what was wrong with it. Also the date and what it cost. This might be useful ammunition with which to write to the manufacturer if the machine develops the same fault three times a year; or it might eventually teach you to empty the lint bag of your tumble dryer, or whatever.

AND SO TO BED

Cooking apart, what a bride needs to know most about – and generally knows least about – is what to look for when buying a double bed.

Apparently most women make three big mistakes when buying their first double bed.

First mistake: They economize. Most of the cost of a mattress is inside, where you can't see it. Women will buy a good bedspread because they – and their friends – can see what they're getting for their money. But faced with two beds which look alike and are the same size, they don't see why one should cost more.

Second mistake: Women buy too small a bed. A 6-foot man needs more than $1\frac{1}{2}$ inches at his head and feet, yet standard beds are 6 feet 3 inches long. Customers rarely ask for anything longer.

Third mistake: They buy a bed because they like its cover, although they see it only when they're turning the mattress.

What do you need to know before buying a double bed?

What is a bed? A bed is a mattress supported by a base, which may be of open coiled springs, wire mesh or laminated wood, which is generally specified for slipped disc sufferers. If the base is upholstered it is made of covered coiled springs.

How long? At least 6 inches longer than the height of the taller occupant. Incidentally, a 5 foot 9 inch bed is called 'Scottish size', which implies that Scots are either small or mean.

How wide? Sleeping alone you need 3 feet width, but two people together need less than 6 feet because, as one expert said, 'Whether or not it's deliberate, there's a certain amount of animal magnetism when two people sleep together.' But unless they snuggle up like a couple of puppies they need a bed 5 feet wide and not the traditional 4 feet 6 inches.

How high? Expert opinions vary between 18 and 20 inches but on one thing they all agree: beds are getting lower. Elderly people find it easier to get out of a high bed and it is certainly easier to make. Mattresses on the floor are very difficult to make unless used with a sleeping bag, which should have an inner sheet or sheet bag, otherwise the sleeping bag will smell fusty. If you buy sleeping bags, get the sort which can be unzipped to use as a quilt or zipped to each other to make a double sleeping bag – you never know.

Castors can be fitted to a bed in order to make it easier to pull out and make it, and easier to clean underneath: buy them from a hardware store.

Which mattress is best?

Latex foam on a laminated wood base is considered smart among the hand-woven set (a disadvantage is that restless sleepers generally hit base). These mattresses are generally 4 inches deep and don't need turning, don't make fluff, and don't attract moths or vermin.

Foam plastic mattresses have the same qualities and keep their shape and resilience better than they used to.

Interior sprung mattresses are made of coiled wire springs, well padded with cotton waste, coiled hair and rubber or plastic foam. Beware of those which are over-sprung: one bed almost threw me out every time I turned over.

Pocketed sprung mattresses – the most expensive – are built to last a lifetime. Each of the hundreds of springs is sewn into a separate pocket, which ensures independent suspen-sion. Everyone moves in bed about four times an hour and man and wife rarely weigh the same. Consequently, unless the mattress has independent suspension the lighter partner often slides downhill. But not on a pocketed sprung mattress.

Flock mattresses are to be avoided if possible. They are made from wool waste or flock, which may quickly become lumpy.

Look for a mattress with a BS (British Standards) label.

How long can you expect a mattress to last? Of course it depends on a lot of variables, such as how much you weigh, how often you lie in bed, and how good it was in the first place, but a rough life expectancy might be as follows:

Flock (considered unsatisfactory by bedding experts because of a tendency to lump) . . . 6 or 7 years.
Latex foam . . . 15 years
Spring interior . . . 15 years
Pocketed spring . . . 20 years

Heals, Tottenham Court Road, London W1 (Tel. 01-636 1666) have a special mattress-making department which will give free, specific quotations for remaking old mattresses.

Bed dress

Pillows: Down is soft and light and expensive. Feathers are heavier and cheaper. Foam is less yielding, more springy, doesn't last as long as down or feathers, can make your neck feel tense and I can't stand it. Comparative shopping is essential with pillows be-cause there are amazing price varia-tions. British Home Stores give good value. Buy at sale time.

Towels: White towels get dirtiest

61

fastest and most publicly. Black towels look sordid. Cigar brown, French blue or olive green towels are a splendid idea for a family with young children.

Buying bed clothes: When buying sheets or blankets, a generous allowance is the width plus 18 inches to tuck in on all sides.

Sheets: Having impulsively and creatively bought patterned bed linen over the years, I gloomily admit that the glamorous, glossy magazine, bed image which I originally had in mind has been shattered. If you scorch a pillowslip here and lose a sheet there, you end up with one rosebud strewn pillow, one scattered with teddy bears, a multi-striped top sheet and a brilliant blue undersheet. If you want to simplify life, buy only white bed linen, which always looks crispest, is easier to launder if badly stained and is *cheaper* anyway. Cheap sheets can be full of filling which makes them feel less thin but which comes out with the first wash. Look closely at your sheets and ensure a tight, firm weave. Crunch a corner between your fingers, you can then see if there seems to be a lot of starchy filling.

Wait to buy linen until the summer or winter sales, then go to stores with a good reputation. I find that John Lewis provides excellent value and a great range of colours. They also take enormous trouble over any complaints. For cheap linen get the Limerick's catalogue. I also buy cheap linen from the Linen Cupboard, 21 Great Castle Street, Oxford Circus, London W1, which have some really dreadful patterns but lots of amazingly good bargains in simply coloured sheets, towels and bedcovers. If you want a lot of cheap bed linen, titled ladies of my acquaintance order in bulk for stately homes from Brentford Nylons, Brentford, Middlesex (Tel. 01-568 9255). Write to them for a free catalogue.

Buying blankets: Warmest and lightest are fine Merino wool, then pure wool, then Acrilan, which is mothproof, easy to wash, quick to dry and will not shrink or 'felt', that is, get thick and stiff. Some synthetics can feel funny – it's difficult to describe, but a bit as if they'd been made from sticky candy floss and not nearly so cuddly as wool. Wool and rayon blankets are less warm and don't wear as well as most all synthetics but they feel better. Wool and cotton blankets are generally cheapest and hardwearing, but heavy and not so warm as all wool blankets. Buy at sale time. Comparative shopping essential.

Sheet and Blanket Sizes Guide

The new METRIC bed sizes

small single, 3' 0" × 6' 3" (90 × 190 cm); standard single (100 × 200 cm); small double 4' 6" × 6' 3" (155 × 190 cm); standard double 5' 0" × 6' 6" 150 × 200 cm).

Blanket and Sheet sizes

Single bed 70" × 108" (180 × 260 cm); 4' 6" bed 90" × 108" (230 × 260 cm); 5' 0" bed 100" × 108" (275 × 275 cm).

Any larger bed or (ugh) round bed requires special sheet and blanket sizes which are (comparatively) fantastically expensive, and as they're generally specially made they generally take months to arrive.

ALL YOU EVER WANTED TO KNOW ABOUT A CONTINENTAL QUILT

A continental quilt almost eliminates bedmaking. A good continental quilt (or duvet) can be the equivalent of at least three blankets and can cost and weigh considerably less than conventional bed clothes.

You're supposed to make the bed only using a bottom sheet and a quilt cover, but I use two sheets traditionally and keep the quilt in its special case until spring cleaning time comes round.

You may want to know the difference between an eiderdown and a continental quilt and whether you can use a double bed eiderdown as a single quilt? No, not efficiently, because the eiderdown is tightly packed and crushed down and there are no air pockets to trap the warm air round you, as does the quilt, on the same principle as a string vest.

What should you look for when you buy a quilt?

Watch out for inferior or inadequate fillings in a skimpy quilt at a 'bargain price'.

A cheap manufacturer's nasty trick is not to put in enough filling: if someone has reduced the recommended filling by 25 per cent then the quilt may be 25 per cent cheaper but it will be 25 per cent less warm. On the whole, in a reputable shop you get what you pay for and if you've found an amazing bargain source of quilts I think I would say *Caveat emptor* (let the buyer beware).

The seven questions to ask before buying a continental quilt are:

1 Is it large enough to keep the sleeper covered?
2 Is it light enough?
3 Is it warm enough?
4 Does it 'drape' well, settling snugly round the sleeper in order to trap the body's natural warmth?
5 Is it free from 'cold spots' caused by movement of the filling (i.e. collecting in a bag at the bottom of the bed?)
6 Is it constructed from good quality materials so that it stands up to the wear and tear of continual use?
7 Can it be easily cleaned?

The warmth to weight ratio is measured in togs, which represent the thermal insulation value. The best merino blanket might have nine togs and a Terylene P3 quilt has about eleven togs. Down quilts vary between ten and fifteen togs, depending whether or not the down has been recycled.

In order to prevent edge draughts a continental quilt must be large enough to overlap the sides and bottom of the bed, while covering the sleeper.

Width: Forget about the bed widths. The minimum width quilt for one adult is 54 inches and for two adults it is 72 inches. Two sleeping on a wide double bed *could* use a single quilt each as they do in Austria. But it doesn't sound very friendly.

Length: Again, don't skimp. Children grow and the same person might not always use that duvet. Minimum 6 foot 6 in to 7 foot for tall people. Forget about the bed length and think about the person.

Stitching: There are several sorts of stitching, but there's no mystique about it. Some channel across, some channel up and down. It doesn't matter how it's stitched as long as there is stitching every 8–12 inches. Some manufacturers of Terylene P3 quilts feel that stitching in channels inhibits the 'plump, soft, angel wing character' of the quilt. Their new versions have only a few spot stitches at the middle.

Quality: Until the new BS standard

is general you had better rely for guarantee on a manufacturer and retailer who are renowned for their quality – and that cuts out cheap chain stores. Avoid sub-standard, inadequate synthetic filling by buying only where you see the ICI Terylene P3 green label standard (which, they say, satisfies four out of five people) or the pink label for people who feel the cold more than most or who live in a very cold area or house.

Synthetic fillings: There are basically two types of synthetic filling, fibres and staple fibre. Staple fibres, which have trade names, are chopped fibre bonded with an adhesive to produce a wad, like cotton wool. Staple fibre hasn't a good warmth-to-weight ratio and doesn't snuggle closely round you. Government hospital contracts generally specify ICI's Terylene P3, a continuous fibre filling. It is used in quilts and sleeping bags and has good insulating quality. For technical reasons it 'settles' easily, cuddling around the sleeper, so has a high warmth factor and excellent drapage. It is produced to a uniform density and placed between two cover cloths which are stitched through in such a way as not to disturb the filling. This is where it scores over feather filling, which can move fairly freely up and down inside the quilt. This means that the insulation properties are never uniform and having to shake the quilt to redistribute the filling means that you lose some of the major advantage – quick and easy bedmaking.

Feather fillings: The first thing you should look for to determine the quality is whether the manufacturers claim that it is NEW, because a lot of fillings are recycled and your local Steptoe could tell you where they come from. The feathers – whether or not they are down – often come from old feather beds, eiderdowns and pillows. Old feathers aren't as efficient as new feathers. In time they turn to dust. The life of down feathers *in careful use* is forty years.

Down is from the breast of a water bird and there's no quill in it, which is why it is very soft. *Feathers* come off any sort of old bird, even cold poultry. In *mixtures*, what counts is the first word. 'Down and feather' has to be 51 per cent down. 'Feather and down' must be a minimum of 15 per cent down. So watch it.

To clean: No one expects you to clean a synthetic quilt often, if at all during its working life. Should you have an accident synthetic quilts should be washed. A quilt doesn't weigh very much, so any suitable washing machine or launderette machine will take it, or send it to the laundry. *Don't dry clean it.* Down and feathers have to be professionally cleaned. Send them to the Danish Express Laundry, 16 Hinde Street, London W1 (Tel. 01-935 6306).

If you get a stain on a quilt cover just push the filling out of the way and sponge the stain as fast as possible with cold water, mopping with a towel.

New cases: Aeonics Ltd., 92 Church Road, Mitcham, Surrey CR4 2AJ, (Tel. 01-640 1113) make an inexpensive, down-proof quilt *case* so that you can simply empty your old quilt into it. You can have any colour you like as long as it's ecru. They also sell the material by the yard, but it's a complicated job to make a case, like a Chinese puzzle, so don't try it if you can avoid it as there isn't a great money-saving.

Do it yourself quilts: Quilts are cheaper by about one seventh if you buy them in a do-it-yourself kit, in down, feather or Terylene P3. There are several different sizes. I've tried a single: it's easy, and sewing by hand it takes about an hour.

The overall look: I don't think much of current cover designs, which tend to be either sloppy, pseudo-modern patterns or else plain colours which look terrific in the pack but a bit school marmish-dowdy on the bed. But there's nothing to stop you making your own cotton cover with pretty or elegant patterns to match your curtains or carpet. Or sew a double sheet together for a single quilt cover or two single sheets together for a double cover. This worked for me, but check measurements first.

Beds might be quicker to make with quilts, but when made, by me, they tend to look a bit wobbly and lumpy, as if there was still someone in there. Cheap heavyweight cotton bedspreads (there are lots at John Lewis) smooth them out nicely.

How to be a Famous Decorator

TRUST YOUR OWN TASTE
(How and why you should develop your own decorative style)

Although money can't buy it, anyone intelligent can learn to have good taste. You can spend like a drunken film star, but you risk an expensive clutter that hasn't quite come off. If you pay someone else to design your home you risk something pretty expensive, lifeless and unlived in, or alternatively, an exuberantly camped-up setting with mouldings picked out in white and in which you feel uneasy.

So the first rule is *Do it yourself*. Because otherwise you'll never learn.

Discovering your own good taste is an unpeeling process, eliminating the layers which other people have impressed upon you. One of the easiest ways to *find out what you like* is to get a pinboard and start sticking up anything which takes your fancy – a scrap of lace, photographs, postcards, a colour swatch, a cartoon.

Then start to *decide what you like best*. Because good taste is the result of severe and constant pruning. Your taste develops and crystallizes. You create your own perfect environment by cutting out everything else.

You might like several styles – art deco, art nouveau, Bauhaus, functional and cottage modern. But, unless you're very sure what you're doing (and very few people in Britain are) stick firmly to one style.

Look at the way you dress: the colours of your clothes will also suit your room, which will then also suit you. If you're a brown and cream woman, go for that sort of room. If you're a silk girl, choose silky rayons. If you're a tailored type, so should your room be.

Use self-discipline: For instance, in a bedsitter or small flat start with one colour theme and allow yourself only two subsidiary colours and two patterns – at the most. If you have a flat, using one overall colour scheme will make it more coordinated and pulled together, so will one floor colour throughout.

If you've got a badly shaped room complicated by writhing pipes or oddly boxed-in areas use a dark colour all over walls and ceiling to simplify the area.

If you've got a horrid little box-shape, low-ceilinged room, pull it together with a small but strong traditional pattern over walls and ceiling.

Be realistic: Just as you can't wear belts if you haven't a waist, or milkmaid smocks if you're six feet tall, you may not be able to indulge in ornate Victoriana in a modern flat, or pristine chrome and glass and fragile ivory figurines if you have five children and two labradors, or bright pink anywhere (corset pink is the only colour allowed nowadays – Aubretia, No. 18 F in Carson's range).

Be ruthless with presents, however kindly given, if they are somebody else's taste and not yours. Sell them, swop, or hide them, because if you don't really like them they only distract *your* style. Say, 'I'm saving it until I've got a bigger place!' or 'My mother's looking after it for me'.

No one's forcing you to be ruthless, but that's the only way to get the best effect.

Don't compromise: Don't settle for second best. Don't have anything that is *nearly* alright. It should be the best or an obvious stand-in; if you long for a glass and chrome TV table, don't settle for one which your mother offered you with cabriole legs. Stand the thing on an orange box or on the floor.

Lack of money need not cramp your emerging style. For seven years I was a designer, producing rooms for other people. However, apart from one antique chandelier, my personal life has mostly been lived on exultant street market bargains, chain store furniture, cheap beds that broke, prototypes which fell apart and painted junk. But as Mae West never said, money isn't everything. The decorative jobs that I've been most pleased with have always been the cut-price, no-room-to-move rooms.

Don't accumulate: Apart from lights, carpet and curtains, the more you remove from a room the better it tends to look.

Analyse your fatal weakness and stamp it out, whether it is for Tudor chandelier light fittings which look as if Errol Flynn should be swinging from them, or a passion for making your own lampshades (I've never seen a home-made lampshade which didn't look wrinkled, tired or slightly drunk).

Stamp out your pretensions, too. You can go out looking like a million dollars when you aren't worth a bus fare and people will only applaud, but you can't fool anyone in your home. Whatever your pretensions – intellectual, social, financial, or moral – they will soon show up in your personal setting.

68

Finally, know what you're good at and emphasize it. Don't try anything else. If you're a patchwork-and-homemade-scones girl with good childbearing hips, you won't give an authentic impression of yourself in an incense-fuddled Biba boudoir. But if plants just grow for you, have banks of massed ferns, if you've got an eye for little objects, collect tables of them. The trick is to know what you're bad at and *not* do it; to know what you're good at and *emphasize it.*

TIME, SPACE AND MONEY

I've *never* been made to work harder than when, for a short period, I was assisting David Hicks, who reputedly charges 1,000 dollars an hour in New York for interior design advice. Here are some tips for those of you who can't afford him.

Never take any book on home design too seriously. Your taste and problems might be different from those of the author. And you want to end up with something which *you* like living in, and which looks as if it was meant to be lived in, not photographed. The civilizing influence in my first home was a small puppy which swiftly grew to the size of a small sofa. By the time the dog had chewed her way round for a week, the place looked far less formal and more relaxed.

From now on buy everything with an eye to maintenance. And when buying furniture lie on beds and sit on chairs and at tables to check that they fit you comfortably.

Upholstery is so expensive that you should try to silicone spray it and don't expect *that* to work magic.

Loose covers are a great investment. Avoid loose weaves which will hole quickly, or hang unevenly in curtains. And avoid regular patterns such as a houndstooth, because these show every mark. A dark or patterned fabric with a dark background is easily the most practicable for upholstery. When you're looking at it in the shop imagine that sofa with two ineradicable small coffee stains on it and you may see what I mean.

Space-making: If you haven't much room, buy space-makers such as stacking chairs, stacking side tables, stacking stools; flap-up, fold-up or otherwise expanding tables; dual purpose furniture, such as bedsettees or beds with drawers beneath or beds with more beds beneath; cupboards with folding or sliding doors (although sliding doors can be maddening); built-in furniture; plenty of shelves: try a bookshelf in a bathroom or kitchen without enough storage space. Have plain, light-coloured walls with matching curtains, fitted carpets and mirrors.

Walls: Do-it-yourself painting is far easier and cheaper to do – and to change – than wallpapering a room.

Moses didn't produce a commandment saying that all woodwork should be white, or even that it should be gloss paint. I've seen many rooms where the emulsion paint is on both walls and woodwork, in beige, dark green, tomato juice or cigar brown.

Always save a jar of paint for emergency touch-ups in every room you paint – and label the jar. When not wielding it, hang your paintbrush by the handle. Stand a paint tin on a paper plate or circle of aluminium foil. *Never* hope that the paint won't splash.

Clear up half an hour before you intended. Exhaustion suddenly paralyses you when decorating.

Curtains: When buying materials allow 10 per cent extra length for shrinkage. Allow for pattern-matching. Ask the assistant to calculate for you because you're almost bound to make a mistake. Allow 12-inch hems in case you move and the next place has bigger windows. There's nothing more irritating than hems 3 inches too short.

Lined and interlined curtains are nicest, but horribly expensive and difficult to make. If you're starting, it's easier and cheaper to make unlined curtains. Use a simple tape suspension method. I don't like using pinch pleat removable prongs because they fall out so easily and are so difficult to put back. I find the easiest, trimmest method is Rufflette's Regis. It is a neat, smart shirr heading with wide tape and draw-strings. Some people don't mind hand-hemming curtains after they've been hanging a month. Other people prefer to take their curtains down five years later, to find the pins irrevocably rusted into the hems.

Flooring: 'Wilton' and 'Axminster' describe the weave of a carpet. 'Broadloom' just means that it was woven on a loom over 6 feet wide. You need best quality carpet where it gets the hardest wear (hall and stairs). You can get away with cheaper in the bedroom. Check whether your carpet is moth-proof, or will burn easily, and what it's made of and how to clean it. Underlays double the life of a carpet, add warmth, and a lush ankle-straining bounce, and lessen noise.

Try to avoid having a fitted carpet under the dining table as it will stain very fast indeed. If you have a fitted carpet, put a patterned rug over it –

easier than the carpet to take away and clean.

Don't have white or very pale floors of any sort – paint, carpet, rugs, linoleum, tiles – unless you are prepared for cleaning headaches. Every home editor I know has had some sort of pale floor trauma before she learned her lesson.

Kitchen floor covering should be non-slip, not cold or hard to the feet, easy to clean and hardwearing. Sealed cork is all of these things. (Wicanders have the best selection). Write for details to 41 Berners Street, London W1P 3DD (Tel: 01-580 1218). Otherwise use good quality PVC tiles or linoleum. Avoid ceramic tiles which are very hard on the feet, though practical.

The Bathroom: If you have a small bathroom or a cold lavatory, a heat and light bulb (cost approximately £1.35) will take the chill from the air and doesn't require a shade.

You can *repaint your own bath,* although you risk it looking oddly amateur, just as home-painted cars look less suave than factory-sprayed models. You first clean the bath with hot water and detergent, then paint thinly with special bath enamel, which can be bought or ordered from do-it-yourself shops. After three coats, drying between each coat, fill the bath with cold water and leave for three days to a week (arrange to bath in a neighbour's bath). The drawback to painting your own bath is that for ever after you should run the cold water in before the hot, otherwise it might wrinkle and peel.

If you have a hopeless, grotty, scratched, dull, greenish, lime scaled nasty old bath you might call for Renubath Ltd, 596 Chiswick High

Road, London, W4 (Tel: 01-994 1325). This is a firm of specialist enamel and porcelain renewers, who will give your bath a spanking new complexion without having to unplumb and disturb it. They will rewhiten a bath for £16.50, or give it a colour change for from £18.50 (not including VAT). Their colour range will match anything the average manufacturer can think of and includes some new subtle pastels: orchid, pampas (a light khaki), honeysuckle (paving stone colour) and avocado green.

Now for accessories: The handyman who helped me on my fifth move in eighteen months said that on the last job he could have accessorized it without any instructions from me. Line up the tops of very large pictures with the top of the doors and treat any slabs of mirrors as pictures. Keep space between them equidistant. Fix aluminium spotlights 4 feet high at the side of the bed, 6 feet on walls. Allow two bowls of ferns or plants or flowers per room.

Mirrors: It's amazing how many people still think of a mirror as something to check their make-up in. I use slabs of 60 × 18 inch as lavishly as I can afford, either vertically or horizontally. A mirror can add space to a room, improve proportions or lighting or simply add glitter and sparkle.

A mirror will increase light, as it bounces it back into a room. A mirror looks good between two windows. Two or three mirrors used either vertically or horizontally can widen or lengthen or add interest to a long, narrow hall, or add breadth, depth and glitter to a small bathroom – especially one with no windows.

If you're using mirrors in a bathroom or other areas where you can expect condensation make sure you get ones with steam-resistant backs, generally copper.

Ready-cut slabs of mirror are far cheaper than custom-cut ones. Verity mirror packs contain all necessary clips, screws, washers, plugs and fixing instructions. Get them from John Lewis.

Standard mirror sizes are:

30 × 18 inch (760 × 460 mm)
48 × 18 inch (1220 × 460 mm)
48 × 15 inch (1220 × 380 mm)
60 × 18 inch (1520 × 460 mm)

The three basic methods of fixing a mirror are to stick it on, screw it on, or hold it in place with beading or frame. I generally screw as I've never been able to find a wall that's flat enough to stick.

Pictures: I would rather have a good reproduction than a bad original, but most of my pictures are etchings, engravings or screen prints. It doesn't cost much to start a real art collection in this way.

Some public libraries have picture-loan collections of both originals and reproductions. Ask at your local library for your nearest source. Bermondsey Library stocks 11,000 reproductions; Holborn Library hires out originals; Rugby and Dagenham lend pictures free to members; in Hove, there's a small charge; Woking specializes in original paintings by local artists.

There are also local clubs which operate like record and book clubs. And don't forget your local art school. Most of them hold an end of the year exhibition around mid-July.

You can buy beautiful posters or reproductions of old masters in poster sizes. The best selection comes from Paperchase, 216 Tottenham Court

Road, London W1 (Tel: 01-637 1121). They also sell cheap, near-invisible silvery metal clips so that you can make your own frames from perspex off-cuts or glass. Or you can buy assemble-it-yourself aluminium frames from Habitat. If you're having your picture professionally framed make sure you know beforehand how much it is going to cost, because these days it could easily be more than the picture.

What to put in an empty fireplace: If you don't like the surrounding tiles, you can paint them. If you don't like the hearth you can take it out, paint the back with black emulsion, then stand a magnificent green fern in it, or any sort of plant in any sort of pot.

EXPECT everything to go wrong and you won't feel quite so bad when it does.

As part of your moving budget plan some selfish treat for yourself after the first week in your new home. Think of this grimly when things get bad. Be prepared for *schadenfreuden*, those who delight in breaking bad news. Remember your private treat to come and fork out your notebooks: tears will get you nowhere.

WHO TO USE

For reasons beyond my control (briefly, money) I once moved five times in eighteen months. The first time I hired a lad and a van and the agony took three days and the breakages were appalling. My slipped disc alone cost £20 to repair. The second, third and fourth time I hired a specialist firm, Cole Brothers. A team of five men, used to working together, moved steadily over the house like locusts, leaving a trail of newspaper in their wake. They packed and moved me out in two hours and were into the new place and unpacked in two hours more and the whole drama was most enjoyable.

The fifth time I couldn't be present, but I engaged the moving department of one of Britain's most famous and expensive stores. A bunch of decrepit, gnarled, near old age pensioners turned up. My husband lost the plan and the whole mess took weeks to clear up.

The moral of the story is: if you can afford it, use specialists. Only the best seems to be cheap enough.

Pickfords provide good leaflets

which cover the difficulties of moving abroad and other non-straightforward moves. Look up their nearest offices from the telephone book. Large removal companies can be cheaper than small companies on long distance moves because additional unloading staff can be made available from nearby branch offices at the other end.

If you can't afford specialists, haven't got anything difficult to move, and aren't moving far, the cheapest way is to hire a van (you can drive a van up to 3-ton capacity using an ordinary driving licence). Hire of van plus man costs a little more.

For anything more elaborate:

Choose your mover carefully and book well in advance, preferably six weeks before (I got the gnarled dwarfs because I didn't do this).

Surprisingly, removal men have peak demand periods: the period before the day the rent is due, at the end of the month or on quarter days, and during the spring and summer – especially in the school holiday period. So these are the most expensive times to move. The cheapest time of the year to move is probably on a Monday in mid-February.

Get the leaflet published by the National Association of Furniture Warehousemen and Removers – if nothing else it's a good thing to wave at the removal men. Furthermore, if you hold it in your hand on The Day you can't hold anything else in your hand, i.e. interfere.

Try to get a removal firm which belongs to the British Standard Association of Movers. Look in the yellow pages.

Estimates and Contracts: Get quotes from three firms. You may be surprised how much they vary (up to 50 per cent in my experience). It can literally be a shattering experience to discover on the day of the move why the price from the firm you accepted is so low, because of their inefficiency.

If there's not enough furniture to fill a van, you will get a cheaper quotation. Some items can be moved as a 'part lot', which means that the firm will fit it in when they have a van in that area, but you must be prepared to wait up to ten days for delivery.

Draw the estimator's notice to any antiques, which will need specially careful handling.

Find out what the conditions of the contract are. In other words, find out what you're getting for your money, and check that it covers insurance while packing and unpacking, loading and unloading and in transit, also whether insurance covers damage to clocks and electrical equipment. The removers won't be responsible for the safety of jewellery, money or documents, so you should pop these in your bank or sew them into your stays or whatever before you move.

Whether it's two students with a bashed-up van or a Coles-style convoy, ask to be sent, recorded delivery, written proof that they are insured for damage to your goods and check with your insurance agent, again by recorded delivery, perhaps after a telephone call to sort out the problem.

Discover whether tea chests and packing materials are provided by the removal firm. Also packing and unpacking. Fixing curtains and carpets will certainly be extra. Find out how many men there will be on the job and ask for separate estimated times of arrival, loading, journey and unloading. Ask if there will be any extra costs?

Read your contract carefully; there are limitations to the contractors' liability. Briefly, the conditions of contract should cover the following points:

1 Acceptance of estimates.
2 Accessibility of premises.
3 Delays caused by events beyond company's control.
4 Responsibilities of a client.
5 What an estimate does not include.
6 What cannot be removed or stored.
7 When charges are to be paid.
8 The company's rights when charges are not paid.
9 Extent of company's liability.
10 The submission of claims.
11 Arbitration procedure.
12 Use of sub-contractors.

Naturally, you will get confirmation of these points in writing, together with a written estimate. When you confirm the estimate send it by recorded delivery and ask for a receipt and make sure that you get it or *you risk being liable for any expensive drama.*

There's generally a time limit – and it's generally seven days – in which to claim or complain. I have endeavoured to avoid boring legal jargon in this book; I stick it in only when it is *vital*. It's so easy for the eyes to glaze over and the brain blank out at paragraphs like the one in bold print below. Only when your Ming is in bits, your saucepans have lost their handles, the crate of your best china is missing and one piano leg has disappeared, may you see the point of it.

IMPORTANT LEGAL POINT: Normally, if a Party 'A' (that's you) accuses a Party 'B' (that's the Removal Firm) of negligence the burden of proof lies with the Accuser. When Party 'A' is the Client (called the Bailor) and Party 'B' is the Remover (called the Bailee for reward) the burden of proof is transferred to Party 'B', who must show that any loss or damage to belongings did not arise through his fault. It is sufficient for Party 'A' merely to claim that the damage was done by Party 'B' and not to establish how, why or where it was done. It is also necessary for Party 'B', if he is to be successful in rebutting the charges of 'A', to prove that he has not been negligent.

If you're moving that interesting little point is worth the cost of this whole book. It can mean that instead of your having to prove that the removers broke your Ming, they are responsible unless they can prove that they didn't.

THINGS TO ARRANGE IN ADVANCE

Traffic restrictions: If any, such as double yellow lines, apply to the area to which you are moving tell the contractor well in advance so that he can ask for police cooperation.

Fixtures and fittings: Make sure you have, in advance, ascertained what fixtures and fittings will be left at your new home. Get it in writing from the old owner of the property.

Amazingly, rose bushes, hydrangeas and doorknobs come into this category, as well as curtain rails, light fittings, fireplace fittings, TV aerial, and fitted cupboards. I have suffered from finding all the above items surprisingly missing upon my entry, and very tedious it was at the time. No use hollering for a lawyer when dusk is falling and you are roaming in the gloaming on a Friday night with no doorknobs and nothing to hang your clothes on.

Also, check the type of sockets at your new home to ensure that cookers, refrigerators and lamps will work on the day.

Services: Gas and telephone offices must be notified of your move a week beforehand (although British Gas *can* cope with forty-eight hours' notice). Electricity and water authorities can be notified forty-eight hours beforehand. Ask for services to be turned on the day before you arrive at your new home (or on the actual day if entry is impossible before you arrive) and turned off and the meters read at your old home on the morning of the day you leave. Be there to see that they are, or complain if they're not. Keep carbon copies (dated) of your letters and send all letters recorded delivery because you can no more assume that the service industries are efficient in your new, unknown area, than they were in the old one.

It is wise to get, and file, a letter from the gas, electricity, and other authorities confirming that you will not be responsible for bill payments after the move. I speak as one who was billed for six months by a single industry for *hundreds of pounds* currently due on houses which I left respectively two and three years ago. It may be relentless maniac computers, but it's still unsettling, time-consuming and very expensive in legal fees.

Locate the local doctor, hospital, bank and police station in your new area, with telephone numbers and addresses. Don't forget to contact the milkman too. Ask your neighbour which one she uses – a good way to meet your neighbour.

Electrical and gas fittings, etc.: Instruct the local authorities to disconnect fittings such as gas cookers, gas fires, water heaters and electrical fittings which should be removed only by a qualified electrician. Removal men won't disconnect any electrical or gas apparatus or take down electrical fittings if wired up to the mains. Nor will they take down or erect TV aerials, so arrange separately for this.

Refrigerators should be defrosted before loading. And you should start to run down any freezer supplies (i.e. eat the stuff) as soon as you know you're going to move, because a freezer is a heavy, delicate item and should be empty when moved.

Change of address: Visit your local post office to tell them of your intended departure. Fill in the forms to ensure that they forward your letters; you pay a small fee for this service (currently £2 a year).

Send change of address postcards to your friends, the magazines you subscribe to, the income tax people, your insurance company and all firms where you have a charge account.

Notification of new address for *premium bonds* should go, together with serial numbers held, to Bonds and Stock Office, Lytham St Anns, Lancs. Similarly, *savings certificates* should be re-registered at the Department of National Savings, Mulburne Gate House, Durham DH9 INS.

Unwanted items: Make an inventory of what you want to (a) move (b) sell (c) throw away. Call a rich charity (poor charities don't have transport) to collect unsaleable items or just leave them on the doorstep with a notice saying 'Please help yourself'. You'll be amazed how fast your junk disappears. Alternatively, telephone the town hall and ask for the refuse department to come and quote for removing the stuff.

Remember that no charity or hospital is thirsting for your broken television set, empty bottles or beat-up old armchair.

On-the-spot removal instructions: Write two copies, one for you and one for the foreman.

Make a neat plan of the dear old home, in red, numbering each piece of furniture. Get sticky trunk labels and stick the number on each piece of furniture, with a letter indicating its site in the new home. Make a neat plan of the new home, using blue pencil, with a letter attached to each room. Write the appropriate letter on the label on each piece of furniture. Each item should end up something like 'Ground floor scullery: Room G Item 29'.

Sleeping and eating arrangements: Organize yourself and family for sleep, preferably in someone else's house, such as that of the nearest grandmother or friends (big present afterwards to hostess). If, as is highly probable, you can't afford to move the family into an hotel during the drama period, fix a list of friends whom you can move to in emergencies. Perhaps you won't like the idea of imposing on them, but plenty of people don't mind putting a sofa or spare room at your disposal for a night. I have often offered mine to friends about to move; they've never taken advantage of the offer (and I refuse to list possible reasons) but it's reassuring to know that you have an emergency plan.

Plan meals also, whether it's a box of sandwiches, a picnic basket or a restaurant – and remember that you will need cash for the latter.

Children and pets: Do your best to get rid of the children. Ruthlessly use a grandmother, a Universal Aunt, or student at almost any cost. Check parks, cinemas, and babysitters in your new area. Keep a predetermined place for a box of placebos: soft drinks, toys, games, books, TV.

One removal expert stresses that parents must be extra kind and considerate during the whole of the removal period. Let calm and patience be the keywords, advises this obviously childless fellow. Keep babies, young children and pets out of the way. Removal men don't like stepping on or tripping over them.

Domestic animals can become unusually aggressive because they are upset by a change in routine and environment. The R.S.P.C.A. (look them up in the telephone directory) provide cheap cardboard carrying cartons for transporting cats, puppies and tortoises. Birds should be taken in a covered cage or a cardboard showbox with airholes punched in, then they won't flap around and risk injury. Carry fish in water in any waterproof container for a short journey, or sealed plastic bags with plenty of air to water. For anything larger consult your vet because, unlike children, pets can be tranquillized for a journey.

ON THE DAY

When the moving men arrive, go round the house with the foreman. Point out to him anything extraordinary which might need special attention. Don't forget outside items such as plants, statues, wire fencing. Give instructions only to the foreman.

What you must remember about removal men is to keep your plan simple, keep out of their way and communicate only with their chief wizard. I may be cynical, but budget for half of a generous tip in advance, give it to the supervisor and hint that the other half may be forthcoming upon your final departure. Allow £1 per removal man per day *at least*.

A good removal firm packs everything – books, china, saucepans, toys – EVERYTHING. (In larger homes the delicate stuff, such as china, glass and small items, may be packed the day before the move.) Bedding should be folded and left for the removal men to pack. Their tasks include taking apart and reassembling large bits of furniture such as bedsteads, wardrobes, desks and kitchen drawers. They take down curtains and take up linoleum. However, they do not rehang or relay it at the new home, except by previous arrangement. Nor do they refix wall fittings such as mirrors.

Very small valuable items, such as miniature carvings, should be packed in cotton wool in a box by the owner. Stereos and Hi-Fi's, say experts, should be specially packed in the cartons in which they arrived. As you will have thrown them away when you originally unpacked them, such items should be carefully packed in tea chests after screwing various screws down on the turntable and playing arm, according to the manufacturers' instructions. I wrecked a good stereo by not doing this on my last move.

Don't pack anything dangerous or inflammable such as matches, chemicals, or a battery gas lighter.

Leaving the old home: Lock the door after you finally leave and make sure that your removal impresario has a key to your new home as well as the address.

If the old house is likely to be empty for a few winter days it is advisable for the mover to drain pipes and tanks, which you do *after* the water supply has been turned off by the water board, by taking all the plugs out and turning all the taps on until the water gives out.

Check that you have left your home as neat and clean as possible: as you would hope to find your new one, in fact.

Upon arrival: Stick large letters on the doors of every room in your new house, according to your plan. Check that every piece of furniture carried in bears a number and a letter. (Tie or tape your furniture keys to the piece to which they belong.)

Your main job: It is your job on the day to keep especially silent. Don't moan, it doesn't help. Don't carry anything, save your strength for cleaning up.

Do *not* bend with the remover to remove. The most exasperating clients, say removal men, are those who tell them their jobs. Keep calm and keep within range, but out of the way.

You should:

1 Keep track of two sets of keys. Keys to the old home and the new should be kept in your handbag, and if possible the chief removal wizard should also have a set.

2 Make notes. Make a note of anything that's been forgotten, lost or broken.

3 Make tea. The last things stored in the first van (and therefore first out) should be the electric kettle, mugs, milk and teabags (cups always get

broken and anyway never hold enough tea).

4 Keep hold of the emergency survival suitcase.

Emergency survival suitcase: Should contain essential items, other than food and drink, such as washbag, toothpaste and toothbrushes, lavatory paper, soap, towels, tin opener and corkscrew, rubber gloves, sleeping pills if you take them, aspirins, a rubber-ended sink stopper, coathangers, a torch, a couple of spare light bulbs.

Keep your head when making, agreeing and checking your list of possessions upon arrival, and getting the removal chief-in-charge to sign it at the in and out stage. This avoids later argument as to whether the Jacobean loving cup wasn't in three pieces when they packed it.

It's the packing crates or orange boxes that make the muddle, so if you're moving without professional help, move them into the new home first and keep them in one room near the front door. Stick a numbered label on each case listing its contents, and keep the copy list of contents clipped to that dratted notebook as well, because then you'll know what's in the packing case which mysteriously disappears. Do not unpack crates until the furniture is in place. Move heavy furniture, such as gas stove and washing machine, before the lighter stuff.

Check that the sink, stove, lavatory, bath and basins work correctly. Check all curtain hanging apparatus is ready and working. Move curtains and carpets. Check light bulbs, light shades and electric plugs.

If all services have not been turned on, telephone and *complain*. Keep cool and reasonable when complaining, do not sound harassed, or you will be written off as an hysterical woman (which, of course, you now are). Always sweetly ask for the name of the person you are talking to at the other end of the line and insist on getting it. You may want to complain about *them* later – which is, of course, why they are reluctant to divulge their name.

Get to know the neighbours fast, so that you can tap them for water, extra milk and teabags. Just take a deep breath and knock on the door; then smile hopefully.

The friendliest way to greet a new harassed neighbour is to offer your telephone and teabags. Also, if you can afford it, give them a bowl of fruit or a bottle of wine on the evening of the first (always worst) day.

The day after: Complain again. Catch up on everything you thought you would be able to finish faster than was in fact possible.

LONG-TERM STORAGE

If all or some goods are being moved into storage, ask in advance what the cost of storage and insurance will be and how goods in store will be covered for loss or damage through fire (for any reason) or flood ? You are responsible for seeing that your goods are insured during the storage period, but the storage contractor can arrange this. Also ask how quickly your goods can be got back to you ?

By far the safest, cleanest, most trouble-free – and expensive – form of long-term storage is the relatively new concept of container loading. This involves prepacking the goods into standard size plywood containers which are sealed with metal clamps, stacked in a warehouse and unsealed only when you want them.

Ask the remover to supply 'Keep Forward' labels to paste on to a *few* items in store which you might need earlier than the rest, such as a desk or a bed or a pram. Once the goods are stored away it can be expensive to locate separate items.

If you pack any woollen garments, blankets or fabrics in trunks and chests, liberally scatter moth deterrent. Storage contractors are not responsible for moths. It's best if carpets and rugs are cleaned before storage and also treated with moth deterrent.

Don't store anything liquid or inflammable.

FOOD

HOW TO SAVE TIME AND MONEY ON FOOD

To shop better and faster the Food Information Centre advises:

1 Plan the week's menus (at least for the main daily meal) one week ahead using seasonal food.
2 Make a shopping list and try to stick to it.

Save time for yourself by cutting your shopping down to twice a week maximum – preferably on Tuesday and Friday, never on Monday because there is less choice and not all the food in the shops is fresh. Also, the more you keep away from the shops the less money you'll spend. You can't afford to see shopping trips as social occasions – it's too temptingly expensive.

The earlier you visit the supermarket, the less crowded it will be and the less time you'll have to waste queueing at the checkout counter.

Try to avoid carrying shopping bags, because they will tire you. Buy, borrow or beg a bag on wheels. Not a basket: they take up too much room and snag your tights, and the basket doesn't lift off from the supporting frame.

Bulk-buy as much tinnery and dry goods as you can afford in terms of money and storage.

Keep a spiral notebook in the kitchen as a *shopping book* with an attached pencil – shopping lists on old envelopes tend to get lost. (You might, like me, also use this notebook for planning meals. Work out menus on the left-hand page: on the facing page write down what you need to buy in order to make them.)

Before you shop, run your eye over your standard food list to check what you might need. Always jot down

FOOD

'marmalade' just *before* you finish the jar.

Make a standard food list by writing down what's in your cupboards *now*. Star weekly necessities like this,*, and divide the list into greengrocer, butcher, grocer, supermarket, baker, sweetshop, or whatever your tastes dictate.

Pin your standard food list on the back of the larder door (I also tape one in the back of my address book). If you haven't a larder, pin it on the back of the kitchen door. (You might also apply to your local authority for a grant to install a proper food store. You are eligible for this if you have no floor-fixed food storage cupboards.)

Stock up with groceries and canned foods once a fortnight, taking advantage of discounts, and cut prices or large sizes. Don't be inflexible with shopping. If you see an amazingly cheap treat, like juicy mussels, that isn't on your shopping list, then get it. *But knock something else off it.*

SHOPPING CHECK LIST

Jeer if you must, but I've used this check list for twelve years, with or without someone to shop for me.

Starred items are staples for quick weekly check.

If you do all your shopping at one supermarket so much the better. I always write out a shopping list from my check list because otherwise I impulse buy.

I sometimes don't make up menus until I've returned from the shops. Instead I put down on the list something vague like two fish dishes, three meat items.

Cross out or add to these lists as you please.

CLEANING MATERIALS

spongecloths, – dusters, – matches, – Brillo scouring pads, – Domestos bleach, – washing-up liquid, – oven spray, – Duraglit brass, copper and chrome, – Pledge spray polish, – Goddard's Long Life silver polish,– Dettol disinfectant, – Ariel biological detergent, – Stergene, – Flash, – Liquid Ajax, – shoe-cream, – Liquid Gumption, – Antiquax, – plastic dustbin liners

CHEMIST

*lavatory paper, – *soap, – *toothpaste and powder, – sponges, – toothbrushes, – *STs, – Elastoplast, – tissues, – vitamin tablets, – *shampoo, – *razorblades

BAKER

*loaves: – Edinburgh, – rye, – Prewitt's stoneground; – croissants, – cake

MILKMAN
  *milk, – sour or fresh cream, – yoghurt

....

....

....

....

PETSHOP
  *dogfood, – *cat food, – *cat litter

....

....

....

....

GREENGROCER
  *parsley, – *mint. *Salad vegetables: lettuce, – cucumber, – tomatoes, – white cabbage, – spring onions, – radishes, – celery, – endive, watercress, – beetroot
  *Basic British vegetables: mushrooms, – onions, – potatoes, – cabbage, cauliflower, – turnips, swedes, – leeks, – carrots
  Other vegetables: avocados, – peppers, – courgettes, – sweet corn.
  *Fruit: oranges, – apples, – bananas, – lemons, – pineapple

....

....

....

....

FISHMONGER
  shrimps, – cod, – herrings, – mackerel, – sole, – kippers, – mussels, – crab

....

....

....

....

BUTCHER
  This list is for when my dazed mind can't think further than lamb chops.

  Grill or fry
  Beef: steaks, fillets, top price but tender; rump, the most flavoursome; Porterhouse, the largest.
  Veal: Best end of neck; fillet, sliced from top of back leg; loin chops; escalopes, to be rolled even thinner and lightly cooked.
  Pork: Chops, spare ribs; fillet – for splendid occasions; sausages.
  Lamb: Cutlets, small; loin chops; chump chops – more meat, less bone.

  Casseroles and stews
  Beef: Stewing steak, chuck steak, skirt, neck, leg, shin, silverside, brisket, mince.
  Veal: Breast, for pies.
  Pork: Belly.
  Lamb: Scrag end for stews and hot-pots, breast.
  Offals: Tripe (beef), sweetbreads (veal or lamb), brains, tongues, liver (lamb or ox), cow's heels, pig's trotters, kidneys (lamb's, calf's, pig's or ox), heart (lamb or ox), calf's head, pig's head.

FOOD

Roasts

Beef: Rib on the bone or boned and rolled for easy carving; sirloin; topside.

Veal: Leg or half-leg; shoulder or half-shoulder; best end of neck.

Pork: leg or half-leg; loin; hand or shoulder (juicy and cheaper).

Lamb: Leg or half-leg; shoulder or half-shoulder (fattish); best end of neck – to carve in 'chop' portions; breast, boned, stuffed and rolled; saddle, more meaty than best end of neck.

Also: Hare, rabbit, game pheasant, partridge, fowl.

GROCER

My list of basics: *bacon, *bread, bouillon cubes, breakfast cereals, *butter, *cheese, *coffee beans, cocoa, *biscuits, *cream, *eggs, *frozen goods, honey, marmalade, jam, ham, fruit juice, haricot beans, pasta, rice, Ribena, sugar, tea, flour, sauces, dried fruit, salt and pepper, olive oil, herbs, packet soups, tomatoes (tinned and tubed), tinned goods, cornflour, nuts, olives.

Vinegars: cider, wine-tarragon; cooking wines, red and white; cooking sherry; brandy essence.

....

....

....

....

SEASONAL FOOD GUIDES

With the help of a Covent Garden wholesaler and a hotel caterer, I've listed the food in a calendar because if you want to know what's fresh and cheap in June, you don't want to start sorting it out for yourself from an alphabetical index.

Food is not generally cheapest at the start of the season, but in the middle, so the food calendar has both a seasonal chart and a good-time-to-buy guide – when there *is* a predictable good-time-to-buy. In order to simplify, I haven't necessarily mentioned when imported, as plentiful availability is what is most important.

I have also included an alphabetical list of some seasonal foods so that if your man lusts for fresh grouse, you can tell him he can't have it until 12 August.

Seasonal Food Chart

Month available	Meat, Fish and Game (including imports)	Vegetables (including imports)	Fruit (including imports)	Preferably cheapest time to buy

All year	beef
	calf
	lamb
	mutton
	pork
	sucking pig
	rabbit
	veal
	cod
	dab
	haddock
	halibut
	herring
	mackerel
	plaice
	prawns
	salmon
	scampi
	skate
	sole
	trout
	turbot
	whiting
		asparagus
		artichokes
		aubergines
		avocados
		beans
		  (broad, french)
		beetroot
		broccoli
		cabbage (hard
		  white or red)
		carrots, old
		cauliflower
		celery
		chicory
		cress (salad)
		cucumber
		garlic
		green pepper
		horseradish
		lettuce (round)
		mushrooms
		onions
		parsnips
		peas
		potatoes
		spinach
		spring onions
		tomatoes
		turnips
		turnip tops (taste
		  like spring onions)
			apples
			bananas
			grapefruit
			grapes
			lemons
			melon
			nuts
			oranges
			pineapple
			strawberries
			tangerines	

January		broccoli, white
		  (until Aug.)
		Savoy and spring
		  cabbage
		  (until May)
		spring greens
		  (until May)		

FOOD

Seasonal Food Chart (*continued*)

Month available	*Meat, Fish, and Game (including imports)*	*Vegetables (including imports)*	*Fruit (including imports)*	*Preferably cheapest time to buy*
February	whitebait (until June)		lemons, best (until Oct.) rhubarb (until Oct.)	
March	crab (until Oct.) fresh trout (until Sept.)	broadbeans (until Dec.) dwarf beans (until Dec.) turnip tops (until July)		spring greens
April	fresh lamb (until May) sucking pig (until May) veal (until May) herring (until Jan.) mackerel (until June)	cucumber (until Sept.) globe artichokes (until Dec.) Jerusalem artichokes (until Dec.) spinach (until Oct.) spring onions (until Nov.) sweet potatoes (until Sept.) Webb's wonder lettuce hooray! (until Oct.)	Charentais melons (until May) ortaniques	salmon broccoli
May	red mullet (until Sept.)	asparagus (until July) Cos and Webb lettuce (until Nov.) mange touts (until Aug.)	gooseberries (until July) strawberries (until June)	mackerel plaice salmon trout whitebait rhubarb

Seasonal Food Chart (*continued*)

Month available	Meat, Fish, and Game (*including imports*)	Vegetables (*including imports*)	Fruit (*including imports*)	Preferably cheapest time to buy
May *contd.*		marrow (until Oct.) mint (until Nov.) peas (until Aug.) radish (until Oct.) summer cabbage (until Sept.) turnips, new (until July)		
June		mint (until Oct.) new potatoes (until Aug.) new turnips (getting positively rare) (until Sept.) parsley (until Dec.) runner beans (until Sept.) broadbeans (until Aug.) French beans (until Aug.) new carrots (until July) globe artichokes (until Oct.) cauliflower (until Oct.) kale (until Sept.)	apricots (until Aug.) blackcurrants (until Aug.) cantaloupe melons (until July) cherries (until Aug.) gooseberries (until Aug.) raspberries (until Aug.) redcurrants (until Aug.)	red mullet salmon trout artichokes asparagus cucumber carrots dwarf beans new potatoes gooseberries raspberries redcurrants strawberries cherries

FOOD

Seasonal Food Chart (*continued*)

Month available	*Meat, Fish, and Game (including imports)*	*Vegetables (including imports)*	*Fruit (including imports)*	*Preferably cheapest time to buy*
July	halibut (until Dec.)	courgettes (until Oct.) endive (until Sept.) fennel (until Sept.) parsnips (until March) shallots (until March) Spanish onions (until Feb.)	apples (until Feb.) blackcurrants (until Aug.) loganberries (until Aug.) peaches (until Aug.) plums, cooking (until Oct.)	salmon trout turbot asparagus new potatoes peas spinach blackcurrants cherries
August	grouse (12 Aug./ 10 Dec.) hare (until Feb.)	aubergines (until Dec.) beetroot (until Feb.) cabbage, red and hard white (until Jan.) celery (until Feb.) corn on the cob (until Oct.) cucumber (until Sept.) leeks (until April) old potatoes (until June) onions, Spanish and pickling (until Nov.) sorrel (until Oct.) tomatoes, English (until Oct.)	fresh figs (until Sept.) limes (until Sept.) plums, dessert (until Oct.) watermelons (until Sept.)	crab halibut trout broadbeans marrow radishes (until Sept.) spinach plums

Seasonal Food Chart (*continued*)

Month available	Meat, Fish, and Game (*including imports*)	Vegetables (*including imports*)	Fruit (*including imports*)	Preferably cheapest time to buy
September	hake (until Jan.) skate (until April) partridge (until Feb.) mutton (best and cheapest from now until Feb.) mussels (until April)	broccoli, purple (until Oct.) brussels sprouts (until March) celeriac (until Dec.) celery (until Feb.) red peppers (until Nov.) swedes (until April) turnips, old (until March)	apples, English (until March) blackberries (until Oct.) grapes (until Dec.) honeydew melons (until Nov.) pears (until Jan.)	haddock mutton (until Feb.) rabbit cauliflower corn on the cob mushrooms parsnips runner beans tomatoes turnips, new apples blackberries pears
October	pheasant (until Feb.)	chicory (until May) new parsnips (until March) primo cabbage (until Feb.) swedes (until April)	apples, cookers (until April) dates (until March)	cod mussels rabbit carrots, old cauliflower mushrooms parsnips spinach turnips apples blackberries
November		brussels sprouts (until March) Jerusalem artichokes (until March) shallots (until Dec.) sea kale (until May)	satsumas (until March) dried figs (until Feb.) dried muscatels (until Jan.)	hare mussels all root vegetables celery leeks sprouts

Seasonal Food Chart (*continued*)

Month available	Meat, Fish, and Game (including imports)	Vegetables (including imports)	Fruit (including imports)	Preferably cheapest time to buy
December		broccoli, white (until April)		hare all root vegetables sprouts

ALPHABETICAL LIST OF FOOD IN SEASON

Meat, Fish and Game

Name	Plentiful	Imported
beef	all year	all year
cod	Oct.–May	all year
crab	March–Oct.	
dab	June–Feb.	
grouse	12 Aug.–10 Dec.	
haddock	June–Dec.	all year
hake	June–Jan.	
halibut	July–Dec.	all year
hare	Sept.–Feb.	
herring	May–Jan.	all year
lamb	April–May	all year
mackerel	April–June	all year
mussels	Sept.–April	
mutton	Sept.–Feb.	all year
partridge	Sept.–Feb.	
pheasant	Oct.–Feb.	
plaice	April–Oct.	
pork	all year	all year
rabbit	Sept.–Feb.	all year
red mullet	May–Sept.	
salmon	Feb.–Aug.	all year
skate	Oct.–April	
sole	April–Jan.	all year
sucking pig	April–May	all year
trout	March–Sept.	all year
turbot	June–Dec.	all year
veal	April–May	all year
whitebait	Feb.–June	

Vegetables

Name	Plentiful	Imported
artichokes (globe)	June–Oct.	May–Jan.
artichokes (Jerusalem)	April–Dec.	
asparagus	May–July	all year
aubergines (import)	Aug.–Dec.	all year
avocado pears (import)	Dec.–May	all year
beans (broad)	June–Aug.	March–Sept.
beans (dwarf)	July–Aug.	March–Dec.
beans (French)	July–Aug.	all year
beans (runner)	July–Sept.	
beetroot	Aug.–Feb.	
broccoli (white)	Dec.–Aug.	
broccoli (purple)	Sept.–Oct.	
brussels sprouts	Nov.–March	
cabbage (hard white)	Aug.–Jan.	all year
cabbage (primo)	Oct.–Feb.	
cabbage (red)	Aug.–Jan.	all year
cabbage (Savoy)	Jan.–Mar.	
cabbage (spring)	Jan.–May	
cabbage (summer)	May–Sept.	
carrots (new)	June–July	March–June
carrots (old)	all year	
cauliflower	June–Oct.	Dec.–May
celeriac	Sept.–Dec.	April–July
celery	Aug.–Feb.	all year
chicory	Oct.–May	June–Dec.
corn on the cob	Sept.	Aug.–Oct.
courgettes	July–Oct.	April–Dec.
cress (salad)	all year	
cress (water)	April–Dec.	
cucumber	April–Sept.	all year.
endive (frise)	July–Sept.	June–Nov.
fennel	July–Sept.	
garlic	all year	
horseradish	all year	
kale (curly)	June–Sept.	
leeks	Aug.–April	
lettuce (cos)	May–Nov.	
lettuce (round)	April–Nov.	all year
lettuce (Webb's)	May–Oct.	
mange touts	May–Aug.	
marrow	May–Oct.	
mint	May–Nov.	
mushrooms	all year	

FOOD

Vegetables (*continued*)

Name	*Plentiful*	*Imported*
onions	Sept.–May	all year
onions (pickling)	Aug.–Nov.	
onions (Spanish)	Aug.–Nov.	July–Jan.
onions (spring)	April–Nov.	all year
parsley	June–Dec.	
parsnips	Oct.–March	
peas	May–Aug.	
peppers (green)		all year
peppers (red)		Sept.–Nov.
radish	Aug.–Sept.	
sea kale	Nov.–May	
shallots	July–March	Jan.–Oct.
sorrell	Aug.–Oct.	
spinach	April–Oct.	
spring greens	Jan.–May	
swedes	Oct.–April	
sweet potatoes		April–Sept.
turnips (new)	June–July	
turnips (old)	Sept.–March	
turnip tops	March	
tomatoes (English)	Aug.–Oct.	
tomatoes (import)	May–Oct.	all year

Fruit

apples (cookers)	Oct.–April	
apples (English)	Sept.–March	
apples (import)		all year
apricots	June–Aug.	Jan.–Aug.
bananas (import)		all year
blackberries	Sept.	
blackcurrants	July–Aug.	
cherries	June–Aug.	
dates (dried, import)	Oct.–March	
figs (fresh, import)	Aug.–Sept.	
figs (dried, import)	Nov.–Feb.	
gooseberries	June	
grapefruit (import)	Jan.–June	all year
grapes (import)	Sept.–Dec.	all year
lemons (import)	Feb.–Oct.	all year
limes (import)	Aug.–Sept.	
loganberries	July–Aug.	
melons (cantaloupe, import)	June–July	

Fruit (*continued*)

Name	Plentiful	Imported
melons (charentais, import)	April–May	
melons (water, import)	Aug.–Sept.	
muscatels (dried, import)	Dec.	
oranges (import)	April–May (Oct.–June)	all year
ortaniques (import)	April	
pears	Sept.–Jan.	all year
plums (cooking)	July–Sept.	
plums (dessert)	Aug.–Oct.	
raspberries	June–Aug.	
redcurrants	June–Aug.	
rhubarb	Feb.–Oct.	
satsumas (import)	Nov.–March	
strawberries	May–June	
tangerines (import)	Dec.–Jan.	

LOOKING FORWARD TO A FREEZE-UP

When my freezer is full I feel a warm, housewifely glow. It's the nearest I can get to an old-fashioned larder with marble shelves, rows of bottled fruit and hanging ham. I used to feel guilty about this before I went to France to interview French farmers' wives and found that the things they were most proud of were their corpse-sized freezers. And they didn't have half an ox inside either. They were stuffed with French pastries. Tiens. Of course I prefer fresh meat and vegetables but there are seven good reasons why I have a freezer:

1 It saves money and effort.
2 It cuts waste. Leftover portions get frozen as a meal for one, not produced the next day to a chorus of groans.
3 It saves cooking time and shopping time.
4 It enables me to enjoy cooking far more, because I do less of it.
5 It helps me entertain without anxiety or exhaustion.
6 I am always ready to produce a meal in emergencies.
7 I rarely run out of everyday food. (I even freeze a sliced loaf in case I run out of breakfast toast. You can toast the bread while still frozen.)

Deep freezing is the simplest natural way of preserving food. Clarence Birdseye started doing so commercially after a holiday visit to the Antarctic. Food-destroying bacteria won't live at very low temperatures and most food, correctly stored, can safely be frozen for months. A deep freeze will store shop-bought food for up to one year (I know an American designer who only shops once a month), and home-made frozen dishes are as different from shop-bought frozen dishes as home-bottled peaches are from tinned ones.

You can also freeze your own or

neighbourhood soft fruit and young vegetables, and a glut needn't rot – it goes straight in the freezer. My father used to fish in the summer and shoot in the winter and his hunting efforts were all immediately frozen. If you live in the country you can, perhaps, profit by buying and freezing local produce when plentiful.

Buying and stocking a deep freeze is generally a major housekeeping investment. So what do you get for your money? Briefly, I found that I recouped the initial cost within two years. From then on I started to actually save money (up to 30 per cent: the biggest saving is on meat).

The first filling can be a heavy expense, but I stocked mine gradually. Others prefer to buy the lot at once, empty it, then start again. I know an architect's wife who got a bank loan to buy a freezer and stock it. She bought a dozen chickens, half a lamb, half a side of pork and half a side of beef. She reckoned she cut her costs by half, after not being able to afford beef for years.

However, it's not necessarily the *folie de grandeur* of laying down a complete cow that tempts a housewife, it's just the thought of having a stock cupboard reserve of extra peas and beans, a positive cornucopia of fish fingers and hamburger meat.

A freezer saves time, and it also means the difference between cookery as a drudge work (three times a day, non-stop, a thousand meals a year) and cookery when I choose, in concentrated wedges of time, when it is possible to cook a batch of dishes. I've accumulated the current pre-cooked contents without even noticing that I was cooking, simply by cooking more than enough for one meal, or by cooking double quantities of everything freezable, such as stew, for a week or two.

I keep lots of food that's quickly thawed and easily warmed up for pop-up children: chops, pizzas, egg and bacon tarts, pies. This means that in the holidays if they are doing something more interesting older children can miss a meal or cook something simple for themselves when they deign to turn up.

Unexpected guests can always be fed without difficulty or mental arithmetic. If more than expected turn up for a meal I put the meal I had planned aside and unfreeze something larger, perhaps *blanquette de veau* or *coq au vin;* thawed out in a double saucepan. Pre-prepared food can be thawed out quicker than a joint or poultry.

If you have a particularly busy or harassing period, or if you are ill, the freezer enables your family to be well fed on balanced meals, whatever the weather or the crisis.

Novelist Mary Stewart told me that when she goes away on lecture tours she leaves a fortnight's supply of pre-prepared, home-frozen food for her husband, with a careful menu for him to follow. Last time I went away I followed her example and stocked up on some trial shop-bought gourmet frozen dishes – *canard a l'orange, ratatouille, boeuf bourguignon, fruit de mer* – that sort of thing. In fact, as soon as my back was turned my husband was invited out every night, so I had the accumulated delicacies for lunch to cheer me up whenever this book looked as if it would never be finished.

I list freezer contents in the back of my menu book. It's easy to write it all in the book as it goes in because

94

I generally do that in big batches, but it's more difficult to remember to tick them off as you remove them, unless you tape your list in the freezer door. I use the freezer list as a menu book. But 'would you like smoked haddock soufflé or grouse this evening?' can be embarrassing if you've run out of grouse and not ticked it off.

Types of freezers: There are basically three types of freezers all of which can be bought on H.P.: (1) chest of drawers (front-opening); (2) cabinet with a lift-up top and (3) combined fridge with freezer on top (not to be confused with a frozen food compartment). In many ways there seems little to choose between them – they are just large white reliable boxes.

A top-opening freezer would seem to invite frozen fingers and slipped discs. You may have to dive in and burrow like a dog at a rabbit for whatever frozen packet you want, which may be right at the bottom under everything else. You will then have to repack the thing. A top-opening deep freeze is said to let in less warm air than a front-opening one, but pay no attention to this fact. Buy a front-opening chest of drawers type and shut it fast.

Some freezers have very useful narrow shelves inside the door, some have adjustable grid shelves, some have pull-out drawers. These last are, of course, the easiest to find your food in. You can get freezers with security locks, quick freeze switches, thermostatic temperature settings, warning lights and interior lights.

Sizes: In general they vary from around 4 cubic feet (the size of a washing machine) to about 20 cubic feet and, as a rough guide, 1 *cubic foot*

stores 25 lb frozen food. If you buy one of the very small ones once you've got the knack you might find it is too small for bulk buying. I happily started off with a 4 cubic foot drawer Bauchnecht that hasn't given a moment's trouble in ten years and, as we live in the city and don't often bulk buy, it has proven large enough for a family of four.

If there's no room in your kitchen, you don't have to keep your freezer there. You can keep it anywhere that's cool and dry and near a suitable electric socket, even in the garage.

What's the running cost? A freezer doesn't cost much to run. A 4 cubic foot freezer uses about five electrical units a week.

What happens if there's a power cut? The food will be safe for twenty-four hours, if the door isn't opened. A well filled freezer can maintain a temperature of 18°F for thirty-six to forty-eight hours. Don't open your freezer for two hours after the power cut is over.

If there's a longer power failure (insure against this as well as against mechanical failure) put on a pair of thick gloves and work fast, wrapping the food in old newspapers. Cover the lot with a blanket. If you can get dry ice it will protect food for three days but, touch wood, power cuts don't generally last that long.

How to freeze:

1 Read the freezer manufacturers' instruction book.
2 Up to one-tenth capacity of the freezer can be frozen at once (say 10 lb in a 4 cubic foot freezer).

FOOD

3 Freeze only clean, fresh food in good condition, as soon as possible after it has been picked, bought or preserved.

4 Package properly, with moisture, air and flavour proof packaging, such as an ordinary plastic bag. The food must be wrapped so that all air is excluded, but leave $\frac{1}{2}$-inch spaces for liquids to expand in. (Suck the air out with a straw.)

5 Cool hot foods quickly before freezing. Set the control to the coldest setting two hours before freezing a batch of food (perhaps when you start to work on it).

6 Label all packages. Frozen jugged hare looks very like frozen beef casserole.

7 Don't refreeze food. It could make you ill.

8 Defrost once a year.

DON'T FREEZE:

MILK, HARD-BOILED OR SHELLED EGGS, BANANAS, MAYONNAISE (pity), COOKED RICE, POTATOES (except for uncooked chips, which seem to freeze well), TOMATOES, ANYTHING JUICY LIKE PEARS, MELON, SALAD GREENS, CUCUMBER (a drooping cucumber looks particularly despondent when defrosted).

Pasta can be frozen, but should be undercooked to allow for the reheating. It is never as good as when freshly made.

Here's my current deep freeze list. All prepared dishes, soups or sauces are for four.

Drawer 1

Sauces, soups and casseroles

Sauces: 6 bolognese, 6 tomato, 6 onion, 4 cheese, 4 bread.

Soup: 4 leek and onion, 2 game, 2 onion, 2 potato, 2 chicken, 4 Scotch broth.

Made dishes: 2 tripe and onion, 2 duck and orange, 4 beef casserole, 2 jugged hare, 2 rabbit stew.

Drawer 2

Meat, poultry, game, fish

7 lb bladebone steak, 6 lb pie veal, 21 hamburgers, 12 lamb chump chops, 2 legs lamb, 6 pork chops, 5 grouse, 8 veal escalopes, 3 chickens, 3 lb chicken livers, 12 cod steaks, 4 plaice fillets and 4 halibut steaks.

Drawer 3

Bakery

12 large vol au vent cases, 6 flat flans, 12 croissants, 6 dinner rolls, 2 Victoria sandwiches, 20 sandwiches (lemon and sardine, shrimp and cream cheese), 6 pizza pies, 12 chocolate eclairs, 1 sachertorte (already sliced).

Drawer 4

Vegetables and fruit

4 raspberries, 2 blackberries, 2 strawberries, 6 sweetcorn, 2 peas, 2 beans, 2 ratatouille, 4 spinach.

Door shelves: In the narrow door shelves, I keep small items and decent-sized single portion leftovers.

96

Door shelf 1
2 parsley, 1 mint (just scrunch the bag over a dish and you don't have to chop it), 1 loaf sliced bread, 12 inches empty space for leftovers.

Door shelf 2
Ice cream (2 orange sorbet, 4 chocolate, 3 coffee, 2 rum, 3 butterscotch).

Door shelf 3
3 brandy butter, 4 chocolate sauce, 4 frozen pastry, 33 frozen whipped cream rosettes.

Door shelf 4
6 packets prawns, 1 carton cream, ¼ lb cheddar cheese, 6 tins frozen orange juice (add a squeezed fresh lemon plus two lemon slices before serving).

PREPARING FROZEN FOOD FOR EATING

Precooked Vegetables: Don't thaw. Cook in a little boiling salted water. How long? Mr. Bertorelli himself told me to take no notice of whatever time the manufacturer puts on the pack. They tend to over-time them. Cook them until *you* reckon they are done, just as you would cook any other vegetable.

Meat and Poultry: When defrosting it's best to leave these in the refrigerator overnight. The meat must be completely thawed before cooking. Fast thawing destroys the taste.

Bakery: Unwrap and then thaw overnight – although frozen croissants can go straight into a very low oven for ten minutes. Bakery freezes extremely well.

Sauces and casseroles: May be heated from the frozen state in a double boiler.

Golden Rule: Monique Guillaume, the famous French cookery writer, told me that whenever she serves anything frozen she tries to add *something* fresh, e.g. a lump of butter on peas, a grating of nutmeg on spinach, cream to a white sauce, lemon juice and a little grated peel on fish dishes, and a dash of wine or cooking brandy for any meat stew (well, she's French).

EQUIPMENT AND SUPPLIES

You might prefer elaborate equipment but you can freeze perfectly well with an assortment of plastic bags, elastic bands, transparent wrapping film, deep-freeze polytape (ordinary sellotape comes unstuck), and wax crayons (ordinary pencil or biro mysteriously dissolves).

You can get a free catalogue of packing equipment from Frigicold, 10 Manchester Square, London W1, who sell a comprehensive selection of containers and packaging for use with freezers.

An excellent pithy little guidebook is *Deep Freezing* by Mary Norwak (Sphere, 40p). She includes good recipes for such easily frozen food as beef in wine, pigeon pie, chicken liver pâté, spaghetti sauce, brandy butter, pie fillings, gingerbread. She also has a most useful list of bulk food suppliers, with descriptions of their mouth-watering wares.

Alternatively look in your yellow pages for your nearest frozen food supplier at catering prices. You can get a wide range of cooked, frozen and fresh poultry, meats, sea food, vegetables, sausages, fish fingers, fruit, pastries, cakes and icecream. Vegetables are obtainable in 5-lb packs, corn on the cob by the dozen.

Smithfield and West, PO Box 26, Orpington, will send by post completely boned and mature sirloins of Scotch beef or best Dutch veal. The cuts are already trimmed to slice into steaks or escalopes. Not cheap, but cheaper than the butcher.

STORE CUPBOARD COOKERY

When, unexpectedly, you have to produce a hostess-type meal and don't necessarily have a deep freeze, it's generally the challenge and the panic which dismays you. But you are perfectly capable. It's the situation which may be unnerving you unnecessarily. *Looking* serene and prepared is half the secret of being prepared, and let no boy scout tell you otherwise.

In an emergency, dress first, then lay the table (shows that they are obviously expected – you can keep guests waiting for food), then start cooking. The worst part of the evening will be the stomach rumbling interlude before dinner, so plan to keep your audience interested. Get your man to bring the boss home via a high grade pub; get the family's five thousand famished friends to help out in the kitchen – they'll enjoy it as long as you pretend it's an enjoyable occasion and do not *bustle*.

The emergencies that send you reeling will fall into two categories. There are the emergencies of quality when the man in your life calls from the office to say he's bringing Mr. Big home to sample your culinary splendours, and there are the emergencies of quantity, when all the family invite their friends in at the same time and expect you to perform the miracle of loaves and fishes all over again.

If *emergencies of quantity* are common in your house keep a couple of these in reserve.

1 Tins of ham, tongue, tuna fish, sardines, frankfurters; rice, spaghetti and other pastas.
2 To go with the above: a packet of Parmesan cheese; tins of tomatoes and tomato purée.
3 Tins of soup, especially Crosse & Blackwell's consommé which can be served cold with a dash of cream or hot with one of the following: a dash of vodka, a squeeze of lemon, a slosh of sherry (and perhaps some green ends of onion chopped small).
4 Packs of long-term carrots or tiny new potatoes (add mint and they'll never know it's Brooke Farm).
5 Bottled and tinned whole courses – not instant curries, but delicacies such as Polish stuffed cabbage, French cassoulet or a whole Polish boiled chicken.
6 Fruit and vegetables in tins, especially red peppers and French beans.

Emergencies of quality need those basics and a few extras such as:

1 Tinned pâté, or bottled gulls' eggs.
2 Tinned prawns, shrimps, crab, lobster (to mix with green salad

98

and French dressing or mayonnaise).

3 Hellman's bottled mayonnaise
(decant into a little dish, add a
squeeze of lemon and stir hopefully).

4 Lychees and other exotic fruit.

5 Chestnut purée (serve in individual
glasses with, if possible, a topping
of whipped cream, or a dash of
brandy).

6 Slowly, one ingredient at a time,
build up a collection of herbs,
spices, garnish and sauce ingredients – things such as anchovies,
stem ginger, crystallized violets,
olives, capers, tabasco and a good
range of dried herbs and spices.

Some things just aren't worth
giving shelf space to: most tinned
minced meats; instant curries or chop
sueys; certain herbs such as chervil
and mint which can't be dried successfully; instant sauces – because
making your own with store cupboard ingredients is almost as quick
and the result tastes better. (However,
Escoffier Cumberland saúce, heated
with the juice and grated rind of half
an orange, is well worth trying with
meat or game.)

It helps with emergency cooking if
you keep a *stockpot*. I kept one last
winter and boiled it up every day
(the only necessary discipline), then
threw it away in the spring.

Don't confuse your stockpot with
your dustbin. The only ingredients
which you throw into a stockpot are
bones, the odd vegetable, herbs and
chopped onions. Bones can smell
nauseatingly funereal. Disguise the
odour by adding chopped garlic and a
slosh of vinegar or white wine.

The most important aspect of
cooking is knowing what you can get
away with and what you can't. What
I have found I *must* have fresh are:
coffee beans, potatoes, onions, cream
and lemons. Also wine vinegar, cooking wine (to add to dishes), butter in
which to toss vegetables, and freshly
ground black pepper, not that beige
dust.

Keep an emergency jar of Nestle's
Gold Blend coffee and Coffee Comple-
ment dried milk buried in the depths
of your store cupboard. You might also
keep some Longlife milk and cream
hidden at the back of your refrigerator.

Suggestions for meals: Tinned peas
or spinach served straight from the
tin are pretty uninspiring; but if you
take a tin of tiny French peas and
butter and spice gently with nutmeg
then serve piping hot pease pudding
with ham or frankfurters it can be
delicious. Similarly serve spinach
pureed with cream and grated fresh
nutmeg.

Serve noodles tossed in butter or
cream with a crushed clove of garlic
as a starter/filler.

Serve egg curry, with sliced hard-
boiled eggs in a tin of Lekari sauce
with an added squeeze of lemon and
hot fluffy, boiled rice.

CAMOUFLAGE

Camouflage is the secret of successful store cupboard cookery. The
principle is simple: use available fresh
windowdressing to disguise the un-
appetizing look, feel or taste of stored
food. A few tips...

For a fresh touch try to have a bit of greenery to chop finely onto whatever you're serving. If you leave onions long enough they will generally sprout. For a chive taste, snip the ends onto soups or omelette.

A fresh pepper, whether red or green, lasts about three weeks and tastes delicious shredded into salad. However shrivelled, when chopped into almost any stew dish it imparts a 'continental' flavour.

A piece of grated lemon peel gives a fresh flavour to almost anything from soup to fruit.

Almost any fresh fruit, from oranges to grapes, tastes delicious when peeled, chopped up, sprinkled with a little white wine then served in individual wine glasses (any old shape or size) with a dab of sugar sprinkled on and topped with fresh or sour cream. If the cream is tinned whip in a dash of something alcoholic.

JADED COOK

There comes a time in the affairs of women when your mind blanks out, you feel resentful, apologetic, apathetic and mutinous and you simply can't concentrate on food. Don't worry. *You are a jaded cook.* It was a jaded cook who once said that the best thing about Christmas was that you never had to think 'what shall I give them for dinner?'. It was a jaded cook who pointed out that the main advantage of spaghetti is that you don't have to peel it. You could deal with this feeling as calmly as Ethel Kennedy, who has a fourteen-day family menu

plan for her eleven children. It is based on simple roasts, grills, omelettes and salads. When she comes to the fifteenth day she simply starts again.

The Kennedy secret is . . . ORGANIZATION. You, too, can have a food plan.

WORD OF WARNING: Keep quiet about it. Don't tell anyone, or someone might complain. Keep your plan for . . .
   . . . when the housework is getting on top of you
   . . . or when you're spring cleaning
   . . . or studying
   . . . or simply lazing, i.e. with your feet up on the sofa reading a bad book.

If anyone *does* notice and upbraids you make it quite clear that you are no longer the enterprising cook that once you were when newly wed and showing off. Life is too short to stuff a mushroom.

So when you've a spare half hour try jotting down your own basic fourteen-day plan and *stick to it*. This is what it might look like. These recipes aren't dull if you serve them prettily. They are no great culinary shakes. They simply stop you going out of your mind and take the minimum time to prepare.

Budgets need slimming as urgently as people, so in both these interests I've left elaborate hors d'oeuvres to your imagination and assumed that puddings are only eaten on festive occasions. Serve fruit or cheese afterwards. The trick with cheese, fruit or salad dishes is to *serve one thing at a time*. A bowl of oranges *au natur*. A dish of bananas the following day. Serve an assortment and you risk the whole family getting jaded by day four.

	Lunch	**Dinner**
Saturday	pea soup, egg mayonnaise	roast chicken and roast potatoes
Sunday	lamb casserole, baked potatoes, and grated cheese	cold chicken and rice, tomato and cucumber salad
Monday	liver pâté, salad, French bread	onion tart, salad
Tuesday	leek soup, baked eggs	spaghetti bolognaise
Wednesday	ham salad	shepherd's pie
Thursday	hamburgers	boiled gammon and mashed potatoes
Friday	omelettes	liver and bacon with onion rings
Saturday	grilled mackerel and grilled tomatoes	steak and kidney pie
Sunday	roast lamb and jacket potatoes	haricot bean salad with hard-boiled eggs and olives
Monday	toasted lamb sandwiches	chicken pie
Tuesday	sausages and chips	baked eggs and vegetable stew
Wednesday	onion and potato soup	lamb chops and spinach
Thursday	egg and bacon flan (quiche lorraine)	meat casserole (using cheap cuts)
Friday	cauliflower cheese	cod steamed with bacon, tomatoes and garlic

Puddings: Choose puddings, if you have them, from:

fruit flan with whipped cream
chocolate mousse
sliced oranges with brown sugar
baked bananas with rum
lemon syllabub

Salads: Say 'salad' to a jaded cook and she will only think 'lettuce'. Here are more suggestions, because salads are easy and healthy and can certainly stretch a meal.

A salad can be served with a French dressing before, with or after any dish. Choose from chicory, endive, mustard and cress, watercress, cucumber, cauliflower, (the flowers only, broken into small flowerets), beetroot, carrot, button mushrooms (slice finely and soak in French dressing for four hours before serving), tomatoes, mixed salad, shredded white cabbage.

Combinations: choose from the following:

lettuce, pineapple and chopped nuts
watercress, and skinned grapefruit segments
lettuce and sliced orange
chicory with peeled grapes
cucumber, chopped apples, soaked raisins and cold rice
sliced new potatoes with chopped spring onions
lettuce and cucumber

French dressing
1 egg cup wine vinegar, 2 egg cups oil, salt, pepper, a dash of French mustard
1 clove crushed garlic, optional
Method: Pour ingredients into bottle, flavour to taste, shake until emulsified. Pour over salad immediately, as emulsion is only temporary. Increase quantities, if you wish, to make enough to last a week.

FOOD

Mayonnaise: If you use a shop-bought one, such as Hellman's, try squeezing a little lemon juice and garlic into it. It will then taste more home-made, especially if you decant it and hide the jar.

ARE YOU EATING POISON?

Many people are becoming increasingly worried about today's polluted and degraded foods. Health food shoppers are no longer regarded as faddists or cranks. It has been calculated that nearly half the people in this country are overweight and under-nourished. We are fast becoming a nation fed entirely on canned, potted, instant-mixed, synthetic, dehydrated, freeze-dried, chemically processed food, tranquillizers, sedatives, sleeping pills and wonder drugs.

There is said to be a potential danger, both physical and mental, in modern processed food, especially those which use the refined carbohydrates (white flour and white sugar to you). Some people think that this is linked with the increased incidence of coronary thrombosis, obesity and constipation, peptic ulcer and other twentieth century diseases.

A dentist, writing in *The Times*, said that we might even be in danger from the lead in our toothpaste tubes, and that childish dental decay in Britain has almost reached epidemic level. He claimed that *25 per cent of today's five-year-olds will be forced to wear dentures by the time they are twenty*. However, I know four children who have used fluoride toothpaste since it became available. The young-est is now fifteen and they have none of them felt the dentist's drill, let alone had an extraction.

I suppose I'm lucky not to be among the one-third of adults over sixteen in this country who have no natural teeth *at all*, but then, although I don't smoke, I use Euthymol smoker's toothpaste, because a cheap box lasts two years, and if it works on smokers, it's dazzling on the rest of us.

There is reported to be an alarming amount of lead in corned beef, sardines, butter, cheese and apples. Other possible poisons on our plate include salts used in bacon, mercury waste in fish, flour bleach, cyclamates, saccharin and monosodium glutamate. Apart from chemical additives you can also be poisoned by agricultural and industrial wastes, defoliates, pesticides, detergents, DDT and anything upon which it has been sprayed.

In addition to the known effects of these, it is also suspected that there are unknown effects on the body and brain, of biologically active substances such as the aforementioned insecticide residue.

What do you do about it? What health food experts advise you to eat is compost-grown vegetables and fruit. If you can't manage that try to stick to fresh meat, fish, dairy foods, eggs, cheese, butter, honey, fresh and dried fruit, fresh vegetables and wheat-grains and raw foods such as salad.

It has been estimated that the average family throws away per year as many potato peelings as are equivalent to five hundred eggs worth of iron, sixty steaks worth of protein and ninety-five orange juice glasses of vitamin C. Steam vegetables or cook them quickly with their skins on so that the water-soluble vitamins and minerals aren't lost in the cooking water. Anyway they *taste* better that way. Don't cook them until they are soggy – serve crunchy vegetables.

Don't eat white sugar or white flour.

Use cider vinegar, sunflower seed oil, dried yeast and barbados sugar, and instead of flour to thicken sauces use gruel, which is a traditional baby food as made by your granny and sold by chemists.

Take vitamin B_{12} for anxiety and three tablets of yeast after each meal. (Which is what trichologists also recommend to make your hair grow long and glossy.)

Make your own stone-ground, whole-wheat bread and yoghurt. Here are recipes for both.

Grandmother's home-made brown bread

Ingredients

1½ lb wholemeal flour	¾ pint water
½ oz salt	(warm)
½ oz yeast	½ oz sugar

Method

1 Warm a mixing bowl.
2 Put half of the flour into mixing bowl.
3 Add sugar and salt.
4 Cream yeast with 2 tablespoons warm water and add to mixture. Add water.
5 Cover the basin with a clean cloth and leave in a warm place for fifteen minutes.
6 Add remaining flour to make a soft dough, using a little more water if necessary.
7 Knead dough on a well floured surface for five to ten minutes.
8 Cut dough in half, shape each piece and place in two warmed, greased and floured 1 lb loaf tins.
9 Place tins in a warm place, covered with a damp cloth. Leave until dough has risen to about double its size. Approximately thirty minutes.
10 Bake at mark 6 for forty-five minutes. 400°F
11 Turn out on to cooling rack.

The Duchess of Devonshire's home-made bread

This is the family recipe. All those 1920 beautiful Mitford sisters, including the Duchess, were brought up on it. It is not only delicious, but easy to make. Use 100% stone-ground wholemeal flour. (The Duchess uses Prewetts). Quantities given are for two 2 lb loaves, or four bun loaves.

Ingredients

3 lbs flour
A little less than 2 oz live yeast
1¾ pts warm milk or water
1 teaspoonful sugar
2 teaspoonsful salt

Method

1 Heap up flour round sides of bowl and put yeast in the middle, a little broken up. Add to yeast the sugar, salt and a little of the warm milk.
2 When yeast is dissolved, stir flour in gradually, adding the rest of the liquid until it becomes a soft dough.
3 Put in a warm place to rise for an hour, covering the bowl with a clean, folded cloth.
4 When risen, turn out on a floured board and knead until it doesn't stick to your hands. Cut in half and knead each piece separately for some minutes until quite firm.

103

5 Put into loaf tins and leave for $\frac{1}{2}$ hour to rise a little more. If you don't have loaf tins, shape the dough into four balls and put on a greased, floured baking sheet.
6 Cook in oven at gas mark 5 (375°) for about an hour until firm and brown.

Easy yoghurt recipe

Put 2 dessertspoons of a good live yoghurt in the bottom of a large pudding basin. (I like any of the French yoghurt which can be easily obtained in most supermarkets.) Pour on 1 pint Longlife milk – unheated, just straight from the packet. Put a plate on top of this and leave in your oven, if it is gas, with a pilot light on. This does *not* mean you light the stove; the gentle heat just contained in the stove by the pilot light is enough to make perfect yoghurt overnight. If it doesn't, leave it longer.

Put it into a fridge, and when cool eat it. Remember to keep back enough to make your next batch. An airing cupboard or the top of a storage radiator will do instead of a gas oven.

RUNNING A PET

Pets are a wonderful idea if you have time on your hands or you live alone or in a superbly staffed country mansion. Pets enhance your lovable earth mother image. They are comforting. They are friendly. They are loyal. They are fun. Children love them. They love you.

BUT think four times before you buy a pet. Think of:

1 The cost.
2 The amount of time which you'll have to spend on caring for and perhaps exercising your animal.
3 What will happen if you go away?
4 Have you enough space in your home and are you prepared to have carpets, curtains, upholstery and furniture scratched, clawed and possibly ruined? I once had to start patching a fitted carpet four weeks

after it had been laid, and before it had been paid for, thanks to an adorable kitten of similar age.

Costs: It costs roughly £48 a year to keep a cat on food, milk, cat litter and vets' fees. To keep a spaniel costs twice as much, i.e. £96 a year, calculate the R.S.P.C.A. Bigger dogs cost a lot more. A dog likes to eat far more meat than a human being.

Vets are very expensive, although if you have no money the R.S.P.C.A. or Blue Cross will care for your beast. But you may have to trek across town to get to them. You think you won't need a vet? Nothing much seems to go wrong with budgerigars, but kittens and puppies need injections when they're small. To get a cat spayed seems to cost more than a vasectomy. Cats and dogs get fleas, mites, pregnant, into fights and run over. Goldfish get mildew. Hamsters and rabbits get more hamsters and more rabbits.

Going away: You can't go away for a weekend without making arrangements for your pet, either expensively with a vet, or with a friend. Holidays are worse.

Pets are as much of a tie as children. They need regular feeding, caring and looking after. Young ones tend to make smelly messes, just like babies only without nappies. Unhappiness is a warm puddle.

Puppies chew everything. Your boots, your husband's boots, your girlfriend's fur coat, your mother's best handbag. You may gain in fortitude what you lose in friendship.

Puppies grow into dogs and they bark very loudly in a way that might go right through your head until you yourself feel like baying at the moon.

It is cruel to keep dogs in flats and often in city houses with no gardens. They need exercise. Having for years been dragged horizontally around the park at dawn in the wake of a Weimarana I can caution others.

A small but tedious point. Bitches on heat can be very messy and, apart from the blood, you'll find every dog in the district at your front door. How often ? Although it varies according to bitch, breed and age, you'll probably have to cope with it twice a year and it goes on far longer than you could possibly imagine. Allow four weeks, but check with your vet.

Kittens grow into cats who look like divine miniature tigers, *but* they can't be put out regularly like dogs, who at least perform like clockwork if well trained. A cat won't do anything you want it to. A cat tray in the kitchen stinks. People are always putting their feet in cats' trays placed elsewhere.

The peculiarly pungent lavender-stink aroma of cat hangs ineradicably around the house and you can't disguise it. I know a girl who for four weeks tried everything from incense and Airwick to Chanel No. 5 (which being aldehyde just worsened the situation) without eradicating the aroma.

Breeding: Another example of false sentimentality about animals which the R.S.P.C.A. want to discourage is thoughtlessly allowing your pet to breed, then forcing the litter on friends who don't really want them. The result is that at least 30,000 stray animals are put to sleep by voluntary organizations alone. So if you're an animal lover make sure that you really are prepared for the responsibility of caring for a living creature.

FINAL WORD OF WARNING : If you have children, never keep a pet if you intend eventually to eat it.

Goldfish: I must admit that goldfish are very little trouble. Give them enough room to swim, change their water once a week and *rarely feed them anything – If you want them to live.* (Having discovered this secret the mortality rate of goldfish went down rapidly in our home.)

NOW READ ON

Dogs: If you still want a dog you can get a mongrel from a pet store or the R.S.P.C.A. or you can buy a pedigree dog from a pet store or an established breeder. Never buy an anonymous dog from a market stall. Get a list of local breeders from the Kennel Club, 1 Clarges Street, London W1. Don't buy a pedigree dog without a pedigree registration certificate.

Don't buy a puppy less than seven

weeks old or more than twelve weeks. Don't buy a puppy that doesn't *look* in good condition, fit and bouncy. Don't accept any explanations for a listless puppy. Don't pick the runt of the litter because it's so tiny and sweet and pathetic. You may be heading for vet's bills.

A pedigree pup should have been inoculated against serious diseases before it's sold and the breeder should provide proof of this. Get a mongrel inoculated. Consult the vet about worming.

Treat your puppy as kindly and gently as you would a baby. Keep him in a blanket-lined box with a ball and a few toys until he's three months old, when he can be promoted to a real live dog basket that will catch on your stockings. Only sporting dogs should be kept out of doors in a kennel.

Housetrain your puppy by saying 'no' in a voice that is not at all kind and gentle, and immediately taking him outside. Exercise him straight away after meals, which is when he's most likely to mess. See he always has fresh water and big bones. Avoid chicken, rabbit or fish bones which can splinter. Dogs need a regular, balanced diet, not just meat. Feed a puppy four times a day until he's six months old, twice a day until he's nine months old, then once a day in the morning or evening. Keep to regular times. Give your puppy dog food or finely chopped meat mixed with puppy meal twice a day, and puppy meal or breakfast cereal mixed with milk twice a day, and perhaps a lightly boiled egg twice a week.

See that he has a licence, a collar and an identity disc, and always keep him on a lead in the street.

Cats: If you've set your heart on a cat, acquiring a kitten seems to be no problem. You just tell everyone you meet tomorrow that you want a kitten and strange kitten owners everywhere will be rushing round in no time. Or you can telephone the R.S.P.C.A., buy one from a pet store, or get a pedigree cat from a breeder. Again, don't get one less than seven weeks old. Don't buy a pedigree kitten without a Cat Fancy Registration Form.

Get your kitten checked by the vet and injected as necessary. Spaying or neutering is done four to five months after birth.

Don't pick up a kitten (or a puppy) by the scruff of its neck or by its paws. Put one hand under his chest and nestle his hindquarters in your other hand.

Feed a kitten four times a day until it's four months old, three times a day until it's six months old, twice a day until it's nine months old and then once a day. Start him off on baby cereal mixed with milk and a little chopped liver, fish or good cat food. By the time he's nine months old he'll need a small can of food a day. Don't feed him fish all the time. As well as milk, a cat needs a constant bowl of clean water.

Housetrain your kitten by putting near his basket a plastic cat tray or ordinary tin tray covered with newspaper, litter or earth. Clean the tray daily. Ugh! Swab it out with hot water and a little disinfectant. You can get a cat panel fixed to your garden door, if you have a garden, or you can have a tiny glass pane which flaps up and down fitted to a suitable window.

AVOID PESTS

Prevention is better than cure: Keep the home clean, avoid damp, meticulously clean up food spills, keep dustbin lids on tightly, and avoid having miles of rotting animal and/or vegetable matter in the garden.

If you find you have a pest, empty and clean all shelves, throw away affected food, such as rice, flour or noodles. Spray shelves with insecticide and leave for half a day before replacing contents. In future keep food in airtight tins.

Don't keep food or grain in the open, at floor level, in the kitchen or the larder. Keep the floor crumbless. Regularly clean out food cupboards.

When you're using a spray insecticide don't spray it on food, drink, animals, or children. Don't breathe it in yourself and don't spray near an open fire. And don't throw a used can into a fire unless you think that an explosion might enliven your afternoon.

Mice: In spite of precautions you may be afflicted by mice. They shred and chew things such as newspapers, corners or clothes, gnaw wire, and leave droppings which are like tiny brown seeds. Cheese in a trap only works for one mouse at a time and they seem to breed as fast as the trap shuts. Telephone the public health department of your town hall. They will kill the mice. Sad indeed, but you can't afford to be squeamish.

Rats: The first time I saw a rat in an empty house I jumped on a chair, held my skirt round my legs and gave a quavery little scream, just like a cartoon. You don't need me to tell you what a rat looks like – your racial memory will inform you.

Rats carry very nasty diseases, so if you see a rat call the town hall and ask for the pest controller or rodent exterminator or public health inspector or whatever he's called this week. If you can, avoid dealing with the rats yourself. If you can't, telephone to ask the inspector's advice about which poison to use to pattern trap the regular rat run. Ugh!

Fleas and bedbugs: Don't panic. These are not necessarily associated with dirt, although they thrive in unhygienic conditions.

Each type of *flea* likes a different sort of host: horses, cats, rats, dogs, humans. Animal fleas will bite humans; some seem to attract them far more than others. Their bites leave itching red spots on the skin, which (counsel of perfection) you should not scratch. They like darkness and warmth, tend to lay eggs in floor cracks and appear in warm wet weather, viz. early summer and early autumn.

If they are infesting something such as the cat's bed, burn it. Buy Bob Martin's Pestroy aerosol and spray the floor, any other places where a lot of dust collects and anything which is infected, such as your bed. If, two days later, you still have fleas, repeat the process. If, in four days, you still have fleas, call the public health inspector.

Bedbugs can enter your home via secondhand books and furniture, as well as beds. They are $\frac{1}{5}$ inch long, roundish, brownish and flattish. Their irritating bites leave large red patches and possible swelling. They suck human blood at night and lay eggs in cracks in the woodwork and behind wallpaper. They are exterminated by burning, by liquid insecticide sprays, or by expert fumigation, when all windows, ventilations, cracks and keyholes are blocked. The room is then left sealed for some time before being aired and cleaned.

Cockroaches, silver fish and other

flying or crawling insects: Cockroaches love moist warm dark places and silver fish love damp, so watch water pipes. Spray with a suitable insecticide, sprinkle insecticide powder liberally where you suspect their 'run' is, and if necessary holler for the public health inspector to trace the source of the trouble.

Flies and wasps: Get a Vapona strip and hang it from the ceiling. You will subsequently find large numbers of flies and any other flying insects lying on your floor with their feet in the air – dead. If you run across a Vapona-resistant strain and they persist, invite the public health inspector round.

Flies love decaying food.

Moths: It's the grubs, which like dark, warm places, that do the damage. They attack wool, fur, skin and feathers. They don't attack rubber, man-made or vegetable fibres, such as cotton or linen. Watch the following for moth damage:

1 Woollen clothes.
2 Blankets, quilts and rugs.
3 Carpets and underfelt.
4 Upholstered furniture and curtains.
5 Stuffed animals, birds, fur and feathers.

All stored articles should be cleaned, frequently inspected and protected by a moth deterrent such as naphthalene, camphor tablets or paradichloro-benzine. Use DDT and pyrethrum to kill the pests.

Where grubs have attacked an item, such as a stuffed bird, you should burn or otherwise dispose of it. If possible send other items to the dry cleaner.

Mosquitoes: Their nasty Brrr can herald a sleepless night for all the wrong reasons. They breed near stagnant water, such as a slimy pond, or in damp leaves which collect in gutters. Use a special spray can repellent.

Ants: Be especially careful in the summer months, when they are likely to invade a ground floor kitchen from the garden. Leave no food spills unwiped, especially if sugary. Keep fruit in a bowl in the middle of a basin of water. Use a special ant killer from garden shops.

Furniture beetle (woodworm): Lays its eggs (which take three years to hatch) in cracks or crevices of *unpolished* wood, such as the undersides of chairs, backs of wardrobes and chests of drawers, flooring, and wooden panels. The baby beetle bites its way through to the open air leaving a $\frac{1}{16}$-inch exit hole. Wood dust beneath a piece of furniture is a sure sign of 'woodworm'. Don't allow into the house any secondhand or 110th-hand furniture which has tiny holes in it, unless you are sure that it has been professionally treated: you risk infecting your other furniture.

You can treat furniture with a woodworm insecticide. The best time is April and May, because then you can get the babies (fiendish chuckle), but DON'T WAIT for April to come round. Brush the insecticide well into the peppery-holed surface. Treatment may discolour light woods.

All insecticides should be available from big stores, ironmongers (fast dying out) or some do-it-yourself shops.

Dry rot is not dry. It is a sinisterly science-fictionish fungus which grows and lives on wood and finally reduces it to a dry crumbling state which sounds 'dead' when hit with a hammer and has a nasty mouldy smell. It starts in damp, unventilated places such as under floorboards and behind wood panelling. It spreads by thin root-like strands which creep over non-nourishing brickwork to reach more appetizing wood. It produces flat growths rather like a cross between a pancake and a mushroom. If you suspect that you have dry rot, immediately call a surveyor or a wood preservation firm.

The first part of treatment consists in discovering the causes. These could be:

1 A damp course rendered ineffective because someone has piled up coal, earth, sand or gravel or something against an outside wall.
2 A broken damp-proof course.
3 No damp-proof course in your home.
4 Not drying out wet boards before laying a floor covering such as cork or linoleum.
5 Faulty plumbing which keeps floorboards damp, particularly hot water pipe joints behind a bath panel.
6 Faulty, leaking drain pipes; possibly combined with worn pointing.

Once the cause has been analysed all rotten wood must be cut away and immediately burned for 3 feet beyond the infected area. All nearby brickwork must be sterilized with a blowlamp then, when cool, treated with a preservative. The timber can then be repaired with new timber, which should also be treated with a preservative.

Wet rot: Not so serious as dry rot, as it is easier to arrest. It is a timber fungus which grows in a *really* damp, wet place where you get leaking water, such as a cellar, shed or Rachmanite bathroom. The fungus, which rarely shows itself on the surface, makes the damp wood darken.

Treatment consists of checking the source of moisture and thoroughly drying the timber, which might have to be treated with preservative. Badly decayed timber should be cut out and replaced.

Expert treatment: If your house timber has woodworm, or wet or dry rot, get expert treatment from a specialist such as Rentokil. It's extremely expensive, but not so expensive as to have the old homestead crumble about your ears.

On no account go only to one firm. Get several quotes. (I have found one firm *ten times* more expensive than another.) If the job promises to be expensive, you may find it economical to employ a surveyor to advise you and possibly supervise the work. I did.

To stamp out woodworm thoroughly they will heave up floorboards, inject every tiny hole in the house with a hypodermic syringe and generally do a thorough job. Don't try to tackle it yourself, the risk is too great.

HOW TO COPE WITH ELECTRICITY

Do you really save money if you turn off the light bulb on the landing, like Dad says? Or do you only save ½p a month, as your kid brother insists?

Movie director Clive Donner has specially asked me to discover what the yearly bill is for a pilot light, because this is what the miser in him resents paying. He doesn't believe the propaganda that says a pilot light costs nothing a year to run. Other mean, magnificent movie directors might like to know that:

An electric red button small neon electric pilot uses approximately half a unit a year, which is less than 1p a year to run.

A gas pilot light costs about £3.64 a year to run, on the cheapest tariff.

Make sure that you won't need electro-cardiac treatment next time the bills come in by switching off the appliances which are rather more likely than a pilot light to cause heart flutter . . . These are your HEATERS. For instance, a two-bar electric fire left on from eight in the morning until nine at night would *alone* cost over £30 a quarter.

THIS IS HOW THE GADGETS BURN UP ENERGY

1 kw electric fire: 1 hour=1 unit.
2 kw electric fire: 1 hour=2 units.
2¼kw night storage heater: 8 hours=between 5 and 18 units, depending on charge controller and room temperature.
Convector heater: 1 hour=½–3 units, depending on size and type.
Water heater: 3 gallons of hot water for one unit.
100 watt lamp: 10 hours=1 unit.

Small fan: 15 hours = 1 unit.

Under blanket for 1 hour a night: 2 weeks = 1 unit.

Over blanket used all night: 1 week = 3 units.

Vacuum cleaner: 2–4 hours depending on size = 1 unit.

Floor polisher: $2\frac{1}{2}$ hours = 1 unit.

3-pint kettle: about 5 boilings = 1 unit, so don't waste money and energy by filling the kettle with more water than you need.

Cooker: allow 1 unit for each person in the family each day.

Refrigerator: 8–24 hours according to size = 1–2 units.

Freezer (7 cubic feet): 24 hours = 2 units.

Dishwasher: 1 load = 1 unit.

Food mixer/liquidizer: 60 cake mixes = 1 unit.

Toaster: 70 slices = 1 unit.

Coffee percolator: 10 jugs = 1 unit.

Coffee grinder: 1 year = 4 units.

Washing machine: average weekly wash = 3–4 units.

Tumble drier: 2 hours = 3 units.

Iron: 2 hours = 1 unit.

Shaver: 1800 shaves = 1 unit.

Heated curler set (allow 20 minutes per day): 1 month = 1 unit.

Hair drier: 2 hours = 1 unit.

TV set: 7 hours = 1 unit.

Colour TV: 4 hours = 1 unit.

Stereo: 12 hours = 1 unit.

Tape recorder: 15 hours = 1 unit.

Sewing machine: 15 hours = 1 unit.

Workshop drill: 15 hours = 1 unit.

The electricity bill: Your electricity bill is made up of a standard charge plus the number of units of electricity you use. The cost of a unit varies under different area electricity boards, but at the time of writing it usually works out at under 1.5p per unit.

A *unit* of electricity is the amount needed to produce 1 kilowatt (1,000 watts) of power for one hour. So a kilowatt fire uses one unit in one hour, and a 100 watt bulb uses one-tenth of a unit in one hour.

To know how much electricity you use in a week, learn how to read your meter: This is much easier than it sounds and modern meters read like the mileage recorder on the car dashboard. Older meters have six sinister little dials, marked 10,000, 1,000, 100, 10, 1 and 1/10 KWH per DIV. Ignore the dials marked 1 and 1/10 because they measure only a fraction of a unit. Write down the numbers shown on the other four dials, from left to right, so you start with the 10,000 dial and work to the 10. If the pointer is between two numbers, write down the lower number, unless it's between 10 and 0, then write down the 9. You should finish with a five figure number such as 18 475. A week later, read the meter again and subtract the first reading from the second. The result of this sum is the number of units you used that week.

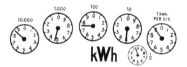

Plan your electricity supply: You can save lots of blood, sweat, toil and tears by getting yourself – or rather your house – fitted with circuit breakers in place of fuses. Circuit breakers are switches which trip to 'off' if the circuit is overloaded. To reset you simply have to press a little button – after you have repaired or remedied the cause of the overload.

If you have a 13-amp ring circuit you will rarely blow a fuse in the fuse box, but the fuse within each plug will give out occasionally (see 'Eight Things Every Girl Should Know', p.117). Keep a stock of plug fuses, with a list showing what colour fuse serves which appliance. You might keep fuse wire and torch on or in the fuse box or hang them in a shopping bag on a nearby wall.

Use BROWN (13-amp) for all appliances rated 750 watts or more, and RED (3-amp) for all appliances rated at less than 750 watts.

13-amp fuses should not be fitted to low-powered appliances, as they might overheat and catch fire. Check the amount of current that the appliance uses (it's measured in amps) and when you buy it ask for the correct fuse.

Be prepared for a power cut. Stock up now on alternative methods of lighting, heating and cooking. Hide box of matches, torch, spare battery and candles where your menfolk can't find them, or in your toolbox.

Lighting: Candles, oil and hurricane lamps, torches, batteries and bulbs. Candles and oil lamps are too dangerous for young children. Give them a torch each.

Keep two torches in the entrance hall. Get a hurricane or pressure paraffin lamp for the kitchen, together with appropriate fuel. Some families live in the kitchen if it's big enough, during a power cut.

Heating: Oil and gas-fired boilers use electric pumps or fans, alas. You're safe with open fires. If you buy a paraffin heater remember that it can be a dangerous fire risk and needs ventilation, but otherwise keep the hot air in as much as possible by not opening windows, which might also cause draughts which can cause fires with candles and oil lamps.

Cooking: Pre-cook at non-peak times for later reheating. Refrigerators and freezers are not generally affected (but insure your freezer contents). (See 'Looking Forward to a Freeze-up', p.93.)

Dishwashers and automatic washing machines will have to be drained and you will have to start again with fresh detergent when power returns.

Auto-timers on cookers or on central heating units or heaters or other equipment and electric clocks will need to be reset.

WARNING! Electricity cuts increase fire risks. Unplug the television, which is a fire risk anyway if left plugged in overnight, and check that electric bar fires, electric blankets and cooker are switched off.

HOW TO HANDLE GAS

1 DON'T strike a match if you smell gas and DO open all windows immediately. Also extinguish fires, naked flames and cigarettes. Make sure that a gas tap has not been left on accidentally or a pilot light blown out. Turn off the supply at the meter control tap and even if you are in doubt telephone Gas Service immediately (look under 'gas' in the telephone directory).

2 Never look for a gas leak with a naked flame. Remember British Gas specialists are the experts when it comes to gas. If there is a leak in the service pipe supplying the meter or in the meter itself, generally no charge is made for repairs. Don't turn the gas on again until the gasman tells you it's safe to do so.

3 A word of warning: Don't have your appliances connected by anyone who is not a specialist. Check on anyone who claims to be.

4 Never use a bath water heater fitted in the bathroom while you are in the bath unless the heater is one of the room-sealed type.

5 Never shut the door or window while the water is being drawn from a gas water heater, unless it is a balanced flue type. Of course, water heaters are safe unless you block up vents, and close windows and doors so that they cannot 'breathe'.

6 Never, under any circumstances, block up ventilators such as air bricks: they are there to help your appliance breathe.

7 If you have any worries concerning the safety of your gas supply or appliances, telephone Gas Service immediately.

8 Make sure that gas appliances have the British Gas Seal of Approval, especially if you're buying a continental model. So get anything you need from a British Gas showroom.

You can save energy and chop your fuel bills . . . here's how:

1 . . . check that you are on the *correct tariff*. If in doubt ask your local showroom.

2 Have your gas appliances serviced regularly and they will stay at top efficiency.

IN THE BATHROOM

3 Make sure that the jacket on the *hot water cylinder* fits snugly. You will then keep your water just as hot but it will cost less.

4 Get *dripping hot taps repaired*. They waste water as well as energy.

5 Fix a *hand shower* to your bath. It will soon pay for itself by halving your bathwater bills. The average bath uses 25 gallons of hot water but an average shower uses only about 10 gallons.

IN THE KITCHEN

6 *Don't wash up* unless you have a sink load. Leave small items for a big wash because an average wash and rinse uses 6 gallons.

7 Never wash up or rinse under a running *hot water tap*, it can run away with 2 to 3 gallons a minute.

8 *Descale your kettle* for faster boiling. Descale with a brand product such as 'Kaydee'. Alternatively, fill kettle with cold water, add 1 level tablespoon of borax and boil. Pour away, rub softened deposit with soft scourer. Rinse and repeat. Then leave a child's glass marble in kettle to prevent future scaling.

9 Don't heat more *water* than you need. If you need 2 pints it is throwing money away to boil 3 pints.

10 Defrost your *refrigerator* regularly and avoid thick ice build-up.

11 Plan menus to make full use of *oven space*. You can cook a whole meal using only the oven burner.

12 Use *grill* to full capacity. It's cheaper to toast 3 slices at once, instead of 2.

13 Use correct sized *saucepans*, not overlarge ones.

14 Cover *pans* to keep the heat in and use the hot steam to cook.

15 Adjust flame on a *fast gas ring* to remain under pans and not come up the sides. After a pan has

reached boiling point, turn gas as low as possible. Cooking will continue, even on a tiny flame.

INVESTMENT

16 Use a *pressure cooker*. It uses less gas and you can cook 3 sets of vegetables on one burner.

17 Consider replacing old, inefficient or broken *appliances* with efficient new ones, which use less fuel to give the same heat.

INSULATION (this applies whatever your heating system.)

18 Hot air rises! Keep the heat in. Save up to 75% of your heat loss by unrolling a 2 inch roll of fibreglass in your loft. In 2 years it should pay for itself, through fuel saving.

19 Fit plastic or metal *draught excluders* to doors and windows.

20 $\frac{1}{3}$ of our warm air is claimed to be lost through the windows. *Double glazing* can reduce this by 50%.

CAUTION! *all fuel burning appliances need some fresh air to work safely. Get your local gas service to check your insulation.*

CENTRAL HEATING

21 If you are going away for the weekend or longer, turn off *water heating* switch and lower *thermostat* to minimum.

22 Set the *time clock* to give heat only when it is needed. Systems vary but I suggest you try half an hour before getting up and half an hour *before* going to bed (because the system will take half an hour to cool down).

23 Switch off *radiator valves* and close *warm air grilles* in rooms

which are not being used. Close the doors which lead to them, of course.

CAUTION! *Leave valves and grilles slightly open in very cold weather.*

24 Most people could reduce the temperature by a few degrees, wear extra warm clothing and still stay comfortable. So whatever you normally dial – turn it down.

CAUTION! *Don't cut the heat where there are invalids, young babies or senior citizens.*

25 Turn a *gas fire* off when you leave the room.

26 Don't open a *window* if a room gets too warm; turn down the heat.

27 Don't draw *curtains* over the radiator or heat will simply be wasted through the windows. If you have full length curtains either shorten them or don't pull them at night. Fit a matching blind to the window.

THE WORKING GIRL'S TOOL BOX

If you can't get a man, you could get a proper tool box fitted with a reasonable set of tools, but I can never fit these instruments back into their neat little places. Instead buy a cheap plastic chainstore tool box with a handle and several self-raising, subdivided trays inside (the Duchess of Bedford uses one as a make-up box); or you can settle for a plastic knife tray in a drawer or even a cardboard box.

Inside this treasure chest you might accumulate the following items. Not all of them are traditionally kept in the tool box but I can't think where else I would keep them.

1 A metric and ancient British steel tape measure with both measures on the same side, if possible, as it's easier to compute.

2 A decent size (10-inch at least) tenon saw. As a tenon saw has smaller 'teeth' and a stiff back one doesn't have to be so strong to use it.

3 A reasonably heavy hammer with a back division claw for yanking nails out. The front is, of course, for crushing rose stems.

4 Pliers for bending wire, twisting wire, stripping wire, cutting wire and grasping small objects.

5 An adjustable spanner.

6 A large and a medium screwdriver, and two small electrical screwdrivers with insulated handles. A Philips screwdriver if you're having to deal with Philips cross-topped screws or one of the newer Posidriv drivers for the new Posidriv cross slot screws.

7 Half-inch cold chisel.

8 A Stanley knife with interchangeable blades for cutting linoleum, etc.

9 A hand drill and masonry drills to match your wall plugs.

10 A Rawlplug punch.

11 Any QA (Quick Assembly) tools you get when you buy a QA picture frame or chair, etc.

12 A penknife – I'm not quite sure why, but I feel safer with one around.

13 A set of adhesives (see 'How to Stick Almost Anything', p. 128). Dunlop's set of five adhesives are claimed to stick 97 per cent of all domestic do-it-yourself jobs. In a box measuring $11\frac{1}{2} \times 6 \times 2$ inches

deep they include a booklet of instructions called 'All about Adhesives'. Dunlop will advise you (free) if you contact Mike Ford, Advisory Service, Dunlop Chemical Products Division, Chester Road, Birmingham 35.

14 Masking tape.

15 Insulating tape and insulated staples for attaching electrical wires to the tops of skirting boards.

16 Spare cards of fuse wire – light (5-amp) and heating (13-amp) and power (30-amp). Fuses and 13-amp plugs. Spare cartridge fuses – 3-amp and 13-amp.

17 Ten yards of 3-core flex.

18 A set of different sized screws.

19 Assorted nails – panel pins, tacks, upholstery tacks, Rawlplugs, hardened steel pins and drawing pins in assorted sizes for fixing new ironing board covers.

20 Assorted different grades of glasspaper.

21 Polycell for filling screw holes and cracks.

22 Assorted balls of string, elastic bands, sellotape, picture hanging wire.

23 Spare curtain hooks.

24 Tap washers, big for bath taps, small for the rest.

25 Soft lead pencil and rubber. Scissors, small, large and serrated: serrated scissors grip what you are cutting, e.g. plastic sheet or bacon.

26 A can of penetrating oil for clearing rust, and a can of 3-in-One for squeaking doors, window hinges, locks, etc. 3-in-One machine oil is for fine machinery.

27 Box of matches, torch and spare battery, and candles for power failure.

28 Elastoplast and Acriflex for burns.

Once you have used something replenish it, so you are not caught in an emergency.

Keep your toolbox where you can get at it.

EIGHT THINGS EVERY GIRL SHOULD KNOW

The hardest part of the simple jobs described in this chapter is to overcome your early conditioning. You were probably brought up to believe that they are not woman's work. But there isn't always a man around when your sink gets blocked, and even if there is it's probably quicker to unblock it yourself than nag him into doing it for you.

Skip this bit and turn to it only in time of crisis. It probably won't make sense until you are forced to do something.

> WORD OF WARNING: Most of us know as much about electricity as Thurber's aunt, who feared that her light bulb leaked it. There's only one main thing the average female needs to know and that is that *electricity is potentially dangerous*, so treat it with respect and keep it away from water.

1 Always switch off the mains before starting a repair job.
2 Never poke a finger or scissors or *anything* into a light bulb socket or wall socket.
3 Never connect an electric gadget to water, especially not via yourself, or you will risk electrocution. James Bond once killed a villain by throwing a plugged-in electric fire into the bath in which his enemy lay soaking. So:

> DON'T hold a plugged-in appliance with wet hands or if you have wet feet or when you are standing in the bath or with your feet in a bowl of water.
> DON'T switch a switch with wet hands.
> DON'T use water to put out an electrical fire in an appliance which is plugged in. Unplug it, then use a chemical fire extinuisher (every home should have one which conforms with British Standards). Smother flames with a coat or blanket and call the fire brigade.

When one light goes out it may

(a) need a new light bulb (so replace it), or
(b) have a broken plug or a blown fuse, if it's a standard lamp or table lamp (so change it).

When a bunch of lights goes out, you have probably blown a fuse in the fuse box. The cable of a wall light, or any other lamp which doesn't have a plug, goes back to the fuse box, so if that light blows then every other light on the circuit will also have gone.

No. 1. How do you discover which, of a number of lights now not operating, is the villain ? You turn them all off. You mend the fuse. You turn them on again, one by one. When the fuse blows yet again you have found the culprit. Switch off lamp and mend the fuse again, then get an expert to deal with the faulty fitting. This is an electrician's job, at your stage of maintenance. Don't call an expensive electrician until you have checked (a) and (b) above.

How to repair a fuse if you don't want to do it.

The theory of the fuse: If you can thread a needle you can mend a fuse. A fuse is a deliberately weak link. It is inserted into an electrical system to stop it from being overloaded. A fuse blows quite easily (then everything stops), because the bit of wire through which the current passes won't carry a strong load, so it melts. Changing a fuse is just replacing that bit of wire. If it melts, you may have overloaded it with too many appliances. If it goes with a bang, there's usually a fault in one of the appliances which needs expert attention.

And how to mend it: Even if you've never been taught to mend a fuse, you don't have to sit in the dark. All you have to remember is to keep a torch, fuse wire and a small screwdriver in or by the fuse box (or in your tool box). Switch off the mains current. Pull out and replace each fuse one by one, until you see that one has a broken bit of fizzled wire in the middle. That's where your problem is. With the aid of a screwdriver, loosen the two screws at each end of the fuse and remove the damaged fuse wire. Insert a new wire of the same thickness and wind it round the screws until the wire is taut. Tighten the screws at both ends and replace the fuse.

If you pull out another fuse you can use it as a guide as to how to twiddle a bit of fresh wire round the broken one. If yours is a new house, you will have cartridge fuses instead of wire. Throw out the old one, and put in a new one of the same colour.

Try doing it now. It only takes ten minutes. You've got to know what size wire to put in (use 5-amp for lighting (thin), 15-amp for heating (thicker), 30-amp for a cooker (quite thick wire). Cartridge fuses are 3-amp or 13-amp. **Don't use the wrong ones.**

If you suspect that your fuse has blown because you have overloaded the circuit, i.e. plugged too many appliances into one socket, unplug everything running off this outlet before you start mending the fuse and don't immediately overload it again – leave one appliance off. Otherwise, after you've mended the fuse, it will simply blow again.

If you have a certain type of cartridge fuse which doesn't have visible wires, what can you do? Keep a spare 5, 15 and 30-amp *new* fuse handy by the fuse box and check each fuse by replacing it with the appropriate new one.

Alternatively, identify your fuses before they blow. Switch on one light only, then remove the fuses, one by one, until that light goes out. Then you know that particular fuse feeds that particular light. Continue with this sort of elimination test until all electrical outlets are identified. Label fuses with stick-on labels.

No. 2. *How to change or fit a plug*

Buy a plug.

Unscrew the plug. It is now in two parts, a top and a bottom. Place the outer case of the flex into the cord grip hole at the base of the plug top. Lay the three wires in the plug bottom in their appropriate terminals, which are marked as follows as you look down at them: neutral (blue) on the left; earth (green or green and yellow stripes) at top centre; live (brown) on the right. (The old colours were neutral black, live red, and earth green.) Twist the wires round their terminals in a clockwise direction. Make sure that the wires lie flat in the plug bottom. Prod them so with a screwdriver. Make sure that there are no loose strands of wire.

Using a knife, peel the outer plastic cover of the flex 1½ inches, leaving the three interior wires exposed (make sure you don't cut them). Cut back the covers of the neutral and live wires about 1 inch leaving the earth a bit longer.

Replace top and screw up. Check cord grip is tight by tugging your flex (hard). Switch off wall socket. Plug in. Switch on socket. Switch on appliance. With any luck there won't be a bang, and, if there is, you've probably got your wires in the wrong place. (Now see 'How to Repair a Fuse'.)

Now for something really creative.

No. 3. How to make your own
     extension cable
     (So that you can vacuum the
     car or iron at the end of the
     garden if needs be.)

Take:
10 yards (approx. 30 feet) of 3-core electrical flexible cable, one 13-amp fused plug,
one 13-amp three-pin socket, and
a cable roll (an electrical shop will give you one free).
Now wire one end of the cable to the plug and the other end to the socket. Unroll the extension and put the vacuum plug into the extension socket.

No. 4. How to stop a tap dripping
If a tap is dripping it needs a new washer. Your local hardware shop will advise on the right type and size.

To change a washer, first turn the water supply off at the mains and let all the water run out of the tap. Then remove the top of the tap – the handle part – and the metal cover which fits over the body of the tap. (To do this you will need the aid of a spanner or wrench: wrap a cloth or adhesive tape round the tap to give a grip and prevent those weapons from marking it.)

The offending washer and the nut should be clearly visible now, so all you have to do is unscrew the nut, remove and replace the washer and reassemble the tap. Some water boards will replace washers free of charge, if you ask.

Alternatively, get a new modern tap. The Supatap has a mixer in the middle, so you don't have to turn the water off at the mains to insert a new washer. You just unscrew the top, slip the old washer out, put a new one in, and then screw it up again.

No. 5. How to stop a tap leaking
If water seeps around the top of the tap, you may need to tighten the gland nut.

You needn't turn off the mains water. Just remove the cover of the tap as described, take your spanner, and tighten the nut about a quarter turn.

Reassemble the tap and test. If it still leaks, the best thing I know is a cheap little tin of Baswhite filler. You just slap it round the leak and leave it. However, if water still seeps, call a plumber.

No. 6. How to unblock a sink (see
     also p. 34)
Mix together equal parts of coarse salt and soda crystals and force this mixture down the sink hole. Add a shake of detergent and pour down one or two kettlefuls of boiling water.

If this fails, use a rubber plunger

which can be bought from any hardware store.

> WARNING! There are two sizes: you want the larger one, the 'C' cup, that is bigger than your sink outlet.

Block up the sink overflow with a damp cloth in order to create a vacuum, grease the edge of the plunger, fit it over the sink hole and pump several times.

If *this* fails put a bucket under the U bend in the outlet pipe under the sink. With a wrench, remove the big screws at either end of the inspection cover in the bend and try to scrape out the blockage with a wooden spoon or similar blunt instrument. Carefully push a thick wire or a thin stick *up* the pipe in order to clear it. If you unblock it, replace screw and turn on water at mains, then at sink, *before* removing the bucket. If you absentmindedly drop a diamond ring down the sink you follow the same routine, because with any luck the ring will have fallen in the loop of pipe under the sink.

No. 7. How to stop a lavatory overflowing

A lavatory cistern overflows for one of three reasons. Whatever the cause, first turn off the water supply to the cistern, remove the top of the cistern and flush the lavatory.

1 *If grit has jammed the lever arm.* Use a pair of pliers to pull out the split-pin which holds the arm in place. Withdraw the arm and ball and unscrew the valve at the inlet end. Clean and grease the valve thoroughly with vaseline and put the parts together again.

2 *If the ball valve is leaking.* Check by removing it and shaking it to hear if there is water inside it. If there is, buy a new plastic one from a hardware store.

3 *If there is a defective washer.* Remove the lever arm, unscrew the end of cap or piston which connects with the end of the arm and replace the washer.

No. 8. How to hang pictures and shelving

Pictures: For relatively light pictures that aren't in heavy frames use two hardened steel pins about 1 inch long. Pencil a tiny cross where you need a hole. Always use a soft pencil because you can, if necessary, rub it off with an eraser.

Bring nail to wall at a downwards angle (so the picture won't slip off). Give a gentle first tap, then hammer it in, getting *gradually harder* until only a quarter of an inch of pin shows. Repeat. Then hang your picture. Always use two nails centred up because it's easier to straighten the picture and it is safer because if one nail comes out there is always the other.

Use picture wire or nylon cord to hang pictures. Never use a natural fibre such as string, or it may rot and your picture consequently fall.

If you are hanging something heavy use screws. NEVER screw directly into a wall, always use wall plugs.

Basically a Rawlplug provides a grip for a screw. Always insert plugs at right angles to the wall. Use either a plug punch which you hit with a hammer, or a masonry drill. Make the hole one-eighth longer than the selected plug. Slide the plug in, then screw in the screw. If you choose plastic plugs pick ones which grip the hole.

Shelves: If you're screwing shelf brackets to the wall always use screws and plugs. It will be quicker if you use an electric drill with a masonry drill inserted. These are quite hard to keep level until you've practised a bit under supervision from one who knows how to do it. Otherwise you might break the drill.

Be careful when drilling walls, that you only drill into *wall*. If you drill into gas pipes or electrical conduit you could be in trouble.

How to repair a fuse

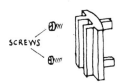

SCREWS

How to stop a tap dripping

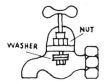

NUT

WASHER

How to unblock a sink

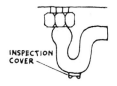

INSPECTION COVER

How to stop a lavatory overflowing

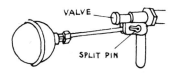

VALVE

SPLIT PIN

THE BASIC BRIDERY
(A home maintenance guide)

If you're lucky enough to have access to a man who can not only fix things around the home but is willing to do so, treat him gently and feed him well. If your man is unwilling do not force him by any method, whether this be a reproachful glance as you nail your thumb, or a list of what your friends' husbands do for *them* (they're probably lying anyway). Men are extremely good at being helpless, the cleverer they are the more helpless they are, and the cleverest ones prove this neatly by making things *worse*. Anyway, you don't want to find yourself patching up a marriage.

The theoretical alternative is to find an odd job man. In fact, although the odd job man is not quite as dead as the dodo, he generally has a sense of time which one can only describe as poetical and knows his scarcity value, which seems to be rather higher than emeralds. In my experience it's quicker, cheaper and less harassing to keep a list of all the jobs that need doing, and keep a day completely free to do a lot of them yourself. Whoever gave wives and mothers the idea that the weekend was time off anyway?

Buy a copy of *Do It Yourself Magazine*, not only to tell you how to do what but also to inspire you with enthusiasm and put over the feeling that it's FUN (which for me it damn well isn't). *Do It Yourself Magazine* covers anything that the do-it-yourself enthusiast can do, from renewing that tap washer to building a home extension or installing your own central heating system. According to them, women are getting more adventurous all the time, and some think nothing of putting in a ring main while the washing is drying or building in a couple of wardrobes over the weekend.

Your first purchases should be a transistor radio and a strong firm ladder, and if possible don't do anything on top of it unless there is someone else in the house to hear you holler for help. You will also need a big box in which to keep your brushes, tins, tubes and tools.

Keeping the cold and damp outside: autumn check list

What not to do: The ultimate in do-it-yourselfery is knowing when *not* to do it . . . when to get someone else. This especially applies to such potentially dangerous check-up jobs as examining the roof and chimneys, which is really a builder's job. You will probably have difficulty finding a builder who isn't about to embark on his biannual Mediterranean cruise, so first make sure that you need his help by checking the roof from outside street level with a pair of borrowed binoculars. You will be surprised how clearly any defects show up.

I also get outside help in the form of an electrician to check all electrical appliances every autumn, whether or not they are giving trouble. Also, check whether you need an electrical time-switch for electric blanket, convector heaters and radiators. Thermostats help too, so you don't waste heat.

LOOK AT:

The chimney stack (with your binoculars): Are there any cracks?

The roof (again with your binoculars): Check broken or missing tiles and flashings beginning to 'gape'.

The brickwork: Does it need re-pointing?

Interior and exterior walls: Check condensation (inside) and cracks (outside). Also basement interior walls and floors, for any sign of moisture which may be news to you. For damp-proofing interior and exterior walls there are solutions such as Aquasol waterproofer or Stroma, a damp remover and preventative, which can also be used for rising damp. There's also Syntheprufe, for interior walls, which you apply with a brush. You can then paint on top with oil-free distemper or emulsion paint. There's an Aquasol damp barrier kit which is a system for waterproofing damp walls and stopping penetration of damp.

Windows: Broken windows can be replaced with putty and glass pre-cut to size by a glass merchant. Ask for glass $\frac{1}{8}$ inch smaller all round than the frame.

Get a carpenter to plane jammed windows, then prime bare wood and paint as soon as possible.

Defective sash cords are, again, a builder's job if you are a do-it-yourself debutante. Replace the hemp with nylon cord which won't rot.

For gaps between window and frame:

Skylights: If they are ill-fitting get a builder.

Persistently rattling window frames should also be replaced by a builder.

Plumbing: No home can be warm or comfortable if pipes are frozen or burst. Lag internal pipes, especially those in an insulated loft.

Gutters: Check gutter outlets, so that autumn leaves or birds' nests don't block them. Put a wire balloon on top (known as a bird cage). It looks a bit like an Edwardian lady motorist's hat and should be sitting atop of all open-ended downpipes and soil pipes.

Check gutters for leaks at the joints. Evidence that water may be running down the outside of a wall may mean that the gutters are broken or blocked at the joints, so that water pours over instead of being carried away. I've only ever met one girl who has mended her own gutter, and she did it painlessly with Plastic Padding (type 'hard'). You mix a hardener with it and just slap it on the cleaned metal. Sylglas tape gives a good temporary repair.

Crack check

Really large wall cracks (more like splits, which open again when you fill them): These generally spell foundation problems. Get a *qualified* surveyor or consult your local borough surveyor and proceed from there.

Small wall cracks: Can be filled with Polyfilla, which mixes like a Betty Crocker cake mix without the added egg. Be sure to brush out all loose and flaking material before starting to fill the crack. Otherwise your patch might wobble loose.

Small ceiling cracks: Can also be filled with Polyfilla.

Cracks where new plaster meets old (the sort that appear when a newly bricked-in fireplace is plastered): The wall looks fine for a few weeks, then cracks appear at the joints between new plaster and old. This happens because the new plaster has shrunk slightly, as is normal. Fill this crack with Polyfilla. If you feel the crack may reopen, wet it with a P.V.A. adhesive such as Unibond or Polybond. This helps the new plaster to adhere to the

old. You can also deal with this by mixing Polyfilla with emulsion paint.

Cracks in timber: Can be filled with Rawlplug Plastic Wood which you squeeze into the crack, let dry and sandpaper smooth. Alternatively, use Brummer stopping, which is in different shades to match the most popular woods. Ask for a waterproof exterior grade, if you're using Brummer outside.

Cracks in brickwork or cement rendering: Can be sealed with Mortar Mix which you can get from Marley shops. All you do is add water like a cake-mix.

Small cracks in cement: Can be sealed with a mastic compound like Sylmasta. You apply it with a knife or small trowel.

A sudden plague of cracks: Expect them everywhere when you have just installed central heating. The timbers dry out and plaster shrinks in the new warm glow. Wait until a whole heating season is over before attempting to deal with them. A humidifier can help reduce the problem and jam jars of water stood on a piano will stop it going honkey-tonk.

Gap check

Gaps where the wood is missing (gnawed by gnomes or rats or cats):

It's a carpenter's job, because the damaged wood will probably have to be cut away and a new piece glued and pinned into place and repainted.

Gaps between floorboards and skirting (where the draught whistles in):

Bridge that gap with a length of quadrant moulding which, in section, looks like a quarter of a broom handle. Use panel pins to keep it in place because they're very fine and won't split the wood.

MAINTENANCE

Gaps between wall and ceiling: Structurally it's rarely serious, but it looks a bit impoverished. Filling the actual gaps is usually a waste of time because they may reappear. You might consider fitting a foam polystyrene cove round the ceiling (it comes in 4-foot lengths, with supplied adhesive from Marley shops) or get a gypsum plaster cove put up. This looks great.

Gaps between timber window frames and brickwork (because of shrinking woodwork): Fill with a mastic compound – not putty or mortar.

Door and window gaps (which can often be the cause of draughts and rattling): Fix weatherstrip round doors and windows. They still open easily after fitting and in my home I found that weatherstripping unexpectedly cut noise and dirt by an estimated one-third.

There are three basic price ranges. If you don't want to do it yourself get a free quotation for fitting bronze weatherstrip from a reliable firm which covers the whole country such as Chamberlin (34 Elm Road, Chessington, Tel. 01-397 1181) who weatherproofed my home quickly, cheaply and efficiently, or Four Seasons Window Co. Ltd (Top Locks, Havelock Road, Southall, Middlesex, Tel. 01-574 7111).

Possibly the most effective do-it-yourself method is fitting Chamberlin draught excluder or a version marketed by Metal Weatherstrip (write for free leaflet), or use Durastrip vinyl and aluminium draught excluder. These are all permanent methods. For weather-and-draught-proofing, the Semaster range of products is considered excellent value.

The third method is fixing plastic foam strip around interior doors and windows. I have never found this method a permanent fixture myself (don't fall for the ads, girls) but I must admit that it is quick, cheap and easy if you're only there for one winter. You might try using Seal, a white self-adhesive foam weatherstrip.

To keep out rain as well as draughts, there is a device called the Sealmaster. This comes in two parts: one fits to the threshold, the other to the foot of the door.

Or you might get draught excluders with an automatic rise and fall mechanism for the bottoms of doors. Ask for the Drydale or the Flip-Flop.

An automatic door shutter fixed on top of the door cuts draughts, banging doors, and also noise, if you count my shrill whines of 'Shut that door'. Try the Gibraltar model.

Bathroom gaps between wall and bath or wall and basin: Can be sealed with Dow Cornings sealant. I've also successfully used Bostik and Seal-a-Round white plastic tape which is supplied with its own adhesive. Remember that draughts are responsible for most heat losses in the average home. Try checking yours with a wet finger on a windy day.

KEEPING THE HEAT IN

Insulation of interior walls and ceilings: Polystyrene expanded foam ceiling tiles not only insulate a room but also absorb some of the condensation and reduce a bit of the noise. The 12 × 12 inch tiles (other sizes available) can be cut with a sharp knife or razor blade. There is a special wire cutter which works off a battery (from Proops, Tottenham Court

Road, London W1). Make sure you stick them on with the correct adhesive (check this with your supplier) and spread the adhesive under *all* the tiles. Thermal foam polystyrene ceiling plain tiles cost very little, fireproofed patterned ones a bit more (from John Lewis).

Expanded foam polystyrene also comes in sheet form for walls or ceilings. It is about twice the thickness of blotting paper and comes in rolls. I don't like the idea of this because little children can push their thumbs into it and indent it and make free form patterns. I know cheaper ways of keeping children quiet. But I am assured it is most effective as an insulator. It can be papered or painted with emulsion paint, but in steamy rooms use an anti-condensation paint such as Silesine's Anti-Con.

Double glazing: I once met a woman whose only claim to fame was that she had made her own storm windows with something unbelievably called Quick-Fix. It's a plastic channel (into which the double glazing slides) which can be cut to fit (without adhesive) a pane of glass. It is then fitted to your window with special clips which screw to the window frame.

For the chilly, idle and impoverished there's also clear, unbreakable, sheet polythene. This can be cut with a razor blade and stuck to the window frame with a transparent double-sided adhesive strip called Duplex Bonding.

Curtain linings: These help to keep in heat and interlining helps even more. Milium curtain lining is aluminium-backed, and although it looks and feels like a normal fabric it is claimed to reflect heat back into the room (from John Lewis).

KEEPING THE AIR FRESH

Once you have your perfectly sealed salon you may have a different problem – *how to avoid a fug-up.* Some might simply open a window, but some might think that if you're spending good money on heating the air, it is better to clean the heated air than replace it with freezing air from outside (which is unlikely to be fresh anyway, more like neat carbon monoxide) which you then start expensively heating up all over again.

Air conditioners are costly and tend to hum like neurotic bees, but they do deal with condensation, clammy bathrooms, kitchen smells, personal odours and stale cigarette smoke. They also enable you to sleep with all the windows closed and not wake up with eyes to match.

The excellent Tampair range by Rootes currently ranges from about £138 for a unit (Phantom 095) for a small room. It measures approximately 26 inches wide × 8 inches deep × 20 inches high and has to be fitted into a wall or window. (From Southern Air Conditioners Ltd, 377 Kennington Road, London SE11, Tel. 01-735 8662.)

Kitchen or bathroom pongs can be extracted with a Vent Axia electric fan.

HOW TO BUY SILENCE

As presidents have found before me this is a very difficult, very expensive and often insoluble problem. You can't do much about traffic, trains or aeroplanes. Whistling errand boys are no longer a problem since they have now died out. And milk carts no longer rattle, they quietly whine away.

However, if the noise in your own home exhausts you, you might try double glazing and draught-proofing. This, plus air-conditioning, plus contract quality carpet on rubber underlay, so thick you could sprain an ankle, plus lined and interlined curtains, should make you feel wonderfully protected from everything in the outside world except your bank manager.

There are also some idiotically simple, cheap tricks which you might try. Eventually, I found that the only way to deal with the dreadful noise of the Barbican (the G.L.C.'s show flat development) was simply to leave the place, but in the final months of our stay I experimented with ear plugs. The wax balls which you roll in your hand until soft and plug into your ear do not harm the ear and they cut down the noise for me, trying to work above a building site, by about half.

There are two disadvantages. One is that someone may come into the room and ask you a question. You ignore it because you haven't heard it. Your silence can upset people who interpret it as dumb insolence or sulking. The other is that if you use the telephone you (a) can't hear it ringing, and (b) have to take one earful out and put it down on some surface where it will be visible. As this little squashed ball is a dreadful knicker-pink colour, like something you bought in a sex shop, it can give strangers a shock, especially if little hairs or bits of fluff stick to it.

Buy soft slippers for small children, deal with the teenage stereomaniacs by buying them headphones for Christmas, with volume control (from Laskys, Tottenham Court Road, London W1).

Put a foam rubber mat on a metal draining board. This not only cuts washing up clangs, but also slipping and chipping.

Refrigerators which vibrate like Mick Jagger can sometimes be kept quieter if stood on rubber or a cork mat.

If water pipes bang and shudder when the cold tap is turned off, the water pressure may need adjusting, but before you call in the water board, check that the pipes are close enough to the appropriate wall and that the fittings haven't worn loose. Sometimes it's possible to fit a plastic paddle device on the ball valve arm in the cold water tank. This kills vibration.

Deal with any embarrassing plumbing noises by putting an equilibrium valve in the cold water storage cistern or toilet cistern.

If the drip of a tap is getting you down, check whether it needs a new tap washer, if so, get one you can use on both hot and cold.

SQUEAK AND RATTLE CHECK

Oil anything which squeaks, from chair castors to curtain runners. Alternatively, rub vaseline on it.

Castors: If a castor isn't moving smoothly check that dust or cotton thread hasn't become wrapped round the wheel or axle. If it has (and you can get at it) cut it away with a sharp knife. Oil the castor while working it around then wipe surplus oil away.

If chair castors are loose tighten the screws. If one of the screws turns maddeningly around insert *spent* matchsticks to jam it. Alternatively, remove screw, insert plastic wood into the hole, and wait overnight while it hardens, then re-insert the screw. If the shank of the castor is loose, remove castor from socket, wrap shank with masking tape or electrical tape and then try to re-insert it into the socket, where it should grip better. Then buy a new castor because it won't last more than a fortnight.

Doorknobs: If a doorknob is loose and rattles there's a good chance that all you have to do is to tighten the tiny screw (it's called a grub screw) behind the handle. That's also the screw you have to wind to remove an antique brass doorknob in order to give it a real polish for the first time in a hundred years. Before unscrewing it is vitally important to open the door wide and wedge it (with a wad of newspaper?). Otherwise, what invariably happens is that you drop the screw, the door swings shut, and you find yourself grovelling for a grub screw in a locked room which no one can open.

Many knobs have vernier adjustment. When you remove grub screws behind both handles and remove handles you will see that the doorknob shanks have more holes on one side than the other, so by varying the grub screw into different holes, you get a different adjustment. Just go on fiddling until one works.

If you tighten the grub screw and the doorknob *still* rattles uselessly, reach for the yellow pages and a workman because you'll probably need a smaller hole in the door or a new spindle.

Floorboards: Squeaking floorboards should be screwed down. If this doesn't work call a carpenter as they may need replacing.

FOR THE PROTECTION OF YOURSELF AND OTHERS

Check your fire escape method and fire extinguisher.

Check that your *burglar-proofing methods* are in order and fit a *peephole* to the front door as well as a chain. Don't feel it's silly to use it.

Manhole covers: Check that they are safe – I once nearly broke my leg in the dark on one, and the girl in front of whose door this woman trap was situated had the sauce to say that it wasn't her responsibility. If it's in front of her door I reckon it's morally her responsibility – no matter whose it is in law – if I end up on a crutch.

WHERE TO GO FOR MORE HELP AND ADVICE

You can get two free booklets on the merits and method of do-it-yourself double glazing from Pilkington Bros. Ltd, St Helens, Lancs. (Tel. St Helens 28882).

The British Standards Institution (2 Park Street, London W1, Tel. 01-629 9000) produces a punchy little free leaflet called 'Protect your Pipes from Frost'.

To repeat, if you should decide *not* to do it yourself, it's vital to get a reputable firm to do the job. The Insulation Glazing Association (6 Mount Row, London W1, Tel. 01-629 8334) will send you a leaflet on their pet subject and also a list of members in your area. The Heating and Ventilating Contractors Association (Coastal Chambers, 172 Buckingham Palace Road, London SW1, Tel. 01-730 8245) will also send you a list of members in your area. They also produce free explanatory leaflets on heating and air-conditioning.

There is a practical little kindergarten guide to household repairs, maintenance and emergencies. It has been said that it is too simple a book, written by an idiot for other idiots; that suits me. Called the *Feminine Fix-It Handbook*, by Kay D. Ward (Macdonald, £1.95, which is less than the cost of one hour of a London plumber), it includes basic carpentry, hanging things on walls, repainting, wallpapering, laying floors, minor plumbing repairs, ditto electrical, how to deal with windows and doors which won't open or close, furniture repairs, exterior maintenance, damp-proofing and some central heating tips.

Unless otherwise mentioned nearly all the above items can be obtained from Selfridges, Oxford Street, London W1, or from good do-it-yourself shops all round the country or builders' merchants.

When applying for any free literature recommended here, please enclose a stamp, *not* an envelope, which may be the wrong shape or too small.

HOW TO STICK ALMOST ANYTHING

In my experience, there is no such thing as an all-purpose adhesive, any more than there is an all-purpose book or all-purpose food or all-purpose shoe. A home needs more than one adhesive to hold it together, because the secret of sticking is to select the most suitable adhesive for the job.

What to stick with what

Main grouping	Trade name	Solvent	Use
Natural rubber	COW GUM	When wet you can rub it off with your fingers if it gets in the wrong place. When dry use dry-cleaning fluid such as BEAUCAIRE	Paper to paper, photographs, artwork, scrapbooks
Natural rubber	DUNLOP'S WALL-TILE ADHESIVE, Water Resistant & BOSTIK No 4	Dry-cleaning fluid	For sticking ceramic wall tiles to all interior surfaces
Nitrile (synthetic rubber)	DUNLOP'S CLEAR HOUSEHOLD ADHESIVE *BOSTIK No 1 CLEAR	Remove with acetone or clear nail varnish remover (*not* oily)*	All-purpose glue for most materials, including flexible PVC. Ideal for handbags, belts, satchels, suitcases, canvas, car covers, braid, lamp shades, picture frames, book binding, and for patching paddling pools, beach gear and mackintoshes

What to stick with what *(continued)*

Main grouping	Trade name	Solvent	Use
Neoprene (synthetic rubber)	EVOSTICK (liquid) or DUNLOP'S THIX-OFIX (spreads easily like butter) BOSTIK CONTACT No 3	Dry-cleaning fluid	For laminated plastics and general purpose do-it-yourself, such as rubber to wood, felt to wood. *Not suitable* for flexible plastics such as PVC or foam polystyrene
Synthetic rubber	BOSTIK'S GLUTAK	Dry-cleaning fluid	Posters to walls
Epoxy resin adhesives (which give the highest bond for the smallest area)	ARALDITE or DUNLOP'S EPOXY ADHESIVE	Remove when wet with hot water and soap. *Warning:* It can set in 10–13 minutes	China, glass, metal, wood, brick, stone, concrete, sticking spectacle frames and shoes, chair legs, teacup handles
For heavy-duty strength			
Polyurethane	7 BOSTIK QUICK SET ADHESIVE	No practical solvent	The recent successor to Epoxys for above items
Latex adhesive	COPYDEX	Remove when wet with cold water	Paper, card, upholstery and carpet, fabrics. It dries fast and repairs almost invisibly
Latex material	DUNLOP'S FLOORING ADHESIVE	Cold water, when wet. Try dry-cleaning solvent when dry	For sticking PVC, cork tiles, felt or hessian materials to floor surfaces
	BOSTIK 10 (glazed wall tiles)		
	BOSTIK 11 (floor tiles)		
	BOSTIK 12 (ceiling tiles)		
PVA (poly-vinylacetate)	DUNLOP'S WOODWORKER BOSTIK no. 8	Remove when wet with cold water, Can dry in 10 minutes! When dry remove with acetone	A woodworking adhesive. Good for most porous materials including hardboard
	DUNLOP'S CEILING TILE ADHESIVE	,, ,,	For foam polystyrene ceiling tiles

How to go about it: Start sticking by making sure, if possible, that you're fixing whatever it is on something that can be thrown away, such as old newspapers. Wear an overall (not an apron), even if you never do, even if you haven't got one. Borrow one from your local midwife or grocer, or whoever you've noticed has one.

Take the telephone off the hook and do not answer the front door bell. Try not to scratch ears, nose or rub eyes, however harassed or itchy you become.

How to come unstuck (if you've spilt the adhesive): Plan pessimistically. Discover, before you start to unscrew, how to get the sticky stuff off. I can't think why They don't print the correct solvent on all containers, but as they don't I give main groupings with their solvents. Treat the disaster area as soon as possible. Some say you should keep an old sheet or teatowel to mop up any mess. As you won't have an old sheet use the old newspapers.

If you have no idea of the chemical content of the mess you've just made, first mop it up, then try to remove with cold water, then warm water, then dry-cleaning fluid.

When spilling latex, epoxy or P.V.A. adhesives remember that once it's dry you'll probably never be able to remove it.

You *may* be able to remove a *small* dried drop of it from, say, a carpet, by softening it with dry-cleaning fluid and then picking it off with a comb or your finger, but it takes patience!

HOW TO KEEP A HAPPY CAR

Most women feel that a car should appreciate in value and give as little trouble as emeralds: but a car depreciates, like a fur coat, so look after it as you would a beloved pet. All you need to know is how and why.

'You can always find a woman who doesn't know how to care for a car,' I was told by the Automobile Association, 'but for every woman you will also find a man.' Sweet of them.

The main reason for joining a motoring organization is for its emergency services: no matter at what hour of day or night the thing packs up, all you have to do is get to the nearest telephone box and ring the AA Emergency Service: help should be with you quickly. When joining you receive a free handbook with map and a key to the AA telephone boxes (but *any* telephone will suffice).

Sudden paralysis apart, if you do not look after it carefully, sooner or later your car will fall to bits and, before the final death throes, you will probably have lots of expensive trouble. Although you don't grease it for quite the same reasons, you should care for your car as you do for your face and have it serviced according to the manufacturer's instructions. As in love, major problems often stem from minor initial causes, so immediately check any trivial fault; you may avoid a more serious one. Do not close your ears to that little clicking noise in the hope that it will go away.

Keep a record of any repair bills and the dates of service (what was done, and when), useful proof of careful ownership when you want to sell it.

Supposedly *every week*, but definitely *before a long drive*, check distilled water in battery, water in radiator, oil level and tyre pressure.

Battery: Check the water level and top up to ¼ inch over the plates with distilled water. Any garage should provide this. Top it up, but do not overfill. If fluid seeps out at the top it may corrode the case.

Make sure that the terminals – the knobs where the thick wires join the battery – are free from dirt and corrosion. Clean them with a little wire suede brush or even with a toothbrush (though onlookers may think you mad) and lightly grease.

WARNING! If you use ordinary water you may reduce the efficiency of the battery, which is the engine room of your engine: everything depends on your battery.

Plugs: Check that the terminal leads to the battery are in good condition and secure, otherwise your engine won't work properly. Replace spark plugs every 10,000 miles. Plugs in good condition will cut your fuel consumption. Plugs in bad condition make you very prone to breakdowns.

Radiator: Check water level (unnecessary with sealed radiator systems). Put anti-freeze in your radiator to prevent the water in the radiator from freezing overnight and cracking the cylinder. Possibly the best thing is a dual-purpose anti-freeze which also helps to prevent corrosion in the summer.

WARNING! The fragrant smell of burning buns sniffed while the car is running may mean that there is no water in your radiator. If there is no water in your radiator your engine will overheat immediately. At the least you will be unable to restart the car for some time, and at the most you will need a new engine.

WARNING! If your radiator steams, the top cap will be boiling hot and the water may be a scalding jet. Wait ten minutes, then use a glove or cloth to ease the cap off, bit by bit, let it cool down for fifteen minutes before refilling. Remember James Watt

and the kettle. If you unscrew it right off while it's still hot, it will probably blow off and scald your hands if not your face.

Oil: Check the level of the oil with the dipstick. Keep oil to the correct level and change it at the intervals recommended by the manufacturers.

WARNING! If there are tiny specks of white metal on the dipstick have it investigated: it may mean that an engine bearing is wearing badly and needs immediate attention. Worn engine bearings lead to a gradual wearing down of the engine.

Replacements: Just as some things, like shoes, men or scrubbing brushes, need renewing from time to time, a car needs the occasional replacement.

Replace *tyres* before they reach the minimum legal requirement of 1 millimetre of tread all round, which is as worn as it sounds.

Treat yourself to a new pair of *windscreen wipers* before each winter. Not only do you risk developing crow's feet as you peer ahead, but it is dangerous to drive with a dirty windscreen because you ought to be able to see where you are going.

Seat belts: Cars have seat belts. The inertia reel sort are easier to slip on and move around in and hold you so comfortably in place that a passenger can end a long journey feeling positively refreshed. For some reason men don't like them: they're supposed to be sissy. But what's so deeply masculine about fiddling around with the bra strap adjustments on the ordinary belt?

Cleaning: You're supposed to keep your car exterior in good condition by cleaning it or getting it cleaned once a week. One way is to drive through a car cleaner. The bliss of yielding self and car to be soaped, washed and brushed by those trembly machines is equalled only by the luxury of having a nanny to wash between your toes.

If doing it yourself, clean the car from the top, preferably with a hose and with warm water. A relatively easy way to swab the thing down is with a softish brush attached to a hose. Cover every bit of the car with the brush or it will look splodgy when dry. With an ordinary bucket and sponge you risk putting back the grit you have just washed off, so make sure you rinse the sponge carefully – and it's quicker if you use a large sponge.

Clean windows with a chamois leather. It doesn't leave scratches on the glass, which is why window cleaners use it.

You are also supposed to *polish* your car three or four times a year. Get the car really clean and dry before you wax it, otherwise it will be twice as hard next time.

There are masses of car-cleaning products available with not much to choose between them. If your car is really filthy with pore-deep dirt a particularly powerful cleaner is Jove, which removes grease, wax and road dirt. For polishing you might use Johnson's Rally Car Wax.

Clean chrome with Solo Autosol, a German product. You rub a little on like toothpaste.

> WARNING! Once chrome is deeply rusted, nothing simple can be done to eliminate it. You have to have it rechromed or buy a new bumper or whatever.

Corrosion: You are unlikely to get salt under your car in summer, unless you race along the beach, blonde on your bonnet, like a cigarette ad. You are far more likely to get plastered with municipal salt sprinkled on winter roads, so get a garage to hose underneath the car in winter if you use the car a lot.

If you think this is unnecessary try soaking an ordinary pair of steel scissors in salt water for a couple of hours, whereupon they will start to rust, whereupon they won't work so well.

What to keep and what not to keep in the car: In the glove compartment keep instruction handbook, maps, torch, boiled sweets (chocolate melts), sunglasses (a genuine safety precaution) and your motoring organization membership card and call box key. Heaven knows where you will keep your gloves.

In the back of the car keep an empty plastic shopping bag to use as a wastepaper basket and another one to contain two sponges, two towels, two dusters and a can of windscreen de-icer and de-mister.

Keep a spare car key in your jewel box.

Cars over three years old must be MOT-tested annually by a garage. Keep the test certificate, the log book and the insurance certificate at home in a safe place, in case the car is stolen. Keep your driving licence on you (in case you want to cash a cheque).

Tool kit: Check you have a jack, set of spanners (or one adjustable spanner), screwdrivers (large and small), spare fan belt, wheel brace (for fitting nuts on wheel), hammer, oil.

Dramas

If your car won't start . . . Have you switched the ignition on ? Is there any petrol ? Does your battery need re-charging ? (Check by switching on the headlights.) Now you can go for help without feeling a real idiot.

Before you skip merrily on to the next page, pause . . . now imagine a lonely road. Night is falling, it is raining. Your tyre has just burst. There is no AA box in sight. Somebody will have to do something and *there is only you.* Now read on.

Changing a wheel: Tyres burst in calamitous conditions, so practise changing a wheel somewhere near your local garage. How that friendly mechanic will chuckle if he has to rescue you!

When you are faced with the real thing:

1 Get the car off the road as fast as possible. Never change a wheel near a drain or the bolts jump down it.
2 Put the brake on and leave the car in gear so it won't slip and run over your hand. Put a block against at least one wheel – a stone or a brick or *something* to stop it moving.
3 Remove hub caps.
4 Loosen nuts with spanner, but DON'T take them off yet.
5 Jack up car (look in your handbook for correct position) until the wheel is clear of the ground.
6 Remove nuts and put somewhere safe, such as the driver's seat.
7 Heave wheel off.
8 Put on spare wheel.
9 Replace nuts and bolts, then tighten.
10 Lower car, until wheel just touches ground.
11 Tighten nuts again.
12 Check you've done them all.
13 Remove jack.
14 Replace hub cap.
15 Remove block against wheel.
16 Drive off and double check fit plus tyre pressure at the nearest garage.
17 Have punctured wheel repaired as fast as possible.

Maintain yourself in good condition – then you will find it easier to stop a lorry driver than change a wheel.

HOW TO SPEND MONEY

Mr Micawber's crisp advice on budgeting hasn't been improved on in the past hundred years: 'Annual Income twenty pounds, annual expenditure nineteen, nineteen six, result happiness. Annual Income twenty pounds, annual expenditure twenty pounds ought and six, result misery.'

If there's trouble in a home, it isn't always in the bedroom – it's quite often in the budget. I wouldn't be surprised to hear that more families fight over money than over sex and mothers-in-law combined, usually because they've built the battleground into their lives by planning their money badly or not planning it at all. (In fact, the Marriage Guidance Council says they find that sex is the main contributor to marriage difficulties, with money in second place.)

The first financial fact that a couple should discover is *what system can be operated by both of them*. One couple might happily operate a system based on a piggybank on the mantelpiece and a two-sided purse. Another couple might positively enjoy running six bank accounts plus an accountant. But woe betide the togetherness when *she* operates the piggybank and *he* divides the laundry bill into his, hers and theirs, with the aid of one of those push-button desk calculators.

According to certain marriage experts, a good test of a relationship is supposed to be whether you can happily operate a joint account. You might feel it would be safer to try going over Niagara in a barrel than to check in this particular way whether either of you is losing out on the domination/submission pattern. All I can tell you is that *no* system will be

135

any good unless you *both* understand and agree to it.

An annual budget is basically two simple lists. One list is of money coming in from different sources over the year, the other list is of money being spent on different items over that time.

Divide the second list by twelve to get the monthly amount you plan to spend (or divide by thirteen if you want four-week periods), or divide it by fifty-two if you want to budget weekly. If you get paid weekly it's sensible to work out a weekly budget. If you are paid monthly, do a monthly one.

Experts say that you should be precise in your accounting – no rounding out sums to the nearest pound. State the actual amount down to the last $\frac{1}{2}$p.

The point of a home budget is knowing what you want to do with your money, keeping track of where the money actually goes (theoretically, these two figures should be the same, but life isn't like that) and making sure that you don't overspend and get into debt without realizing it.

In working out the budget everyone should be absolutely clear where even the smallest expenses fit in and make sure that everything fits in somewhere. For example, cigarettes. Are they a necessity, to be bought regularly and paid for on the weekly supermarket bill? Or are they luxuries to come out of individual personal allowances?

'Mistakes and contingencies' is the disaster fund (unpredictable, act of God stuff). Leave a really pessimistic amount of the budget to go into the disaster fund. After all, if you don't use it you can divert the money into savings or a spree at the end of the year. But you will use it. The budget for saving should *not* be lumped with the disaster fund, or your savings will just melt.

Save what you can in a deposit account or building society or by purchasing investments or cream part of the savings off into mortgage repayments (since bricks and mortar are also an investment), or buy potential old masters, or silver or similar items.

If you can't seem to save, you could make yourself save by taking on savings commitments and having your bank enforce them by banker's order, or you might firmly commit your money in a direction other than a piggy bank. H.P. can be a great way to force yourself to save up for things, but *only* if you don't allow more than 10 per cent of your annual income. I know a girl who bought a diamond tiara this way. It's the smallest tiara in captivity and she's never worn the thing because it's always in the bank guaranteeing something. But it certainly was a glamorous way to save and the value has increased six times in ten years.

If you are self-employed allow for tax and national insurance stamps when budgeting. Work out what your tax should be and deposit this money in a savings account where it will earn you interest until the taxman needs it, as he eventually will.

Working out the budget: Allow for items such as the following in your outgoing budget:

rent or mortgage payments
rates
maintenance
H.P.
food

fuel
services
insurance
medical and dentistry
household expenses
clothes repairs and replacements
child costs, such as football boots
schooling or coaching, school extras,
    such as stationery
personal allowances
entertainment
holiday
christmas
charity
pets
garden
telephone
domestic help
transport
savings
mistakes and contingencies

Sorting out the income: If there is more than one contributor, either (a) sort out separate responsibilities or (b) pool the family income – whatever its source – family allowances, dividends, earnings, legacies or whatever – and add it up. Then try redistributing it under headings such as I've suggested.

Some think it is important that the chief earners should not allow themselves to think that because they bring in the money they have a greater right than the rest of the family to determine how it should be spent. A husband might work and get paid and a wife may work full-time in the home and not get paid. He is the breadwinner for the family but she is not just a bread-consumer. Some wives feel that he gets paid (to a greater or lesser degree) for both their work. That's certainly the main reason given by men for unequal pay. But the days

are gone when you could get a woman to work for a week merely for full board and a roof over her head.

Where a young husband and wife both work they often feel it is better not to learn to rely on the wife's pay in case she has children or stops working for any other reason, so that there would not have to be a painful adjustment to a lower standard of living. Provided there is some compensatory form of security for the wife, such as a joint mortgage, it seems reasonable that the extra money which comes into the kitty because of her work should be earmarked for major but slashable items, such as central heating and household appliances.

Separate bank accounts: You cannot afford to be sentimental about money. If you and your husband are madly in love, well that's wonderful, but statistically you have a one in six chance of falling out of love and divorcing. If you were married before you were twenty the possibility is one in three. So without being offensively self-protective, avoid entwining your money or goods (assuming that you have any) with those of your husband (or any other member of the household). Not to be mean – just to keep things clear.

I consider that only one joint account for two people puts the budget at risk as well as the relationship, and so does the judge who lives next door. His non-working wife has a personal account and a housekeeping account.

If you have a separate income, get your tax assessed separately and run the housekeeping on a third joint household account.

If your housekeeping money is paid into a joint bank account in this way you might like part of it in a cash sum

MONEY, MONEY, MONEY
YOUR HOUSEKEEPING BUDGET

Item		Cost		Cost per Week		Cost per Year	
£	p	£	p	£	p	£	p

sent to you weekly or monthly *on standing order*. This means you have only once to tell the bank what to do and then it just keeps coming. This helps to keep some control over your cash spending.

If more than two earners are sharing a home (husband and wife, mother and son, two or three friends), each might pay an agreed sum regularly (every week, month or quarter) into the joint household account, for the purpose of running the home.

Keep your own private money apart from the housekeeping money: It could be by having two purses, or a purse with two pockets, or two separate bank accounts and cheque books.

In fact for me, the secret of keeping track of home budgeting is to reduce as many outgoings as possible to a regular basis, and for this I've opened a number 2 housekeeping account. First, add up all your regular payments for *everything*, from the milkman to the dog licence. Estimate what fuel and telephone bills will be by looking up last year's costs. Take a deep breath and don't panic at this point, because the total amount will be truly staggering. Divide it by twelve, prune, then arrange to have the resultant sum paid monthly into a *number 2 budget account*. All *regular* bills are paid from this account, so I don't feel faint at the *thought* of opening the electricity bill. If I am overdrawn one month it should theoretically balance out in following months. Food and unexpected or unbudgeted expenses are paid from the number 1 account. This means I have three bank accounts in all: a personal account, a housekeeping account and a second housekeeping account for regular payments.

It's expensive but I prefer to pay for clarity than having to keep doing little sums to find out whether I can afford to buy a window box.

Book-keeping: I do as little as I can get away with and so might you. Stop reading if you wouldn't dream of organizing your money. Come back to this page again if you start raising Corgis or cucumbers or get in a money muddle.

The easiest form of housekeeping or business book-keeping is to get a *cash book* because this has lines and columns conveniently ruled for you. Fill in the date of entry, money that comes in and money that goes out. I don't mean the cost of every lettuce. . . I just fill in 'food' as such. This book not only calms you when you wonder where on earth the money went or when someone sends you a second bill for something you've already paid for or when you want to check how many times the vacuum cleaner has been repaired since you bought it, but it is also a good indicator of where you can economize.

It is a good idea to make a point of entering cheques in the book *before* filling them in, otherwise you tend to forget to enter them at all. To pay bills, sort them out alphabetically, enter them in your accounts book, fill in the cheque stubs, then nerve yourself to make out the cheques.

For the advanced muddler: If you want to know exactly where you are financially you can do a satisfying little sum which grandly calls itself a cash flow statement. An average thirteen-year-old child who is weak on maths could do one. First telephone the bank and find exactly what is in each of your accounts, then write them down on a line as follows:

MONEY, MONEY, MONEY

Date: 1.4.1984	*Me*	*Housekeeping*	*2nd account*
State of play	+£2	+£20	+£200
Deduct bills to pay	0	− 17	− 120
Deduct cheques not yet presented	− 1	0	− 32
SUB TOTAL	+ 1	+ 3	+ 48
Add cheques not yet paid in	+ 13	+ 10	0
FACTUAL TOTAL	+ 14	+ 13	+ 48
Add, tentatively, money due in	+ 25	0	0
THEORETICAL TOTAL	£39	£13	£48

Business book-keeping: If you have your own little cottage industry steaming along nicely (embroidering blouses, making cushions or cakes or fibreglass sculpture or breeding Burmese cats) then keep separate accounts of what you spent exactly as above.

In a second, separate cash book on the left-hand page keep a dated list of the invoices you send out (how else will the accountants of other firms know that they owe you money?). Enter the date on the right-hand page when payment is made. Anything undated on the right-hand page is unpaid.

When you send someone an invoice, which is an exact account of what they owe you money for, you should send a short summary, or statement of it at the end of the month. You can normally expect payment at the end of the month following that, i.e. in five weeks at the earliest after delivery of goods and eight weeks at the latest. You may have sensibly made arrangements that the goods should be paid for *before* delivery, in which case you send a PRO FORMA INVOICE, which is just the same as an invoice. It means 'cash in advance, please!'

It is inadvisable to sell goods on a sale or return basis. Your goods are gone, and the shop hasn't invested in them, so it might be less keen on selling them than some other product in which the shop's money is tied up, and the position about possible dirt or damage is unsatisfactory.

I mention these points because though they are simple I have seen many housewives, who have never been in business, muddle a good start by not understanding the procedure.

FAMILY FUNDS

Involving the family: Some families have regular conferences about money – once every three months, say. Get the children in on these as early as possible, even though they may be bored, and treat their contributions with respect. After discussing the budget, analyse disasters to find out why they happened and how to prevent them, suggesting amendments to the budget (more pocket money may mean a less expensive holiday) and take account of future changes, such as rising prices. After this the family should all go out to dinner – even if it's only fish and chips – to cheer themselves up again.

This may sound horrendous, but my pretty cousin Corinne, a comparatively new bride, says she's eternally grateful to her father for doing this. Not only did she, as a little girl, see the point of switching lights off (more money for holidays) but she sailed into marriage able to run a budget, without ever realizing she had been taught to do so.

Major expenditure in the house should, ideally, be discussed and approved by all the family. If he wants a scarlet sports car, if you want a dishwasher, if your eldest son wants to spend a year travelling before settling down, it's a matter that all the family should know about, if paying for it will affect the finances of the whole household. This is what the quarterly conference is for.

If one adult member of the family tries to explain a major change which the rest can't see the sense in (i.e. how the aforementioned sports car will actually *save* money), get him/her to explain it in front of the family bank manager who can then act as an impartial adviser.

WHAT TO DO IF YOU'RE A CASHAHOLIC

A cashaholic is someone who's hopeless with money. Psychologists say that hopeless extravagance is inculcated in children by parents who don't give their children a proper allowance and make them responsible for their own expenditure, but who only give pocket money for treats and presents. The result of this is that the child, when grown up, thinks of cash as meaning treats and money for personal pleasure and never for dreary things such as rates and electricity bills.

I've never really found a cure for this condition, but you can survive solvently as a cashaholic by treating yourself as an alcoholic and hiding the bottle – i.e. don't own a cheque book, certainly don't own a credit card, deal only in cash and when your purse is empty stop spending. Form a Cashaholics Anonymous with a similarly minded friend and telephone her when you get the urge to spend – she will then reel off a litany of bills and responsibilities and, in theory, deter you. Don't go out of the home, stick to your shopping list and don't add one extra item. If you can't do this, shop by telephone to avoid temptation. Yes, it's a bit more expensive, but you're avoiding larger areas of temptation.

Finally, commit your money firmly in other directions (see p. 136).

How to bring up more sensible children: You won't raise a second generation of cashaholics if you teach your children how to handle money as soon as they can buy their own ice-creams.

Involve them in the family affairs as soon as possible, as I have suggested, and give each child an allowance– yearly or monthly – to cover all he or she spends; older children can have clothes on their own budgets, plus hobbies, sports, travelling, school expenses, going out to the cinema, sweets and ice-creams. Expect drama in the first six months, when they learn that early over-purchasing of ice-cream leads to later lack of model-making glue. *Be firm at this point.* Kindness will not equip your offspring to stand on their own feet in later life.

As soon as possible put the allowance in the form of a post office savings book or bank account and arrange with your bank manager to make the most almighty fuss if there's an overdraft, accompanied by extremely stiff letters from the bank.

My children have had bank accounts since they were eight. I pay their allowance on standing order and they sort out everything for themselves, including mistakes and contingencies. Although I advise them I never bail them out. Accidentally, this seems a good method for parents and children alike, once the children have recovered from discovering the hidden disadvantages of a cheque book.

HOW TO CUT THE COST OF LIVING

No matter how tight your budget there is room in it for economy.

Cut down on big things: Don't economize on things which will hardly save more than a few pence – margarine instead of butter, unless your butter consumption is gargantuan (although, as I write, butter is cheaper than marge). This will not be much of an economy and will make everyone feel pinched.

And never cut down on what makes your life worth living: if you have chocolate cake for Sunday Tea, don't switch to buns; if your one joy is playing squash don't hang up your racquets. The trick is to economize in a big way on something boring, not to bring down the whole family by being miserly and making yourself miserable.

If your troubles are not likely to be temporary, you might consider moving to a smaller house. You might trade the car in for a smaller one or put the

family on bicycles – which is anyway more sensible in cities.

I've just sold my car and bought one of those funny French motorbikes called a Velosolex. You can bicycle it with your feet (my thighs are disappearing!) then flip on the engine when you get tired. And as it does 200 m.p.g. I feel virtuously patriotic as I sail along with the shopping at 30 m.p.h.

Don't be sentimental or afraid of what the neighbours will think if you have to move for money reasons. You won't be around to hear them. On the other hand, do go into your economies carefully before you make them – moving to the country may save money in some ways, but with the dearth of big supermarkets and the increase in travelling costs it entails it may not help you at all. And moving itself is a great expense.

It isn't easy. When Doomsday hit me I moved home five times in eighteen months. Oddly enough I was cheered by my solicitor telling me how difficult *everybody* always found it, not just me. 'One of the most difficult things you can do,' he said, 'is to cut your budget drastically, because nobody ever thinks that he is personally being "extravagant", or he wouldn't live that way.'

I was also cheered and urged on by another lovely man who said, 'Come on Shirley, see it as a challenge. I mean, you could have the most marvellous garage in London, if only you put your mind to it.' From then on I upset my mother dreadfully by drawing garage conversion designs on the backs of envelopes and working out how three of us could live in an area 12 by 14 feet. But the point had been hammered home. Everything is easier once you face it and get interested in the situation, as opposed to being appalled by it.

HOW TO AVOID PAYING A BILL *OR* WHAT TO DO ON DOOMSDAY

Doomsday happens in every family sometimes – the day when Father is made redundant, Mother's secret extravagance comes home to roost, the accountants turn out to have been crooks, or whatever. The essential feature of the situation is that the money just won't go round, there are too many bills and not enough money to pay them.

When Doomsday comes to your family you *can* cope with it, if you remember two basic facts. Firstly, all the people you owe money to are chiefly interested in getting their money not in suing you, which will only cost them more money. Secondly, as these disasters happen to everyone it's nothing to be ashamed of, but something to be calmly explained in your dealings with your creditors as soon as possible.

Make a list of all your major creditors – building societies, service industries, HP companies, tradesmen and so on – and how much you owe each of them. Then work out how much you can afford to pay each of them – thinking in terms of paying off what you owe in instalments. This is called 'keeping your credit good' and it ensures that you don't get blacklisted by credit investigators, which might mean no more HP or mortgages.

Then write each creditor a letter, addressed to the chief accountant, explaining that your family is in a financial crisis (no need to go into details)

and it would help you enormously if they would accept payment by instalments, quoting the sum you have decided you can afford. Almost all firms will accept this offer, and then it's simply a question of slog and cutting down expenses until all your debts are paid off. Two things to remember are:

1 Always get your letter off *before* the creditors start demanding money.
2 Don't over-estimate your income or under-estimate the cost of living when working out what you can afford to pay off. Offer less rather than offering more and risking not being able to live up to your promises.

NEVER, NEVER, borrow money to pay off debts unless you borrow from your bank. By handling your crisis yourself you will avoid paying heavy interest on your debts.

But never ever run up an overdraft without asking permission from your bank manager. Apart from anything else, it's only polite to ask before you help yourself to his money. Don't think that it might pass unnoticed. And you don't want to jeopardize your credit rating on that little pink card they keep with your name on it, on which they note every letter or telephone call you make to them.

Although, as from 1974, financial matters can never be straightforward, it's useful to have a simple guide for money matters. Sheila Black, the financial expert who writes in *The Times*, recommends the *Save and Prosper Book of Money* (edited by Margaret Allen, published by Collins, costs £1.25). It ranges from taxation problems and buying a car, to how to borrow and save. It also covers bank accounts, mortgages, pension and hire purchase and other dreary subjects which you might be forced to deal with.

If you have difficulty getting it, write, sending 25p extra for postage and packing, to 'The Save and Prosper Group', 4 Great St Helens, London EC3P 3EP.

ORGANIZATION

DO YOU SINCERELY WANT TO BE ORGANIZED?

A tycoon millionairess once told me that she found a business easier to run than a home. I'm sure she's right. I've never yet been able to make the house-keeping show a profit, but my system is to run it in the same way as I run an office, with a planned budget, purchasing and filing department (all me). This is not nearly as clever or complicated as it sounds. Any sane woman in a perfect world wouldn't bother, but if like me you've lost two vacuum cleaners and £140 worth of laundry in one year you'll know it's worthwhile.

The equipment: All you need to get organized is a writing surface, a chair, a kitchen drawer, a large cardboard box or a bit of shelf space on which to store two wire office trays or a couple of shopping bags (IN and OUT),

eight double-sided envelope files with which to start a filing system, a duplicate book, two notebooks, envelopes and writing paper, a handbag diary and notebook, an address book – and some pretty postcards.

Shopping lists: Sellotape a shopping check list of food and household items you often buy in the back of your address book.

Expect – or rather, exact – no co-operation from your family; it will result in a restful state of non-expectancy and consequent non-nagging, non-resentfulness for everyone. The only family rule is: Everyone must write in the shopping list notebook what is *about* to run out. This works, because the family doesn't see it as a chore but a sensible necessity. They know if they don't do it, we will run out of peanut butter or whatever they're about to scoff.

ORGANIZATION

The mail: I throw incoming mail in a wicker basket on top of the refrigerator and outgoing mail in a string bag hanging by the kitchen door. I open the mail immediately after breakfast and deal with small items by postcard.

It's easier to write a line than a letter. Try to write thank yous on pretty postcards as soon as you get home, while you're still feeling grateful. Also use postcards for Christmas thank yous: last year's list was polished off in half an hour. I know a barrister who keeps her postcards *already stamped* in an elegant basket by her bed.

Weightier things such as bank statements get thrown into the IN tray for Monday morning, when I do all my office work, tardy thank yous, and general organization. Anything which doesn't get done on Monday doesn't get done. There is always another Monday.

Bills: Always save business letters, bills and *receipts* (otherwise what proof have you that you paid cash to the man who mended the sink, when his firm sends you an invoice for it six months later?). This is especially necessary in this unnerving age of automation: computers *do* go wrong, and people with (or without) computers *can* be even more inefficient than you.

I may be paranoid but I've noticed that computers never go wrong in my favour. And, when you've been invoiced for £66.32 for a real pigskin bidet which you haven't dreamed of, let alone bought, remember that it can take six weeks for a computer to answer the simple question: 'What proof have you that this was ordered?' Keep a duplicate book in your bill file for letters about bills-in-query. Don't send them the receipt which proves you've paid; if you do you may lose your proof. Trace the signature or quote the reference.

Work lists: My work notebook is just a list of non-food work to do and reads 'buy nametapes', 'order lampshade', 'get new sink stopper', etc. I never promise to do anything unless I have scribbled it down in a handbag notebook or work book.

Go through these every Monday morning, ticking off a job when you've done something about it, and crossing it out when it's completed. Write work lists on right-hand pages only and make any notes about the job on the left-hand side of the page. So when the laundry promises it will return the purple towel, tick the note, but not until the towel has been welcomed home do you cross it off completely.

Supposing the right-hand page says 'Query telephone bill', on the left-hand page jot the date and name of the person you have discussed it with. If the argument goes on for weeks you can *always* flip back to that left-hand page and make dated notes of the continuing saga (it helps to have a wrist watch with a day and date calendar).

I go through six notebooks a year and I keep them (they take up little room in a grocery box under the sofa, and it's amazing how useful they are).

Always check everything in and out of your house, getting someone to sign in your work notebook for anything they remove. Date it. As service gets worse, people get more harassed and work is skimped or rushed. The busier you are the more you should make it a rule always to keep check of who has what and where. When signing for any parcel always add 'not inspected', or 'not tested', whichever applies.

146

Jeer if you must, but this sort of efficiency takes no time, only care, and can save a lot of trauma.

The only New Year's resolution I keep is to look at my yearly list – things to do on 1 January. Sometimes you may feel too frail to cope with things on 1 January, in which case do them as soon as convenient. The list may look dreadful, but I find that mine (reproduced here for your inspiration) took only two hours to sort out last year. On 1 January? No, on 14 February.

NEW YEAR CHECK LIST

Apply for car licence with M.O.T. certificate, registration book and insurance certificate (or solex or whatever).

Insurance, personal, house, etc.
Check national insurance card is stamped. (If you're running a business, even the smallest business, consider sending accountant one year's stamp money in advance.)
AA membership renewal.
Check bank standing orders.
Check passports up to date.
TV licence.
Service central heating and Ascot. Also all electrical appliances such as dishwashers and washing machine.
Check roof and gutters, chimneys.
Service car.

Fill in your check list overleaf.

Income tax: If you use an accountant (perhaps, like me, you work at a part-time business) at the end of your financial year the minimum you should send him is the following:

1 Cheque books, up to date, with stubs properly filled in and list of entries from current cheque books.
2 Bank paying-in book and other bank correspondence.
3 Invoices for work.
4 Order books.
5 Receipts in date order.
6 Diary.
7 Cash flow position at end of year.
8 Other items as follows:

....

....

....

....

....

....

....

....

....

If you haven't an accountant, deal with any income tax work.

New address book: Some people write out a new address book every January, sadly weeding out the dead and discarded. Not a bad idea to do this occasionally because then, when you lose your handbag, you can go back to your old address book.

New diary: In my new diary I jot down all seasonal items: transferring them from year to year. (Sow 18 lb. coarse shade grass seed every March, rake up lawn, ignore existing grass which will look messy for a few days

ORGANIZATION

CHECK LIST

....

....

....

....

....

....

....

....

....

....

....

....

....

....

....

....

then springs to life. Hose well immediately after.) I also jot odd notes in
the back of the diary, knowing that I
won't read them until the year's end: a
Christmas present list, a list of the current medicines the family is dosing itself with, the collar sizes of my favourite men and the overall size of my
mother-in-law.

Writer Katharine Whitehorn wants
me to recommend her one and only
organized habit. Write your name and
address and 'please, please return' in
front of every single notebook, diary or
address book you ever use. These
have frequently been returned to her
by bus conductors, taxi drivers, friends
and strangers.

THE DRAWER WITH THE
ANSWER TO EVERYTHING
and what to put in it

Filing is a word that makes most
women look mutinous, but it's not
only a good idea, but in home emergencies absolutely essential. Don't be
frightened by the idea of filing. The
verb only means putting things in a
sensible place where you can find them
quickly and easily. Four years of my
filing fit into a suitcase.

Know your limitations and don't
plan a filing system that is better than
you are, as you won't stick to it and you
will find that even more depressing
than doing it.

What follows sounds amazingly
neat and tidy, but it isn't. Most of my
key work seems to be on the front of old
envelopes (backs already used for
key work). If I stopped to type or
write them out they would never get
done; it's easier to shove any old

scrap of paper into its correct place in
the system than to have it lying around.

The simplest filing system: This
might just be an alphabetically indexed
document wallet. Or a Twinlock personal file suitcase.

My humble system started with
two cardboard mushroom boxes labelled 'IN' and 'OUT', and one kitchen
drawer that deserves its peeling label
'The drawer with the answer to everything'. It contained eight standard
office cardboard files, with two pockets
each, providing sixteen compartments,
which should be enough for any fun-
loving, file-hating harassed housewife.

What to put in your files: Everyone's
individual filing system is a different
sort of organized chaos. Once you've
started it the only thing you will have
to remember is that this repository,
whatever its size or situation, is from
now on the *one and only safe place in
the house*. Any scrap of valuable paper
(except money) should be in it, even if
it's just saved in the huge envelope
labelled 'For sorting out sometime'.

File roughly as follows, according to
your circumstances and tidiness potential, in the eight double pocket
files you have bought. I never file anything in alphabetical or date order or it
would never get filed.

File 1 (A) **Guarantees.**
(B) **Instruction leaflets.**

File 2 (A) **Health** A little notebook
listing children's illnesses with dates,
health certificates, family National
Health cards.
(B) **Licences** for yearly renewal: dog
licences, television licences.

File 3 **Household** (A) Hopeless
gardening schedule, with plan of

ORGANIZATION

garden, so when next spring's tulips
fail to appear, you can check that you
were at least looking for them in the
right place.

(B) Linen, cutlery and china list, if you
care about these things. I do. I like to
know how much disappears each year.
Also a list of the different strength
light bulbs used in the house.

File 4 **Personal** (A) Recipes and diets
and all their magic appurtenances, like
the note you wrote to yourself saying
'One slice of bread a day equals
365 slices a year, which equals huge
hips'.

(B) Useful things torn out of magazines, such as how to clean your
jewellery, and how to get to Delhi for
£5, what revives a cyclamen and a list
of all-night rave places in Paris. This
file is never used, but I find it a comfort.

File 5 (A) **Important documents.**
What's important is a highly personal
decision. My file contains passports,
children's post office savings books,
premium bonds (we have one), marriage and birth certificates, insurance
certificates, tax coding notices and similar potential drama, along with the
first (and only) love letter my first husband wrote to me. Ah well, on with the
filing.

(B) Overspill from 5 (A).

File 6 (A) **Money** file. Stick bills in one
pocket, leaving the other side for bank
statements, used and unused cheque
books, and paying-in books. As my
official paying-in book meant entering
everything twice, I now use a little
stationer's duplicate book with numbered pages and carbon paper. So far
it hasn't jammed the bank's computer.

File 7 (A) and (B) **Receipts** Just put
them in and sort out only when someone's accusing you of not paying the
parking fine for which you bitterly
remember writing a cheque. (No one
ever puts that seven-figure reference
number on a cheque stub; partly
because there isn't room for it and
partly because you're so cross at the
time.)

File 8 (A) **Household addresses** This
file contains a sheet of paper with a list
of names, addresses and telephone
numbers that are important to you,
and anyone else who is temporarily
in charge. For example:
doctor; dentist; vet; garage; A.A. or
R.A.C. emergency numbers; taxis;
police; hospital; child welfare/ante
natal/family planning clinics; telephone engineer, directory enquiries
and telegrams; drain cleaner; plumber;
builder; local town hall (for complaining about non-removal of dustbins or eccentric reshaping of same;
local fuel sources (i.e. coal or oil
supplier); British Gas; Electricity
Board; electrical repair shops (incidentally, I vaguely believe in buying
all electrical appliances from one firm,
if possible (depending on what *Which?*
recommends) as you can then establish
a friendly Christian names relationship
with *one* complaints department instead of several); TV repair men;
window cleaner; local shops; laundry;
railway station, coach station, airport;
nearest all-night chemist, if you're
lucky enough to have one; local cinema
and theatres, ditto; odd job man.
And so on, according to your own
idiosyncrasies and odd job men. (See
'How to Get Hold of the Men in Your
Life', p. 189.)

(B) **Photographs** of any good silver

or other portable valuables and antiques. With crime on the increase and insurance premiums soaring at the rate of the latest Apollo, the prompt supply of these details to the police can often lead to their recovery. Could you describe such things from memory at this agitated moment, including the brand name of radios and watches?

In fact, you might, given the strength, time, patience and a rainy Sunday afternoon, draw up a list of your **family numbers,** so you won't have to forget to fill them in the beginning of your diary every year. These range from national health numbers, national insurance numbers, passport numbers, driving licence numbers, insurance policy numbers, transistor radios, cassettes, stereos, TV, cameras, watches, bicycles, slide and cinema projectors, cars: almost anything mechanical and stealable has a serial number somewhere on the case. Note these numbers with a description of the object. Also include any car or scooter numbers. For some reason the police think you need slapping straight into a straitjacket if you can't remember your car number: but some brains are pondering mightier things, such as whether to file love letters under X for kisses and did you remember to put the plastic losable key to the washing machine in your jewel box, where the baby can't grab it to teethe on.

It's a good idea to add a list of the items which you keep in your handbag, together with their *serial numbers:* credit cards, Barclay card, Access card, £30 cheque card, cheque books, union card, library card, driving licence, car insurance certificate, National Trust life membership card. In case of theft you can quickly inform the police and cancel or replace these items.

If there is still room in your drawer keep an envelope or plastic bag full of assorted sticky labels, for files, jam jars, etc., and if you can bear it, wander round your home with string and labels and remove unused keys from furniture and suitcases, labelling the keys as you go and putting them in a plastic bag. This saves time when you are trying to keep, find and/or identify keys which are rarely used. In this container I also keep a list of anyone who has a front door key, however temporarily. Burglaries are most upsetting and unsettling.

That is the minimum efficiency method. Read on if you feel you can take something slightly more grandiose. If, for example, you have complicated home help or do stalwart voluntary work or are running a cottage industry (I know a girl who started a thriving lunch business by selling pizzas out of her kitchen window to the office workers in the factory opposite).

More advanced filing: The advanced filer uses a proper filing cabinet. You might – as I did – use an old orange box or a wire crate, until I bought a secondhand filing cabinet and resprayed it scarlet. Now, if anyone asked me what I would save in a fire I would say that cabinet.

I was encouraged to buy that filing cabinet (of all ridiculous things to have in the house) by the beautiful historian Lady Antonia Fraser. She said that it took her two years to get around to buying one and another year to summon up the energy to fill it, but that it really does work and she can find something like the television licence in a minute. But only *she* can find it, because Lady Antonia believes in surrounding herself with a certain amount of uncertainty, if not mystery. So, she has a secret system which only she understands: bills, for instance, are not filed under B but under U for unpleasant.

My filing cabinet is a four-drawer clanger. The top drawer is for boring business; files labelled 'Insurance', 'Accountant', 'Receipts', 'Bills'; the second drawer is for my writing works; the third drawer has files labelled 'In/Out', 'Pending', 'Stationery', and 'Voluntary Work'; the fourth drawer holds family things such as photographs, letters and school reports.

You think that's going too far? American matriarch Rose Kennedy kept a card index on *each* child.

How to be a Working Wife and Mother

YOUR ATTITUDE AND YOUR FAMILY'S

I've read a lot about women who serenely cope with the three roles of full-time working woman, wife, and mother. However, I've never actually met one. All the ones that I know feel inadequate.

Going back to work after having children is a practical and emotional problem and both are interdependent. You risk worrying about them when you're at work and about work when you're at home, and end up being happy in neither situation.

Two requisites for a working mother are stamina and an understanding family. Sympathetic they may be until it comes to your interests versus theirs, but they still want their evening meal on time and they don't want to hear about the bus queue which made you late. A husband who doesn't mind the occasional snack meal in a crisis – or even cooks it – is worth his weight in platinum. What a working mother risks if she goes out to work is her health. She needs to be an exceptionally well organized person to survive and even if she manages the mechanics she will probably have emotional problems. Her biggest unrecognized problem will probably be to get a certain amount of private time to herself every day.

Your attitude

It is important that you shouldn't feel guilty about working – and this is impossible. You have been conditioned to feel guilty. Accept it. Children instinctively know that your guilt about your work is your Achilles heel and will use it, when they are bored, or cross, to have a crack at you. 'Why

153

don't you ever make *cakes*, like *other* mothers?' once nagged my son, who hates cakes.

A doctor once told me to do as much as you can for your children, but never make gargantuan sacrifices for them because they will resent it. He also told me that children have a very good basic set of priorities. They don't care about mess or dust as long as they feel they are loved and if they feel secure in this then it doesn't matter much what else you do, because that's the only thing which really matters. This seems so obvious that one is left wondering what you've been so worried about all this time. However, it's a good thing to remind your eldest of it when, raising an eyebrow, he runs his forefinger along a window ledge like a music hall mother-in-law.

The family attitude

Your family will probably never regard your work as anything but tiresome. There are certain occasions when you would, of course, never think twice about asking for time off work: for anything special which involves your husband's boss, any special occasion involving your child at school, or when a child is ill. Before you start a job you may have to sort out that odd days such as these come out of your holiday time.

It helps to realize that husbands can be *unconsciously* selfish, emotional and unreasonable about the working wife situation and that therefore it may be unreasonable of you to expect him to be reasonable. If you can't be insensitive then be sensible enough to shut up and put up with it when the caveman in him surfaces.

You must be unobtrusive about your work, and *never* expect your husband to help you do it: that's really baring your breast for the dagger.

I find that it is difficult to slow down my working pace to a child's pace. Except for emergencies I have also found it easier not to expect any help from my children and then I don't irritate them or rely on them. Small children are *no use* in an efficient domestic routine. They are slow and messy and they break things. What children over seven *can* be expected to do is to provide a certain amount of self-help. They can make their own beds and tidy their rooms. Over ten they can wash up, but I find it's not worth the effort to get them to do it, and then have to check it, and then redo it. Teenagers can be careless and reluctant, if not downright resentful, and they've probably got their own full quota of school work. I found that as my children grew into teenagers, they needed *more* of my time and undivided attention. Their needs were more complicated, and obviously at this stage they want *you*, not just your services.

Your child's teacher is tremendously important to you because he or she has a balanced, objective view of your offspring and their problems. My sons' teacher once offered to sew nametapes on their clothes, but she was rare. Ask his or her advice if your children develop any anti-social habit, such as bullying, or if they seem to be doing badly at school, or if you have any misfortune such as divorce, which will affect the children.

ADVANTAGES OF A WORKING MOTHER

There are obvious disadvantages to a

child in having a working mother but there are less obvious advantages. Children with working mothers certainly don't suffer from smother-love – over-fussing. They learn to be realistic, independent, responsible and sometimes stoical, no mean preparation for the toughness of life.

Your children risk having a mother who's not permanently on tap for them but who is likely to have a younger outlook and be more tolerant and open to new ideas (although I *did* hear myself saying to my older son during that craze, 'I don't know how you can walk on those high heels').

A working mother may turn out to be a more respected and valuable adviser in later life (you have to rely on reason, not authority, if you hold down a job) and in turn (I am told and hope) a working woman is not so likely to cling to her children when it's their turn to leave the nest. A working mother has her own interests.

YOUR STAND-IN

If you employ home help make sure that your stand-in likes and is liked by the children, whether or not she is particularly efficient with the housework. Don't be jealous of your children's affection for their minder. You want them to feel affectionate towards lots of people. Check on your child minder. There is no reason to trust her until she is proven trustworthy. If you can't hop home unexpectedly yourself, get someone else to do so. This sounds nasty, but they're *your* children and you can't take risks. Also check carefully with other parents about your child minder, play group, or nursery school. *Never stop checking.*

If you have no home help, here are some of the organizations which might help you.

A pre-school playgroup: A centre organized by parents in premises which have been approved by the local authority. It takes children from three to five for about three hours in either morning or afternoon, so it's only suitable for mothers doing part-time work. Nominal fees pay for heat, light, toys, modelling clay, paints, books and other equipment. The children are taught no formal subjects but learn to relate to other children, to accept authority and to be imaginative and unselfish.

If there isn't one locally, how about starting one, either on a cooperative basis with other mothers or as a business venture?

Get advice from your local health department and information and advice from the Pre-School Playgroup Association, Alford House, Aveline Street, London SE11.

Local authority day nurseries: Non-educational in the same way as playgroups. These are for priority cases – the children whose mothers must work or who are ill. They take children from three months and for up to eight hours a day. Get further information from your local health department.

State nursery schools: For three- to five-year-olds, but there is a great shortage. They come under the Department of Education and Science and keep normal school hours. You can get a list from your local education office. Priority is again given to the children of mothers who have no option but to work.

If you haven't a local authority day nursery or state nursery school start campaigning for one.

Private local nursery schools: You can get details of these from the local authority health department.

A registered child minder: Can look after your children for up to eight hours daily in her home. Costs can be from £5 per child per week including food. There are bad child minders and there are good ones.

The only working mothers of schoolchildren who seemingly don't have problems in the yearly fifteen weeks of school holidays are schoolteachers. Mothers who have no home help might pay a non-working neighbourhood mother to cope with their children as well as her own. In the lower income groups there's still sometimes a granny or aunt to look after the children, but nowadays there's a good chance that granny is running her own boutique and aunty is a trainee computer programmer.

In London there's a private agency licensed by Westminster City Council and called Child Minders which specializes in trained nursery nurses and nannies for London homes. You can get a day babysitter for a minimum of four hours or a living-in or -out nanny. Child Minders is at 67A Marylebone High Street, London W1 (Tel. 01-935 2049.)

The best place to advertise for a mother's help seems to be the *Nursery World.* For any other sort of living-in help the best place seems to be *The Lady.*

HOW TO RUN A HOME AND A JOB

Women hate being efficient in the home. Lists and routines simply do not

fit into the pink-check-gingham-and-lace mental picture of the soap opera mother, which so many of us were brought up to be. When you become a working mother with any luck you will get twice as much out of life, but you can't run your house as if you weren't working. A working mother has to work faster and more efficiently in the home. She has to be *twice* as reliable outside it because people expect her not to be.

I have evolved my own system, which I slowly slip away from, but it pulls me back to reality at regular intervals, and heaven knows what I would be like without it.

1 Disregard what you're *supposed* to do.
2 Consider what you can't avoid doing.
3 Consider what you *can* avoid doing, e.g. daily cleaning, drying up, most of the ironing, and producing *two* hot meals a day. Remember that evening candlelight or soft lamplight is kind to your face and your standards of housework, but they can't disguise tinned spaghetti ad nauseam.
4 Everything you dread doing you must do *straight away*, then things seem immediately much better, so says Lady Dartmouth, who seems to have four children and nine lives.
5 Try to evolve a basic lifestyle which allows for the fact that you can't get a quart out of a pint pot, and plan around your own capacity and weaknesses.
6 Your lunch-hour is for lunch and relaxation. Try to keep shopping out of it. Try to relax and do nothing but count your blessings for ten minutes around lunchtime.

Just to shut your eyes and stop thinking will help a bit. If not at lunchtime, then at some other time during the day. I seem to collapse around 6.30 p.m. daily and I've now learned to combine this with a bath and rest. If I stubbornly totter on I won't recover my strength all evening.

7 We are all too often too tired, but try never to let the phrase cross your lips. Try going to bed really early once a week immediately after work. It's amazing what a treat it feels.

Writer Ann Scott-James once told me that she never took her coat off until she had laid the table and the evening meal was well under way. Otherwise she would have flopped into an armchair with a drink and the meal would have been extremely late, if indeed, it appeared at all. A famous architect told me that she never entertained. Never, ever. She sent flowers, notes and gifts to her hostesses, but she never asked them home, and eventually this was accepted by all the friends she had left.

Penelope Perrick, who wrote *The Working Wives' Cookbook*, told me: 'For me the clue to being successfully organized lay in realizing that my work must be my hobby.' She believes in a once a week preparation time for food and realizes that the best day to do the bulk of the shopping and a good bit of the housework is Saturday. (The only day? For most people, yes.) 'Any meals that have to be prepared on Saturday must be fitted in between painting the ceiling and washing the dog. Reserve Sunday morning for fixing casseroles and baking pies and all the other things that result in stacks of washing up. Then tackle this chore in one fell swoop.'

A few useful ideas which may also work with you and your family: Never rely on your memory. Nobody has one good enough to retain all the tedious daily clutter that your work involves. Keep a notebook in your handbag and don't let anybody get at it. Keep a notebook and biro (pencils break) *attached* to the telephone. Train the family to write in it. Everything they want you to know or do. Look at it as soon as you get in.

In my wardrobe I keep an emergency clean set of clothes for each child, even if it is only cotton underwear, jeans and a T-shirt. Also a spare shirt, set of underwear and cuff links for my husband.

Never return to an unmade bed, it's so disheartening. Make it fast rather than not at all.

A few family mottoes:
DON'T PUT IT DOWN, PUT IT AWAY
IF YOU LEAVE THINGS ON THE FLOOR
THEY GET TRODDEN ON BY CLUMSY
GROWN-UPS
FIRST THINGS FIRST, SECOND
THINGS NEVER

Making more time: The choice: Get up early. Go to bed late.

According to Mary Wilson, she and I are larks, not owls. Owls can't open their eyes in the morning, but they cheerfully perform amazing feats such as laying breakfast and putting everyone else's clothes out the night before. If you are not a lark you might have to invest money in getting up: try a costly telephone alarm call or one of those weird tea-making machines. I know a poet housewife (not Mary Wilson) who works from 5–7 a.m. Perhaps only someone with the soul of a poet can do that, but if you can't summon up enough energy to get up early then you can go to bed later, a regular 2 a.m. owl. If you do neither, then you don't really want to be a poet or study English or whatever. Bernard Levin told me this and I was furious with him for months, because he was right.

WHAT IF YOU CAN'T COPE?

What should you do if you can't manage a husband, children and full-time office job? Signs of overwork are nervous tension, irritability, harassment, indigestion, severe headaches. If you reach this point, not only you will be suffering, but your children too. Try to simplify your job or take a part-time one near your home – one, two or three full days, say. This is especially easy if you have secretarial qualifications.

An *Observer* reader once wrote asking me what she should do because at night she was too tired to make love with her husband. A serious question. I trotted round town getting advice from various experts and what it all seemed to boil down to was: chuck the job, cut the luxuries, live on spaghetti and have a nap in the afternoon.

What a working woman needs is a fast and unerring sense of priority.

WHICH WORK PATTERN IS EASIEST?

Should you work part-time or full-time? It depends on your needs. When I had my first baby I did part-time

design work at home. Then I worked full-time from an office with resident home help. Then I worked full-time at home with no home help. Now I work at home, full-time during the term and theoretically not at all during school holidays. I have found it easiest (but not always possible) to go out to work full-time, and pay for adequate home help. For me working part-time seemed to involve twice the work for half the money with none of the office perks and protection.

I am not the only woman to have found that part-time work from home is ten times more difficult than it sounds. It is because you are trying to do at least two jobs at once. Of course the children interrupt you, and so does the milkman, whether you're trying to start a business or write a short story in your own kitchen. Of course you answer the telephone, the door, take in your neighbour's laundry and stave off a Jehovah's Witness. It's certainly easier to work part-time if you leave home to do it.

I know a Cambridge professor's wife who writes detective stories: she leaves her house every day at 11 a.m., catches a bus to a room she has hired, and works until 2 p.m. If you can't afford to rent a room for your work try swapping homes with a friend who also wants to work. You'll have less difficulty in not dealing with *her* home life. Or advertise locally.

After my business got groggily on its feet, I could afford a secretary, who comes in one day a week to help me. I now feel I'm not struggling along entirely on my own, and *knowing* that I am going to have Nicola's help on Monday acts as a good discipline to get all my office work ready in time for that day – no matter how early I have to get up – when it gets polished off in one go.

THE HIGH COST OF WORK

There's nothing more satisfying than doing the work you love. Work is a wonderful antidote to misery and grief and it can be a constant stretching of your mind and capabilities. Was it not Freud who said: 'Love and work bind people to sanity'?

Are you sure, however, that you can afford to work? In terms of money that is? Working can be expensive. Add up the weekly costs of doing your job then multiply it by fifty-two to get the rough, real annual cost. Include tax, fares, lunches, union dues and contributions, hairdresser, make-up and clothes (although you wear *something* wherever you are, you undoubtedly spend more on clothes, etc., if you work), extra laundry, and food costs. This last is also a difficult figure to calculate, but convenience foods, weekend shopping or late night supermarkets can certainly add 15 per cent to food bills and you have to accept the fact that some food is bound to be wasted.

Then there is the cost of home help and/or child care, especially if you have living-in help. Home help is very expensive when you do a proper accountant's costing on it and include wages, insurance, room, light and heat, food and general extravagance, such as not switching off the electricity because she isn't paying the bills. *And* you have to deal with her neuroses when you've just got back from the office and want to nurse your own.

Add it up here:

Add to your total a third of gross income for tax. Although you may not be working primarily for money, how much of the year do you have to work before you start to show a profit? When you've actually made some money, do you have time to spend it carefully?

Working wives who don't bear the financial responsibility of being the breadwinner often feel exhilaration. Mothers who have no option, who are bound to work because their husbands are ill, or just not there, or whose husband's earnings don't cover the family needs, are more likely to feel tired and anxious all the time. In order to avoid anxiety I took out a crippledom policy when I became the family breadwinner. It is *not* tax deductible and costs £125 per annum. If I lose my legs under a bus or am incapacitated in any more interesting manner, I shall be paid £3,500 p.a. When I was ill for a longish period they paid up £500 immediately, which was a pleasant surprise.

Accountants don't consider it wise for a mother with an earning husband to depend on her earnings, in case she has to stop work; she is best regarded as a supplement to the wage earner's contribution. Generally husbands pay rent and running expenses of the home. The wife pays anything she incurs, and extras and luxuries. A fun-funding cornucopia – in theory.

Sometimes the wife works for a specific purpose, say the down payment on a house. If so, it's best to thrust it fast into a *separate* deposit account. If it goes into a joint bank account, there's the risk that the family will quickly get used to a higher standard of living and nothing much will be saved. On the other hand, I know a famous writer whose family live entirely on her income, while her husband is working all the hours God gave him to set up his own publishing business.

CAREERS FOR MOTHERS

Training: If you have had training you can probably find job opportunities through your professional body or through reading or advertising in your professional journal.

Assuming that you haven't had any training prior to marriage and aren't coping with pre-school age children, what is available? Most women are unskilled. Only 6 per cent receive any further training when they leave school. However, there are suitable training courses for 'mature students', the official description of any woman over twenty-three. You can exploit a talent which you already possess and are practising in your home (sewing or cooking) or be trained by a firm who wishes to employ you, or at one of the many courses at a local technical college. Generally what is difficult to acquire isn't really the training, or even the job, but the determination to forget embarrassment, laziness or shyness – and go out and get it.

Get advice from your local employment agencies and watch the columns vacant in your local press. Don't mind taking a low wage to get some fast experience, or to get your foot in the door. And once you have discovered how your job is done, you might improve on it and get promotion, or even start your own business.

For instance, Freelance Work for Women Bureau was started by a married woman who needed a job. I know a divorced woman with two teenage children who took a part-time typing job at one of the best secretarial schools in Britain and became the principal within two years. They seemed ordinary housewives – but they had never before tried to be anything else!

Careers Research and Advisory Centre, 25 St Andrews St, Cambridge (Tel. Cambridge 54445), will give advice on further education courses throughout Britain. Also The National Institute of Adult Education (England and Wales), 35 Queen Anne St, London W1 (Tel. 01-637 4241).

Twinning. National Westminster Bank are pioneers in this field, where two friends share one job, such as cashier, and do a full-time fortnight each. Get your twin before approaching an employer, appear together at the interview and explain how you will tackle the drawbacks. Don't both talk at once.

GETTING A JOB

Here are a few ideas:

Beauty therapy: Visiting people in their own homes or in hospitals or having them come to your home.

Travelling sewing machine consultant.

Travelling sales consultant for beauty products, a fast-growing field. A tactful woman can be really helpful.

Travelling representative for a wig manufacturer or a corsetiere. Can be quite exciting: all you need is a deep breath and a brass nerve.

Demonstrator of appliances at exhibitions, stores or showrooms.

Cooking weekday meals for an office, factory or boardroom.

Cooking evening meals in other people's homes.

Cooking or serving school meals.

Gardening in a market garden or nursery. Or starting your own window box servicing business, like another friend of mine.

Working in a florist, if you don't mind getting up early and have a flair for flowers. Susan, Lady Pulbrook, a brilliant florist who works for Buckingham Palace, started because she was lonely after her husband died.

A local government job: There is scope for women in welfare, child care and education. There are day release classes and training schemes. You can get more information from the National and Local Government Officers' Association, NALGO House, 8 Harewood Road, London NW1 (Tel. 01-262 8030).

Market research: Interviewers and research assistants are needed; married women and part-time workers are welcome. You need a neat, cheerful appearance and good handwriting. Plenty of training schemes.

Freelance journalism for newspapers or magazines. (Well, I'm doing it.)

Interviewer on TV or radio.

Nursing, if you have the Florence Nightingale temperament and strong feet. The Department of Health offers training to older women because there is serious understaffing in hospitals.

Nursing auxiliaries help nurses with their basic duties without the long training of a qualified nurse.

Midwifery: A woman with no nursing qualifications can take a two-year course up to the age of fifty. What could be more satisfying? And a mother has one pretty essential qualification. When trained, she will know what she's talking about. She's already had at least nine months' experience. Apply to your local Regional Hospital Board for details.

Office work: Just look at the shortage of secretaries! Every firm needs them. Offices often prefer an older responsible, reliable woman. You then have your pick of jobs, at home or outside it, one, two, three, four or five days a week, mornings only or afternoons only. Very flexible. Pitmans training is considered best. Your local educational officer can advise on others.

Schools often employ part-time secretaries who work only in term time.

Receptionist: There are plenty of opportunities in big cities, and, again, friendly, responsible, reliable women are increasingly preferred to young dollies.

Telephonist: ditto.

Clerical work: The Civil Service recruits up to the age of sixty, and they are probably going to start new working programmes to suit married women. Get the address of your local government offices from your post office.

Office machine operators for duplicating machines, adding and calculating machines and computers. There is a great shortage of computer staff and much of the work is taken on part-time or freelance by married women.

Full-time or part-time shop assistant: Hard on the feet but can be more interesting than office work if you like meeting people. Part-time work is often easier on Saturdays.

Stocking shelves in supermarkets, to prepare for the next day, is one example of evening preparation work. Ask the manager of your local supermarket if there's anything going.

Welfare workers are largely women. Child care officers are needed (training from one to three years necessary) so are youth club workers, youth employment officers, young people's advisers (being marrried is a qualification and it's possible to do as little as thirteen hours a week work). Details from Social Work Advisory Service, Information on Training and Careers, 26 Bloomsbury Way, London, WC1 (Tel. 01-242 5654).

Babysitting, emergency child care (such as when a mother has to go into hospital) and *child minding.*

Primary school helpers and school care work: The main qualification here is that of a good, tactful, sensible parent. For details write to the education officer of your local education authority.

Teaching: Minimum qualifications of five O Levels or three O Levels and an A Level, but you can take a Special Entry Test if you lack these qualifications but nevertheless strongly feel that you could teach. A teacher training course takes three years to complete although mature students are sometimes allowed to take a two-year course. The thirty-five-week college year is similar to that of a school.

Working in kindergarten and nursery schools: Mothers have obviously had experience of working with children. Kindergarten and nursery schools are short of staff. Qualifications are not essential, but some previous experience is useful. Get details from the local chief education officer.

Running a playgroup: If you want to run a playgroup you must comply with the standard conditions laid down by the Department of Health and register with the local health authority and town planning committee. Your local health officer will advise you on the necessary requirements, which are mainly such obvious ones as an outdoor play area, safety catches on windows, adequate light, heat and ventilation, sufficient lavatories (one to every eight children).

> WARNING! Make sure your initial charges are adequate; play equipment can cost more than you think. Make sure you won't mind noisy activities.

You can find other mothers in need of a playgroup by asking among your friends, or writing a letter to the local paper or putting a postcard in your local newsagents.

Further details from: National Association of Pre-School Playgroups, Alford House, Aveline Street, SE11 5DJ (Tel. 01-582 8871).

Far more detailed information concerning these jobs can be found in an invaluable book *Late Start: Careers for Wives* by Penelope Labovitch and Rosemary Simon (published by New English Library). There is also The Over Forty Association For Women Workers, Grosvenor Gardens House, Grosvenor Gardens, London SW1 (Tel. 01-828 2867). Also get *Women and Work*, a BBC leaflet for women who want to return to work, *Out of the Rut*, a book for £1.50p, and *Careers for Girls*. Only read the parts which tell you what part-time or seasonal work is available. Write to 'Out of the Rut', BBC TV Centre, Wood Lane, London W12 8QT.

STARTING YOUR OWN BUSINESS

If you're thinking of starting your own business . . . the queen of the financial writers, Sheila Black of *The Times*, agrees with me that the most practical way to go about it is simply to *start doing it*.

Most of the home employment offered to housewives is naked exploitation. Avoid like the plague any sort of piece work or commission-based schemes (envelope-typing, telephone-selling) because you will have to work like a slave, the work may be disheartening, and you may very possibly make very little money or even end up out of pocket.

If you have a special skill, typing, translating, accountancy – advertise it in places where the people who might employ you will see your ad. A skilled *qualified* home worker gets the best deal from employers, so stick to an area you know. If you were trained as a secretary, you might start a home typing agency.

Buy an electric typewriter on HP as soon as you can afford it. Make sure you are efficient, neat, professional and reliable. No jam stains on translations or letters unposted because your husband put them in his pocket and forgot them. No home life intrusions of any sort.

You might start a home industry in your bedroom. Sew cushion covers, do knitting, with or without a machine, or crochet work. Or invisible mending for the dry-cleaners. Or, if you have a hairdryer, set hair. You're not the only woman who can't afford to go to a hairdresser and can't see the back of her own head in order to set it. Printing personal book plates, making dolls or, like Laura Ashley, printing tea towels on the kitchen table, are other possibilities.

Whatever you decide to do, keep a dated record of everything you pay out and everything you send out in two duplicate books; tick items off when you are paid. In order to avoid confusion with your personal life, open a new bank account. (See 'How to Spend Money'.)

You will soon find out whether your business is going to pay or not. After six months stop and review the situation. If you want to continue you will want to consider regulations concerning tax, planning permission, registering your company and employing other people. At this point you may need to get a lawyer and an accountant. (The accountant will find your two duplicate books provide him with a simple record of what has happened to date.)

The Department of Trade and Industry can advise you and, possibly, direct you to the various associations which help small businesses, their address is D.T.I., Victoria St, London SW1 (Tel. 01-222 7877).

SEX ManiaCs and the SinglE Girl

By 'Single', I mean a woman who is unmarried, divorced, separated, or whose husband is temporarily absent.

Sexual aggression from a stranger may take the form of:

1 Obscene telephone calls.
2 Frottism (such as being rubbed up against in a crowded train or bus).
3 Indecent exposure (such as showing genitals to little girls in a park).
4 Letter threats to rape, maim, or kill.
5 Odd burglaries involving violation (such as urinating on the bed) or the theft of fetish objects such as frilly knickers or black suspender belts.
6 Peeping Toms.
7 Unintentional rape (sometimes called 'going too far').
8 Attempted rape.
9 Rape.
10 Child molestation.

A man, or any woman who has not experienced any of these forms of sexual aggression, might find it difficult to comprehend why minor cases are so frightening and why women are so unreasonable about them. About telephone calls, one woman said: 'I found the unreality, the nightmare lunacy aspect, the most difficult because the police didn't seem to understand *why* I was frightened, because nothing had happened.' A strapping, normally self-assured 6-foot blonde said: 'What I most hated was being instantly turned into a gibbering idiot by some cowardly twit on the end of a telephone.'

Other comments were: 'It's the unprotected feeling. You feel stark naked and vulnerable. It might happen any time of the day or night. You're powerless to stop it and you're at his mercy. You're helpless.' 'The police don't seem to think that threatened sexual assault is important. Assault doesn't seem to be an important crime unless it's on a policeman. Motoring offences and smoking pot, that's the sort of thing they seem to take seriously.'

What a woman wants when she is being sexually threatened by a stranger is PROTECTION. She also wants sympathy and understanding. Often it is not possible for the police to give her any of these things to the degree that will allay her fright.

A senior C.I.D. officer commented: 'If a person has been offended against, no matter in how minor a way, that person feels aggrieved, therefore, as far as the police are concerned, it is an offence and the duty of the policeman to investigate and assist the aggrieved person inasmuch as he is able.' '. . . inasmuch as he is able.' That's the crunch.

Policewomen may, but policemen in general can have no conception of *why* a woman is frightened by a mystery prowler or heavy breathing down the telephone. This is because they are the wrong sex: they are not frightened of a man because they *are* men. This attitude is apparent in some of the things they say, some of which are hurtful. DO NOT LET THESE PHRASES UPSET YOU.

'Is he a friend of yours?'

'Have you broken up with a boyfriend lately?'

'What makes you think this man is threatening you?'

'Are you sure you weren't encouraging him?'

'Well, you must have been doing *something*.'

'We'll keep an eye on the place' (i.e. drive past now and then).

'We'll have a squad car over right away' (twenty-three minutes later at the earliest, with enough flashing lights to announce a royal wedding procession).

'Don't you worry now.'

'You're perfectly safe inside.'

The police certainly get plenty of frivolous complaints or complaints made by women who are unnaturally nervous or mentally disturbed and which, when investigated, prove groundless. For instance, steady footsteps behind you at night across the darkened common might not necessarily mean that a man is following you. His route from the bus stop might be the same as yours.

To expect automatic protection in every case is impractical. Be sensible. The police haven't got the men or the money. They can't give twenty-four-hour protection to the recipient of every obscene telephone call or it would cost at least three policemen's salaries per year per protégée. Sympathy you may get but not always protection or understanding.

So what should you do if you or one of your family is frightened by sexual aggression from a stranger? Senior C.I.D. officer, Barbara Kelly, helped me to compile the following answers.

Try to deal with *obscene telephone calls* by putting the phone down *at once*. Then he's lost 10p (apparently they hope and pay for a long call) and got no satisfaction.

'The call may be to assist masturbation,' explained Miss Kelly, 'and that's one good reason to slam the phone down. Of course he may ring again. The essential thing is: *don't reply to him*. Leave the receiver off the hook and cover it with a cushion or a rug.' The second you reply you are becoming involved and could even be inveigled into connivance.

The main reason for slamming down the phone is to avoid giving the pervert at the other end the satisfaction he achieves by frightening and flummoxing you. Such people are often sexually inadequate and do not feel they are 'men'. They feel they lack power and potency. So the more distressed you get, the happier they are to be proving to themselves that they *do* have a sort of sexual power over you – the power to upset you. So replace your receiver immediately.

Telephone or call at your local police station and ask to speak to the duty officer, to report what has happened. It is then up to the police to decide objectively on the gravity of the situation, and what they can legally do. Remember that, for good reasons, the police are trained to keep calm, keep a poker face and proceed methodically. They should be unbiased towards one side or the other. They can't do much about a frightened woman, but they understand that in these cases a woman can't always control her emotions.

Understandably, Scotland Yard have asked me not to reveal their methods of dealing with obscene telephone calls, but if a pattern starts to emerge then action is taken. One of the obvious things that the police can do is get your telephone number changed fast and kept secret. Inconvenient, but generally effective.

If you receive *obscene, anonymous letters* try not to talk about them. Take them straight to the police.

Obviously you would contact the police as soon as possible after a burglary, so they would quickly learn of any details other than theft, such as messing the carpet. Burglary can feel like a minor sort of rape. It results in the same sort of shock of uncleanness, of being violated, of sudden, unexpected violence.

The best way to treat *indecent exposure* is to ignore it and walk on. Try to move away from the man who is pressing against you in a train, bus or lift.

The way to deal with *peeping Toms* is to cover yourself up and inform the police. If you haven't any curtains to draw, pin a sheet over the window until you can make curtains.

Stealing knickers is a well recognized minor fetish, so the police advise you never to leave any underwear on the washing line. It's asking for trouble, they say.

If you feel a *groping hand* in a darkened cinema or other closed space you could say loudly and clearly 'KINDLY TAKE YOUR HAND OFF MY KNEE,' whereupon he will skid off. Alternatively, change seats *at once*, keeping an eye on the man. 'If he thinks you've merely moved and aren't going to report him he'll probably stay in the cinema,' says Miss Kelly. '*Then* slip off and ask the usherette for the manager, go back and point him out.'

Miss Kelly also advises: 'If a woman can see that she's going to be left alone in a train carriage with a man, she would be wise to move before the train leaves or at any rate at the next station. Similarly if a man gets into a carriage with a lone woman he might think of moving: there are unbalanced *women* as well as unbalanced men you know.'

SEX MANIACS AND THE SINGLE GIRL

RAPE

What is the likelihood of your being raped? At time of writing rape is the fastest growing crime on this side of the Atlantic. The figures for England and Wales during the past sixteen years show a 56 per cent increase, and in America there has been a startling increase of 172 per cent.

Avoidance is best: Easily the best method of dealing with rape, say the police, is avoidance. Particularly after dark, avoid lonely places such as commons, churchyards, alleys and waste land. On the street, especially at night and in unfamiliar surroundings be alert at all times. If a bad or potentially bad situation starts developing, the safest thing to do is run. Head for a shop building or lighted area where people are likely to be. Yell 'HELP', go to a nearby house, knock on the door and ask to telephone the police. Don't feel silly.

You've only got to read the newspapers to see what can happen to hitch-hikers. A girl who's a passenger might have no means of escape other than jumping out, maybe while the car is travelling at speed. 'A woman driver should also be careful: it's always taking a risk if you don't know the person, not only of sexual assault or an uncomfortable situation, but of robbery. A car can be a moving prison cut off from help from the public,' commented Miss Kelly. 'You wouldn't invite a stranger into your house but you do so in a car where you're likely to be more vulnerable.'

The majority of situations of possible attempted rape, situations which can get out of hand, are with pick-ups who don't *seem* to be pick-ups to the woman: 'She might ask a purely casual acquaintance back home for a cup of coffee without knowing his background,' said Miss Kelly. Be wary, not sympathetic, of any stranger who says that he's lonely: there might be a good reason for this sad state. 'A woman who goes anywhere alone, to a garage, a flat, or any closed place, at the invitation of an unknown man or casual acquaintance, *is putting herself at risk.* In fact, unless a woman knows a man very well she must remember that many cases of complaint have been lured somewhere on a simple and innocent pretext.'

When you're alone in the house, never open the front door without looking through a peephole and operating a heavy chain. This sensible precaution costs less than a restaurant meal.

Try and make your house as secure as you possibly can. 'If it's terribly difficult to get into a place and a sexual marauder has to make a noise, he's less likely to persist.' A burglar opportunist is a minimum risk.

But what if you're actually attacked? Predictably Miss Kelly said, 'I can't tell women whether or not to defend themselves: all situations are different. So is the timing, the woman's ability and strength, and her level-headedness.

'To introduce more violence into the situation may be disastrous. If you yell, whether it's a scream for help or a blood-curdling battle cry, he may put his hands round your throat to stop you and squeeze too hard and too long.

'However, should you wish to defend yourself don't be afraid to hurt someone who's hurting you. If you're caught by surprise and don't think you can run away or have nowhere to run to, you might use something you're wearing as a weapon. Probably the

168

best thing is the heel of your shoe (holding the shoe by the sole) or maybe your belt buckle, umbrella or handbag. If your arms are free you might try to stick your fingers in his eyes and if you scratch him hard the marks will be unmistakable as a later possible means of identification.'

If you're grabbed from behind don't try to flick him over your left shoulder unless you really know what you're doing. Try to stick your elbows backwards and upwards into the top of his solar plexus, just under the centre of the rib cage. Try it on yourself with your left fist and you'll see that just a little thump leaves you gasping.

What if you're attacked at home? Should you invest in knives or airguns?

'I can only tell you the law,' said Miss Kelly, looking a trifle uneasy. 'If someone's *trying to enter your house by force* you can eject him by force or stop them entering by force. There are certain cases where it is justifiable homicide and one is if it's the only way to stop a really outrageous crime such as an attempt to murder or rape when a woman uses whatever she has to hand, such as an umbrella. Anyone else who comes upon the scene can do likewise.'

I personally think that knives, guns, fake guns and bedside empty milk bottles are dangerous to use against somebody stronger than you since they can be turned against you. It's introducing violence into a situation which *might* have become violent and uncontrollable, and now *certainly* will.

Going to the police: If you are raped you are supposed to report it to the police as soon as possible.

If you want to prosecute don't change clothes, don't take a shower, and don't wash away any evidence because you feel unclean. You should be prepared to recount the horror, because the police will (as soon as you feel able to talk coherently) want every detail of what happened, where he touched you, etc. This may be humiliating, but it is necessary if they are going to try to trace a man (who has perhaps raped before) and then prosecute him before a judge and jury.

Don't expect tea and sympathy from the police. It's not their job to provide it. It's their job to get your statement, get evidence and get after the villain as fast as possible.

A police station is not a hospital. If it's four o'clock in the morning don't expect them to have hot milk at the ready, or a spare greatcoat, or a spare police doctor waiting to examine you. They may need your clothing for scientific examination for blood, seminal and other stains, tearing or other similar evidence for possible use in court. They might have a blanket.

You can only be medically examined to support your statement with your consent. Rape is very difficult to prove medically. What does a doctor look for? Evidence of semen in the vagina and on clothes, as well as evidence of internal and external trauma, such as lacerations. You can telephone a friend or relative from the police station, and normally they would be allowed to telephone you back.

See a doctor: After you have informed the police go, or get someone to take you, to a hospital or doctor. You have three worries:

1 Venereal disease. A hospital may give rape victims preventative penicillin.
2 You can wait until six weeks after your last period, get a pregnancy test, and possibly arrange for an

abortion if necessary. In case of extreme anxiety the 'morning after' pill can be taken. This is Oestrogen which is only available on a doctor's prescription. If taken within twenty-four hours of intercourse, this should prevent implantation of the fertilized egg. The oestrogen drug can make some people nauseated and violently ill for the five days it is taken. These factors have to be weighed against the dangers and anxiety of pregnancy. It's preferable to wait and see whether pregnancy has occurred.

3 If you are bruised, cut or even just generally shaken, you may want to get a medical check-up.

If you want a man convicted, possibly deterred from raping others, you have to be prepared to go to court. The proceedings are no longer public. But you may not get a conviction.

Mr Justice Melford Stevenson was reported in *The Times* to have summed up one rape case saying, 'It was, as rape goes, a pretty anaemic affair', as he awarded the guilty party a two-year suspended sentence.

This appears to be a male attitude not confined to judges. If a man's home has ever been vandalized by a burglar, you can tell him that is a tiny little bit like the shock of rape. This compounded of surprise, then fear, with growing horror, followed by terror, pain, exhaustion, disorientation, and fear of possible disease or actual disease and/or pregnancy. It's an unclean feeling that you perhaps can't wash out of your head for weeks or months and which may cause grave psychological damage.

Mud sticks. Rape myths abound.

'No decent girl ever gets raped.' 'Every woman really wants to be raped.' 'A girl only gets raped if she wants to be.' (But how would an 8-stone boxer fare against a 14-stone boxer?)

So if you're raped that's sad. But what follows when you report it to the police could make you feel worse, unless you are prepared for it. I know it may be considered antisocial, but I feel that a raped woman may suffer less in the long run if she does not go to the police first, but gets to a doctor or casualty ward as fast as possible and then informs the police.

WHAT SHOULD YOU TELL THE CHILDREN?

The single girl bothered by sexual perverts can sometimes be very young indeed. What can you tell children to protect them without frightening them about any possible child molester?

It's best to be as short, clear and factual as possible, in order that there may be no misunderstanding, and no mystery. Don't beat about the bush no matter how embarrassed you are. Come out and say it calmly and firmly in a matter of fact voice.

Don't merely inform. Try to set up a dialogue so that the child knows that it can ask you or tell you about such things. (If one thing leads to another, two good sex education books for older children are *Boys and Sex* and *Girls and Sex* by W. B. Pomeroy, published by Penguin.)

Exhibitionists and child molesters commonly called 'dirty old men' are not always dirty and old. Although they can be frightening they are rarely dangerous and generally act the way they do because they are sad, lonely, depressed, frustrated and immature. A child who comes across one should be told not to panic but to immediately tell a grown-up person whom she trusts, even if she would rather not tell a parent. But a child may not be sure. If in doubt . . . TELL.

Children who are old enough to travel to school on their own should be taught never to be alone in a lonely sort of place, if possible, and to report as soon as possible anything nasty, silly or upsetting to the nearest grown-up in charge, such as the bus conductor. They should also be told:

1 Never talk to a stranger *who approaches you*. (If a child is lost and asks someone the way that's different.)

2 Never take sweets or presents from any strange men or women.

3 Never let a stranger touch you anywhere. Not lay a finger on any part of you. If anyone tries, get home as fast as you can, or find a policeman.

4 Never get in a strange car or go to a strange place unless it's with someone you know well.

5 Usually adults have the bottoms of their bodies covered. If you see an adult unzip his trousers, move away fast and tell a grown-up. Always immediately report any 'rude behaviour' to the nearest person in authority, whether it be a schoolmaster or policeman. In fact, anyone in uniform will do, or even a taxi driver.

6 What if it isn't a stranger, but a schoolmaster or uncle who is behaving in an undesirable fashion? Tell your mother as soon as possible. It can be most difficult for a child to inform on someone he knows, so this must be emphasized.

The police add that a child should be taught that whenever he or she is in trouble, lost, without any money, or upset in some way, always ask a policeman. If you can't see a policeman ask someone where a police station is. As soon as possible teach a child to dial 999 and be able to read out the telephone number from which he or she is speaking.

HOW TO PROFIT

FROM A CRISIS

There are two sorts of crisis: there is the personal one, such as the loss of a job or of a loved one by death or divorce, or the communal one, such as a motorway threat to a village, or a war. But there always seems to be some sort of crisis.

When personal disaster strikes, you probably need sympathy and practical help; but there is a distinct possibility (especially if everyone else is also swimming for the lifeboats) that the only person who is always interested in you, and able to provide you with sustained help is . . . YOURSELF.

Don't think 'somebody ought to do something about it' or 'the government should see to it'. Start thinking in terms of self-reliance. What *you* can do and what *you* can't do – that may be all you can count on. Whatever your crisis, force yourself to look cheerful. Shakespeare said: 'There is nothing

either good or bad, but thinking makes it so', and Napoleon added that 'the moral is to material as three to one'. I would also say that the quickest facelift is a smile. Go on – try it, just for today SMILE and try to find something good instead of something bad in every new situation.

Look on the bright side, because there always *is* a bright side, however minor. If your husband disappears, at least you won't ever again have to watch Match of the Day.

Face your crisis and don't hide your head in the sand, ostrich-wise. Don't cross your fingers and hope for the best. Face what it is here and prepare for what might be coming.

Be constructively selfish. Think of yourself first. If you're not healthy and functioning efficiently, you can't look after your family or do your job. Ignore accusations of selfishness, egotism or ruthlessness from those who resent that you won't do what they (selfishly) want you to do. The need for self-preservation forces everyone to be selfish.

Don't hope to change anyone or their attitudes: it will probably be an exhausting waste of time.

Don't hate anyone: It's a destructive waste of energy. Try to ignore that person and try to make sure that you are no longer vulnerable to him or her.

Recognize your practical and emotional limitations. If you can't control your temper, look for ways to avoid losing it. Don't allow yourself to be tempted or bullied into any emotionally upsetting situations which you can avoid.

Don't hope. Hope is dangerous if it is over-optimistic, and can stop you viewing your situation realistically.

Try not to worry. It can't do any good and it's often only a habit. ('Your mother's a worrier'.)

Don't go on about it. People may get bored or embarrassed. So keep it to yourself.

Don't be self-pitying. You don't need pity; you need clear thought and action.

'Thought must be the harder; the heart the keener.

Courage must be greater as our strength grows less.'

A fighting Anglo-Saxon chieftain said that; whoever he was, he sounds like a survivor.

Make allowances for your weaknesses: It's unrealistic to give up smoking to save money now, if that's the only thing that takes your mind off your problem. Just make sure you don't start smoking more.

Count your friends: Whatever your

crisis, it is important to realize that it has happened before. Trust your true friends to understand and sympathize, although it may not be within their power to help in practical matters. Don't mind asking for simple practical help when it is needed. At the worst, they can only say no. Some people in this world *are* selfish, but it *helps* most people to give help when it's in their power. Those who have been through hard times are glad to pay back the help they've had from others. This is the way the help chain works.

Don't ask too much of your rights. The less you rely upon them the less you risk disappointment – when a few pounds takes months to come through or someone else's inefficiency negates your claim.

Count your resources. Your money, time, talent, possessions and family help. Write them down in a list. Mine started with 'mother' and ended with 'continental quilt'. I looked at this long list (there were other things in between) and thought 'How dare you feel sorry for yourself?'

Get expert advice: A survivor must be practical. Assess your immediate problems, write them down and seek objective advice to clarify your situation. No one can think clearly when disaster strikes. You might need to visit a specialist, solicitor or accountant.

You must also realize that you might be in a state of shock, which is a physical illness. Don't hesitate to go to a doctor if you have any unusual symptoms and be sure to tell him the whole problem, not just the physical symptoms. Again, don't be proud or ashamed, or feel that you are wasting his time. He's heard it all a million times before and your problems will obviously be treated as confidential. To pride yourself on *not* going to the doctor or to think you are making a fuss, might harm you and might impair your efficiency for dealing with your crisis.

Make your own decisions: Although specialists may be useful to analyse a situation and suggest solutions, they cannot run your life for you. Once your choices are clarified, use your common sense to make your own decisions. Then force yourself to be pessimistic, to look for the snags in the arrangements and face them. Don't opt out because you don't understand your position. Make your adviser explain it all again until you *do* understand it, and so can be responsible for deciding which path you want to take. Be prepared to be responsible for your own decisions. Life is a risk. Nothing is certain in this world and there is no guaranteed security, financial, intellectual or emotional. Security lies in your own self-reliance to deal with the problems of life. You will make some right decisions and some wrong ones. Pay the penalty for the wrong ones, cut your losses and start again.

Make a rule *never to take a decision if you are upset*. Wait at least twenty-four hours until you can think more clearly. Also wait twenty-four hours before sending an emotional letter. Then tear it up.

Cut out waste: Don't waste money, resources, time or friendship. You can now stop feeling obliged to do things just because others expect them from you. There are now plenty of reasons and excuses.

There are a lot of things in life that you needn't do. You don't have to cook a hot lunch on Sunday or return the Jones' invitation, or attend parties if they make you nervous, or functions if they bore you.

Don't waste time: And if you've suddenly got more of it than ever before, try to look upon it as a life-enriching bonus. If you've wished for more time in the past – now's your time to use it.

Use that time for more creative leisure, active sports and hobbies, doing things *with* your children instead of *for* them, or taking an inexpensive, stimulating course. Think of something rewarding to do and start DOING IT NOW.

Stop wanting things. Are you wasting time, effort and money doing things and buying luxuries that you don't really need? After all, your grandparents got along without a Teasmaid or an Instamatic. Try switching off the sound on the TV commercials for a start and then start trying to tell the differences between a wish and a want. A wish is not a true need, but an artificially stimulated status symbol. In other words, unnecessary.

THE ADVANTAGES OF A CRISIS

A crisis can be a blessing in disguise if it makes you stop and take a long look at your life, and then cut out the clutter.

IN A COMMUNITY CRISIS

Share your troubles and share the solutions to them, whether it's grouping together to buy groceries in bulk or passing on a good recipe. All over the country people are having the same problems. Pool your resources. Start lending things, the way people did in the war.

Advertise in your local tobacconist's right now for a swop babysitter; babysitter-swopping is *far* more liberating than wife-swopping. If one person answers the ad you can take turns to sit for each other. If two or three people answer it you might as well be a bulk babysitter if you're stuck doing it anyway. You could each of you look after three babies a morning, or afternoon or day and have the rest of the week free. Wouldn't that be nice for a bit? If more than one person answers the advertisement, start a rota. Don't wait for someone else – *you* do it.

Nothing gets started unless somebody starts it, and if nobody else seems to have thought of it, why shouldn't that someone be you?

Today we are threatened on all sides by financial, industrial and political crisis. However, you aren't the Prime Minister or the President of the U.S. Let those people continue to shoulder all *their* responsibilities. What *you* can do is mind your own business, check the store cupboard and the hot water bottles (crises are always cold) and start digging an allotment. Voltaire said, '*Il faut cultiver nos jardins*' and I'm sure that if that sensible man were alive today he'd tell us to turn it over to vegetables.

What to do with the time you've SAVED

First, take a good look at yourself (body, soul and inside skull). Decide what areas could stand a little pleasant improvement. Decide what your life lacks. New friends? Less weight? More fun? Once you've decided what you want, stand up, take a deep breath, and START.

WHAT YOU CAN DO INSIDE YOUR HOME

Make yourself more beautiful: This is basically taking better care of yourself, encouraging healthy narcissism, learning to love and take care of your body, condition your skin and hair. Learn to relax. Take care of your clothes.

Make yourself healthier: Do exercises every day – find the sort that work best for you. Grope your way out of bed and *do* them straight away.

Get better educated: Home can be the best place to study. Do you want to know more about anything? Did you get enough O and A levels? Do you need a degree, in order to get out there and work at something that is fun and lucrative? Write to the Open University, PO Box 48, Walton, Bletchley, Bucks.

WHAT YOU CAN DO OUTSIDE YOUR HOME

Go to evening classes or daytime classes: Do you realize just what you can learn in the evenings? Wouldn't you like to know just a bit more about at least one of the following? Antiques, art, astronomy, beauty culture, boat-building, chamber music, chess, citizens' rights, cookery on a shoestring, drama, dressmaking, French, Russian, German, Greek or Italian, guitar-making, jewellery, model engineering, photography, pigeons, psychology, toy-making, wine-making or woodwork.

If you can't find locally the class you want, you and nine friends or family members can persuade your local council to run an evening class on *anything* – they're likely to operate quite a selection anyway. Ask in the town hall or library for the appropriate leaflet.

If you can spare a *lot* of time you could sign on for a full-time course in something you like and/or something useful; you may even be eligible for a grant to help you study. You can also sign on for plain recreational courses of lectures on the arts, archaeology, music or whatever; again, badger the town hall for full details.

Get into physical activity: By which I don't necessarily mean play netball, unless you really like netball.

Visit your local library or town hall to find out what's on. Admittedly I live in a city, but there's a local council-sponsored choice of eleven sports, including judo, golf and fencing to Olympic standard.

If you were always hopeless at games at school don't allow yourself to continue your career as a physical wreck. Go in for something gentle and uncompetitive like yoga or dancing.

Your local council might easily offer classical ballet, modern ballet, ballroom, Latin American or 'Old Time' dancing, so check on it.

Half the battle is forcing yourself to organize it. If you want to, do it now.

Help somebody who needs you: All charities are gasping for your help. Working for others can be the most fulfilling of all out-of-home activities – it can also be the most demanding. Most good causes are well advertised and all you have to do is turn up or telephone and offer your services. If you would like to do charitable work and really don't know where to offer, ask your local vicar for advice. You needn't be a churchgoer.

Meet men: If this your specific aim in your free time, just go about it methodically and intelligently, like any other project. Lady Docker who was once a salesgirl at Debenham and Freebody said that she married millionaires because she mixed with them. Go where the men are: to work first and foremost; to educational courses in man-filled areas such as accountancy, science, maths or engineering, to two-sex sports that men prefer, such as skin-diving or fencing. Do not allow yourself to be conned into amateur dramatics, tennis clubs, charity work or artistic evening classes for the purpose of meeting men – all these areas are full of beady-eyed man chasers (not like you, of course) and weedy unchaseworthy men.

Get a job: see p. 161.

SKIP this section till you need it, except for the rough shopping guide for liquids.

THE METRIC SYSTEM: A ROUGH CRIB

The great point about the metric system is that it is logical and not based on the length of the big toe, pole or perch of somebody's Saxon ancestor. The French worked it all out according to reason, just after the Revolution in 1791.

The decimal units of calculation are: temperature in degrees; solid weight in grammes; liquid volume in litres; length in metres; area in square metres. All calculations are made in units of ten and interrelated.

Here's an example in LENGTH:

10 *millimetres* (mm)	= 1 *centimetre* (cm)
10 centimetres	= 1 decimetre (dm)
10 decimetres	= 1 *metre* (m)
10 metres	= 1 dekametre (dk)
10 dekametres	= 1 hectometre (hm)
10 hectometres	= 1 *kilometre* (km)

Most people only use the measurements in italics.

179

A FEW HOME TRUTHS

HOME TRUTHS

It's useful to know:

Weight

25 grammes (g)	=just under 1 oz
100 grammes	=just under 4 oz
400 grammes	=just under 1 lb
1 kilogramme (kg)	=about 2¼ lb
1 kilogramme	=1,000 grammes

Volume

1 litre (l)	=10 decilitres (dl)
1 litre	=1¾ pints
½ litre	=just over ¾ pint
¼ litre	=just under ½ pint
1 decilitre (dl)	=6 tablespoons
1 centilitre (cl)	=1 dessertspoon
5 millilitres (ml)	=1 small teaspoon (standard medicine spoon size)
1 millilitre	=a few drops
4½ litres	=1 gallon, so a 5-litre tin of paint holds just over 1 gallon.

4.54 litres=1 gallon=8 pints

Length

1,000 metres	=1 kilometre
1 metre=100 cm	=3 feet 3 inches
90 centimetres	=1 yard
30 centimetres	=1 foot
2½ centimetres	=1 inch

Area

1 hectare	=10,000 square metres=2.5 acres 4,000 square metres=about 1 acre
1 square metre	=10.8 square feet

Temperature

Normal body temperature=98.4 Fahrenheit=37° Centigrade or Celcius (same thing) which is what most people's temperatures are if they are healthy.

100°C (212°F) is the boiling point of water.

0°C (32°F) is the freezing point of water.

15°C (59°F) is the temperature of a cool summer's day.

20°C (68°F) is the temperature of a warm spring day in Britain.

30°C (86°F) is the temperature of a hot summer day in Britain.

22°C (72°F) is central heating living room temperature.

43°C (110°F) is hot bath temperature.

50°C (122°F) is hand-hot water temperature.

ROUGH SHOPPING GUIDE FOR LIQUIDS

This comparative fluids chart has been duplicated in case you want to cut it out and keep it in your purse.

If you shop with a slide rule don't read on.

Comparative shoppers *are* confused by bottles of different shapes and sizes. They know that they must look on the label for the quantity of shampoo, olive oil, Caleche or whatever.

Unfortunately you often find yourself comparing 200 cc of the pink shampoo at 21p with 14 fl oz of the green one at 28p. At this point you stop trying and crossly grab the cheapest one (which is, in fact, the one which costs more in that example).

ROUGH SHOPPING GUIDE FOR LIQUIDS

Them (Metric System) cc or ml (g for gramme)	Us (Imperial System) fl oz (or oz for ounce)	
600	21	
570	20	1 pint
540	19	
510	18	17½
500		
480	17	
450	16	¾ pint
420	15	
400	14	
370	13	
340	12	
312	11	
300	10½	½ pint
255	9	
230	8	
200	7	
170	6	
140	5	¼ pint
114	4	
85	3	
57	2	1½
50		
30	1	

ROUGH SHOPPING GUIDE FOR LIQUIDS

Them (Metric System) cc or ml (or g for gramme)	Us (Imperial System) fl oz (or oz for ounce)	
600	21	
570	20	1 pint
540	19	
510	18	17½
500		
480	17	
450	16	¾ pint
420	15	
400	14	
370	13	
340	12	
312	11	
300	10½	½ pint
255	9	
230	8	
200	7	
170	6	
140	5	¼ pint
114	4	
85	3	
57	2	1½
50		
30	1	

Fairly scientific footnote: This is only a rough guide. It is impossible to relate volume and mass because of the density difference of products. Even I can see that a pint jar of treacle weighs more than a pint jar of methylated spirits, so only use this chart for comparing similar items, such as several brands of treacle.

You probably don't want to know – but these measurements refer only to *water-based* fluids. Some liquids are heavier than others. Other lighter liquids (such as methylated spirits) or denser liquids (such as treacle) may be weighed differently.

1 cubic centimetre = 1 millilitre (these are measurements of volume) and 1 cubic centimetre of water weighs 1 gramme (this is a measurement of weight). But the same equivalents won't necessarily apply to non-water-based fluids. The same goes for translating fluid ounces (volume) into ounces (weight).

WHICH IS WHY THIS IS ONLY A ROUGH SHOPPING GUIDE.

Fairly scientific footnote: This is only a rough guide. It is impossible to relate volume and mass because of the density difference of products. Even I can see that a pint jar of treacle weighs more than a pint jar of methylated spirits, so only use this chart for comparing similar items, such as several brands of treacle.

You probably don't want to know – but these measurements refer only to *water-based* fluids. Some liquids are heavier than others. Other lighter liquids (such as methylated spirits) or denser liquids (such as treacle) may be weighed differently.

1 cubic centimetre = 1 millilitre (these are measurements of volume) and 1 cubic centimetre of water weighs 1 gramme (this is a measurement of weight). But the same equivalents won't necessarily apply to non-water-based fluids. The same goes for translating fluid ounces (volume) into ounces (weight).

WHICH IS WHY THIS IS ONLY A ROUGH SHOPPING GUIDE.

QUIETLY GOING METRIC IN THE KITCHEN
(translating us to them)

For converting your own recipes from imperial to metric. Recipe translators generally use 25 grammes as a basic unit in place of 1 ounce, 500 millilitres in place of 1 pint. Use the new British Standard 5-ml and 15-ml spoons in place of the old variable teaspoons and tablespoons; they will give slightly smaller quantities. Translated recipes are rounded off – either upwards or downwards – in quantity, but the *comparative* quantities should remain the same.

Weight

Pounds and Ounces to nearest Grammes

1 oz=	28 g	(say 25 g)
2 oz=	56 g	
3 oz=	85 g	
4 oz=	113 g	(say 100 g)
5 oz=	141 g	
6 oz=	170 g	
7 oz=	198 g	
8 oz=	226 g	(say 200 g)
9 oz=	255 g	
10 oz=	283 g	
11 oz=	311 g	
12 oz=	340 g	(say 350 g)
13 oz=	368 g	
14 oz=	396 g	
15 oz=	425 g	
1 lb=16 oz=	453 g	(say 450 g)
2 lb=	907 g	(say 900 g)
3 lb=	1.36 kg	(say 1.400 kg)
4 lb=	1.81 kg	(say 1.800 kg)
5 lb=	2.27 kg	(say 2.300 kg)

A FEW HOME TRUTHS

Volume

Use decilitres, millilitres and litres

$\frac{1}{4}$ pint=142 ml (say 125 ml)
$\frac{1}{2}$ pint=284 ml (say 250 ml)
$\frac{3}{4}$ pint=426 ml (say 375 ml)
1 pint=568 ml (say 500 ml)
2 pints=1.14 litres (say 1 litre)

ANCIENT BRITISH VOLUME MEASURES

A level teacup of flour=$5\frac{1}{2}$ oz=156 g
A level breakfast cup of flour=$6\frac{1}{2}$oz=184 g
A level teacup of castor sugar   =$7\frac{1}{2}$ oz=212 g
A level breakfastcup of castor sugar=10 oz=283 g
A level teacup of rice   =$6\frac{1}{2}$ oz=184 g
A level breakfast cup of rice=$9\frac{1}{2}$oz=269 g
A level teacup of breadcrumbs=$3\frac{1}{2}$ oz= 99 g
A level breakfast cup of breadcrumbs=$4\frac{1}{4}$ oz=120 g
A level teacup of butter=$7\frac{1}{2}$ oz=212 g
A level breakfast cup of butter=11 oz=312 g
A level teacup of olive oil=7 oz=198 g
A level breakfast cup of olive oil=$10\frac{1}{2}$ oz=298 g
A level teacup of icing sugar=$5\frac{1}{4}$ oz=148 g
A level breakfast cup of icing sugar=$8\frac{1}{2}$ oz=240 g
A level teacup of golden syrup/black treacle=$11\frac{1}{2}$ oz=326 g
A level breakfast cup of syrup/treacle=$15\frac{1}{2}$ oz=439 g

183

A FEW HOME TRUTHS

WEIGHT TRANSLATIONS

Pounds and Ounces to Grammes

1 oz= 28.3 g	1 lb 1 oz=481.9 g	2 lb 1 oz= 935.5 g	3 lb 1 oz=1389.1 g
2 oz= 56.6 g	2 oz=510.2 g	2 oz= 963.8 g	2 oz=1417.4 g
3 oz= 85.0 g	3 oz=538.6 g	3 oz= 992.2 g	3 oz=1445.8 g
4 oz=113.3 g	4 oz=566.9 g	4 oz=1020.5 g	4 oz=1474.1 g
5 oz=141.7 g	5 oz=595.3 g	5 oz=1048.9 g	5 oz=1502.5 g
6 oz=170.0 g	6 oz=623.6 g	6 oz=1077.2 g	6 oz=1530.8 g
7 oz=198.4 g	7 oz=652.0 g	7 oz=1105.6 g	7 oz=1559.2 g
8 oz=226.7 g	8 oz=680.3 g	8 oz=1133.9 g	8 oz=1587.5 g
9 oz=255.1 g	9 oz=708.7 g	9 oz=1162.3 g	9 oz=1615.9 g
10 oz=283.4 g	10 oz=737.0 g	10 oz=1190.6 g	10 oz=1644.2 g
11 oz=311.8 g	11 oz=765.4 g	11 oz=1219.0 g	11 oz=1672.6 g
12 oz=340.1 g	12 oz=793.7 g	12 oz=1247.3 g	12 oz=1700.9 g
13 oz=368.5 g	13 oz=822.1 g	13 oz=1275.7 g	13 oz=1729.3 g
14 oz=396.8 g	14 oz=850.4 g	14 oz=1304.0 g	14 oz=1757.6 g
15 oz=425.2 g	15 oz=878.8 g	15 oz=1332.4 g	15 oz=1786.0 g
1 lb =453.5 g	2 lb =907.1 g	3 lb =1360.7 g	4 lb =1814.3 g

Imperial and Metric Equivalents Liquids Translations

3 litre — 5½ pint
2·7 litre — 5 pint
2·5 litre — 4½ pint
2·2 litre — 4 pint
2 litre — 3½ pint
1·7 litre — 3 pint
1·5 litre — 2½ pint
1·2 litre — 2 pint
1 litre — 1¾ pint

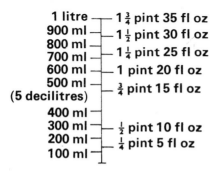

1 litre — 1¾ pint 35 fl oz
900 ml — 1½ pint 30 fl oz
800 ml
700 ml — 1¼ pint 25 fl oz
600 ml — 1 pint 20 fl oz
500 ml — ¾ pint 15 fl oz
(5 decilitres)
400 ml
300 ml — ½ pint 10 fl oz
200 ml — ¼ pint 5 fl oz
100 ml

TEMPERATURE CHART

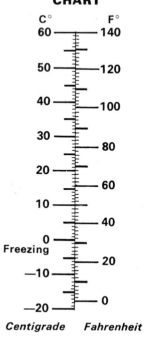

C°	F°
60	140
50	120
40	100
30	80
20	60
10	40
0 Freezing	20
−10	0
−20	

Centigrade   Fahrenheit

THE MAD HATTER'S TEASPOON TABLE
(approximate liquid measures)

To measure cookery ingredients, Talaware manufacture an excellent metal measuring cone. However, don't abandon a recipe if you haven't a measure. The age old table below is workable and better than nothing, although it is approximate and has no accurate arithmetical progression. (It's like the Calendar before they invented Leap Year; you keep going progressively wrong by a few drops.)

You may, like me, have four different sizes of teaspoon in your drawer. However, you're not splitting the atom for lunch and, generally speaking, cookery measures need not be so precise as laboratory ones.

A pint bottle is what they say it is but don't think that an average wine bottle is a litre; it's about 9/10 litre. A hock bottle contains even less.

	METRIC	IMPERIAL PINT	FLUID OUNCES
1 teaspoon=	8 millilitres		$\frac{1}{4}$ fl oz
3 teaspoons=1 dessertspoon=	15 ml		$\frac{1}{2}$ fl oz
2 dessertspoons=1 tablespoon=	30 ml		1 fl oz
3 tablespoons=	1 decilitre (100 ml)		
5 tablespoons=1 sherry glass=	150 ml	$\frac{1}{4}$ pt (1 gill)	5 fl oz
2 sherry glasses=1 British breakfast cup=	$\frac{1}{4}$ litre	$\frac{1}{2}$ pt	10 fl oz
2 sherry glasses=1 American cup=	$\frac{1}{4}$ litre	$\frac{1}{2}$ pt	10 fl oz
2 sherry glasses=1$\frac{1}{2}$ British teacups=	$\frac{1}{4}$ litre	$\frac{1}{2}$ pt	10 fl oz
2 sherry glasses=1 mug=	$\frac{1}{4}$ litre	$\frac{1}{2}$ pt	10 fl oz
2 sherry glasses=1 tumbler=	$\frac{1}{4}$ litre	$\frac{1}{2}$ pt	10 fl oz
4 sherry glasses=2 tumblers=	$\frac{1}{2}$ litre (6 dl to be precise)	1 pt	20 fl oz

A FEW HOME TRUTHS

OVEN TIMING

Oven temperatures

SOLID FUEL	GAS	ELECTRICITY	TO COOK
Very cool	¼ – ½	240°F = 116°C	Stew
Cool	1	275°F = 135°C	Casseroles, slow roasts or milk and
	2	290°F = 144°C	egg dishes
Slow	3	325°F = 163°C	
Moderate	4	350°F = 177°C	Biscuits
	5	375°F = 190°C	Fruit cake
Mod. hot	6	400°F = 200°C	
Hot	7	425°F = 218°C	Soufflés, short pastry, flan, sponge cake
Very hot	8	450°F = 232°C	Fast roasts, bread
	9	475°F = 246°C	Puff and flaky pastry

All cookers aren't the same: some tend to be hotter than the temperature at which they have been set: allow for the idiosyncracies of your oven in using the table above and follow manufacturer's instructions.

MEAT ROASTING

A meat thermometer takes the guesswork out of roasting, but if you haven't one, here's a timetable guide. It allows for wrapping meats or poultry in foil and unfolding the foil during the last twenty minutes of cooking so that it will brown.

These times are for average British taste. If you like your meat rare cross out this timetable and pencil in your own. It's also for meat joints of average family size, i.e. 3–5 lb.

	Quick Roast at High Temperature	*Slow Roast at Low Temperature* (*reduces shrinkage*)
	(Gas 7. Elec. 425°F = 220°C)	(Gas 3. Elec. 325°F = 160°C)
Beef and venison	15 mins per lb + 15 mins (rare) 20 mins per lb + 20 mins (well done)	25 mins per lb + 25 mins
Lamb or mutton	20 mins per lb + 20 mins	30 mins per lb + 30 mins
Veal and rabbit	25 mins per lb + 25 mins	35 mins per lb + 35 mins
Pork	25 mins per lb + 25 mins	Can't cook it this way, if you want crackling, but if not 35 mins per lb + 35 mins
Chicken and Duck	15 mins per lb + 15 mins	25 mins per lb + 25 mins

Quick Roast at High Temperature (Gas 7. Elec. 425°F=220°C)	*Slow Roast at Low Temperature* (Gas 3. Elec. 325°F=160°C)
Goose and turkey 15 mins per lb+15 mins	25 mins per lb+25 mins (under 14 lb)
(Before cooking a fat goose stab the bird with a fork so that the fat oozes through and bastes itself)	20 mins per lb+20 mins (over 14 lb)

Game (Gas 6. Elec. 400°F=200°C)
Woodcock 15 to 20 mins
Grouse, guineafowl, partridge and young roasting pigeon
        35 mins for small ones
        45 mins for large ones
Pheasant 15 mins per lb+10 mins

HOW TO GET HOLD OF
THE MEN IN YOUR LIFE

(*You* fill in these telephone numbers)

Police station ....

Hospital...

Doctor...

Dentist ....

Chemist ....

Local gas emergency ....

Local gas service...

Local electricity emergency ....

Local electricity service...

Heating fuel supply ....

Heating repairs..

189

HOW TO GET HOLD OF THE MEN IN YOUR LIFE

Railway stations ....

Garage ....

Taxi-cabs ....

Town hall (also refuse collection) ....

Bank manager ....

Insurance broker ....

Vet ....

Milkman ....

Builder ....

Decorator ....

Plumber ....

Carpenter ....

Electrician ....

TV repairs ....

Telephone repairs ....

Domestic machine repairs ....

Special machinery repairs ....

Newspaper delivery ....

Laundry ....

Dry cleaner ....

Drain cleaner ....

Window cleaner ....

Florist ....

Local odd job agency ....

HOW TO GET HOLD OF THE MEN IN YOUR LIFE

Fill in the following according to your needs, i.e., piano tuner, contract cleaner, carpet cleaner, curtain maker, babysitter, off-licence, flower nursery, local paper advertisement department.

And So Farewell...
with the joke which never fails

As WE bashed out lunch for twenty teenagers, when only seven were expected, an old schoolfriend of mine hissed that what she wanted to read in this book was a joke that she will continue to think funny every time the milk boils over. So here's my favourite cartoon:

An astonished husband has returned home from the office to an amazing scene in his kitchen. Two little children are murdering each other while another tot is garotting the cat. There is a pile of last night's dirty dishes and a heap of dirty laundry. Saucepans are burning, clouds of steam are rising, the floor is covered with smashed crockery and the dog has just upset the litter bin.

In the middle of this chaos is his wife, sitting in an easy chair with her feet up on the table. She is reading a novel and dipping into a box of chocolates. She says, 'I thought that the best way to let you see what on earth I do all day was not to do it.'

Index

INDEX

INDEX